P9-DFY-129

TORTURE
TEAM

TORTURE TEAM

*Rumsfeld's Memo and
the Betrayal of American Values*

PHILIPPE SANDS

First published in 2008 by
PALGRAVE MACMILLAN™
175 Fifth Avenue, New York, N.Y. 10010 and
Houndmills, Basingstoke, Hampshire, England RG21 6XS.
Companies and representatives throughout the world.

PALGRAVE MACMILLAN is the global academic imprint of the Palgrave Macmillan division of St. Martin's Press, LLC and of Palgrave Macmillan Ltd. Macmillan® is a registered trademark in the United States, United Kingdom and other countries. Palgrave is a registered trademark in the European Union and other countries.

ISBN–13: 978–0–230–60390–5
ISBN–10: 0–230–60390–4

Library of Congress Cataloging-in-Publication Data
Sands, Philippe, 1960–
    Torture team / Philippe Sands.
        p.   cm.
    Includes bibliographical references.
    ISBN 0–230–60390–4 (alk. paper)
        1. Torture (International law)—History.   2. Human rights.   I. Title.
K5304.S26   2008
341.4'8—dc22

                                                                    2007041092

A catalogue record of the book is available from the British Library.

Design by Letra Libre

First edition: May 2008
10 9 8 7 6 5 4 3 2 1
Printed in the United States of America.

For my parents, Allan and Ruth

"*We also have to work, though, sort of the dark side, if you will. . . . it's going to be vital for us to use any means at our disposal, basically, to achieve our objective.*"

—Vice President Dick Cheney, Meet the Press,

September 16, 2001

"*In situations like this you don't call in the tough guys; you call in the lawyers.*"

—former CIA director George Tenet,

At the Center of the Storm, 2007

ALSO BY PHILIPPE SANDS

Lawless World: Making and Breaking Global Rules

CONTENTS

Acknowledgments	viii
List of Illustrations	xi
Principal Characters	xii
List of Abbreviations	xv
Kick-Off	I
The Path	28
Comeback	III
Responsibility	155
Chronology of Events	233
Notes	237
Index	250

ACKNOWLEDGMENTS

I begin by thanking all those who shared their experiences and views on the events described in this book. No one was under any obligation to do so, since I was not armed with any form of subpoena. Whatever reason each may have had, it is a mark of the openness of American society that people are willing to talk. The interviews took place between September 2006 and September 2007, mostly in the United States. Several interviews were recorded, but in others the interviewee preferred me to take detailed notes. In some cases I met the individual on only one occasion, in other cases I made repeated visits. I have also relied extensively on material that was in the public domain, even if sometimes obscurely so. On matters that appear to me to be significant I have, in general, tried to ensure at least two sources. In some instances off-the-record conversations provided important confirmation, but for reasons of professional etiquette I have made no reference to the contents of such conversations. I was constantly struck by the strong sense of public service and professionalism in so many of the people I met. It may be unfair to mention any group in particular, but I cannot avoid expressing appreciation for the career military lawyers I talked to around the United States, women and men of integrity and professionalism whose attitudes reflect the best American traditions of valor. For everyone, I hope to have reflected the contents of the conversations and interviews in a way that is fair and balanced. If I have failed to do so, the responsibility is mine alone.

Several friends and colleagues generously agreed to review draft chapters or passages and make suggestions. I am especially grateful to Jane Mayer, whose brilliant and brave articles in the *New Yorker* are a source of great inspiration, and whose assistance and collegiality was constant. I hope one day to be able to do the same in return. For insights and critique I am grateful to James Cameron, Adriana Fabra, Nick Hornby,

Scott Horton, David Kennedy, Robert McCrum, Tim Owen, David Rakoff, Susan Talalay, and Don van Natta. My brother Marc gave unstinting support, as he always does.

A number of individuals, some occupying senior positions, provided invaluable assistance and have asked to remain in the background. Anonymity cannot obscure the depth of my appreciation, not least for their principled stand on matters of real human importance.

Others have assisted in a range of different ways. My sincere thanks to Daniel Alexander, Moazzam Begg, Sidney Blumenthal, John Bush, Professor Andew Clapham, Professor David Cole, Ernesto Ekaizer, Bart Gellman, Gay Gill, Tim Golden, Katherine Gorove, Karen Greenberg, Ann Hennigan, General Sir Mike Jackson, Jonathan Klein, Professor Dawn Johnsen, Professor Marty Lederman, Leanne Macmillan and Sheila Melzak at the Medical Foundation for the Care of Victims of Torture, Professor Kate Malleson, Henry Mayer and Dr. Juergen Matthaeus at the Holocaust Museum in Washington, Donna Mcmurray, Jonathan Marks, Brenda Moski, Dr. Christopher Mueller and Dr. Peter Spaengler of Altstötter & Spängler, Ed Pilkington, Paul Reichler, Simon Rooke (for providing a copy of *The Memory of Justice*, Marcel Ophüls' classic film), Professor Beate Rudolf, Michael Scherer, André Schiffrin, Leina Schiffrin, Günter Schulze-Weckert, Dr. Constanze Stelzenmüller, Professor Richard Stewart, Brenda Tuttle, Erin Voto, Diane Wachtell, Colonel Kelly Wheaton, Laurence Wilkerson, and Ed Williamson.

I have benefited greatly from first-class research assistance. Chanda Betourney at Georgetown Law School guided me around U.S. Congressional documents, and Mirja Trilsch from Düsseldorf and the Université du Québec à Montréal provided invaluable assistance on German historical materials. I am also grateful to Joel Gregorio, Hejaaz Hizbullah and Mustafa Qadri from University College London and Keith Chapman at NYU Law School. Julie Albrektsen at Matrix Chambers organized the voluminous materials and assisted on the footnotes, both important tasks carried out with great skill.

At UCL, Professor Ian Dennis generously allowed me a year's sabbatical to complete this book, and Cathy Brown provided consequential support; thanks to Ruth Mackenzie for taking on additional teaching commitments and being a terrific colleague, and to all at the law faculty for their encouragement and support. Thanks also to friends at Matrix Chambers, in particular Kate Cook, James Crawford, Zachary Douglas, Alison Macdonald and Blinne Ni Ghralaigh for holding the fort, and to my practice managers for living with the consequences of putting my practice on hold for a few months.

I have had the great fortune to be assisted by two wonderful administrative assistants. Jenny Bromley transcribed some of the taped interviews and, as reflected occasionally in the text, I benefited from her perceptive insights on their contents. Kate Barber has once again demonstrated why she is indispensable, and probably the only person in the world who can decipher my writing in reasonable time and maintain good humor.

In London my agent Gill Coleridge provided all the support one could conceivably ask for, and far more. Her knowledge of, and interest in, the issues and her constant enthusiasm and ideas provided great support. In New York, Melanie Jackson performed an equally admirable role, having to go to bat on a sticky wicket (saturated market) and she delivered up trumps. It is difficult to imagine a more committed team than Gill and Melanie, or one that could be better placed to contribute in this subject area.

At Penguin in London, as editor and friend Margaret Bluman has continued to nurture my writing and provide insight and encouragement for which I am deeply grateful. Jane Robertson was meticulous as ever in her copy-editing. At Palgrave Macmillan in New York, Alessandra Bastagli decided to go where others were more hesitant, and provided a degree of detailed editorial input that has undoubtedly improved the text, and Yasmin Mathew assisted in translating my prose for an American audience. To all four I express my appreciation.

Finally, I owe much to my family. To my parents Allan and Ruth for putting up with my peripatetic ways. To Leo, for providing useful input on the relative merits and demerits of various techniques of interrogation and for creating the table of characters during a school holiday. To Lara, for taking the most important phone messages, even from generals (retired), and standing firm on the title. And to Katya, for inviting me to her makeshift restaurant and a restorative meal at a moment of particular anxiety, and for teaching me tic-tac, her own card game. Natalia keeps the whole thing going, in every way. She is my most important and intelligent reader, critic and supporter: thank you, again and always.

London and New York, January 2008

LIST OF ILLUSTRATIONS

1. Alberto Gonzales
    Counsel to President George W. Bush (Photograph courtesy of the U.S. Department of Justice) (p. 17)
2. William J. Haynes II
    General Counsel to U.S. Secretary of Defense (Photograph by Scott Davis, U.S. Army, courtesy of U.S. Department of Defense) (p. 17)
3. David Addington
    General Counsel to Vice President Cheney (Photograph by Richard A. Bloom) (p. 17)
4. Doug Feith
    Undersecretary of Defense for Policy (Photograph courtesy of the U.S. Department of Defense) (p. 28)
5. Doug Feith and Jim Haynes at U.S. Department of Defense press briefing, March 21 2002 (Photograph courtesy of the U.S. Department of Defense) (p. 28)
6. Major General Michael E. Dunlavey
    Commanding Officer, Joint Task Force 170 (Photograph courtesy of U.S. Department of Defense) (p. 38)
7. Lieutenant Colonel Diane Beaver
    Staff Judge Advocate, JTF-GITMO (Photograph courtesy of the author) (p. 56)
8. Jay Bybee
    Assistant Attorney General, Office of Legal Counsel, U.S. Department of Justice (Photograph © PA Photos) (p. 73)
9. John Yoo
    Deputy Assistant Attorney General, Office of Legal Counsel, U.S. Department of Justice (Photograph © Karen Ballard, Redux Pictures) (p. 73)
10. General James T. Hill
    Commander, U.S. Southern Command (Photograph © PA Photos) (p. 79)
11. General Richard Myers
    Chairman, Joint Chiefs of Staff (Photograph by Ron Hall, U.S. Air Force, courtesy of the U.S. Department of Defense) (p. 88)
12. Paul Wolfowitz
    Deputy Secretary of Defense
    (Photograph courtesy of the U.S. Department of Defense) (p. 105)
13. Major General Geoffrey D. Miller
    Commander, JTF-GITMO (from November 2002) (Photograph © PA Photos) (p. 108)
14. Alberto Mora
    General Counsel to the U.S. Navy (Photograph courtesy Tom Fitzsimmons/JFK Library Foundation) (p. 132)
15. Josef Altstötter
    Circa 1945–46 (Photograph by U.S. Army) (p. 197)

PRINCIPAL CHARACTERS

(POSITIONS HELD IN 2002)

THE WHITE HOUSE

George W. Bush, President of the United States
  Alberto Gonzales, his Counsel
Dick Cheney, Vice President of the United States
  David Addington, his General Counsel

DEPARTMENT OF DEFENSE

OFFICE OF SECRETARY OF DEFENSE
  Donald Rumsfeld, the Secretary of Defense
    William J. Haynes II, his General Counsel
    Dan Dell'Orto, his Principal Deputy General Counsel
    Jack Landman Goldsmith, Special Counsel to Mr. Haynes (from
      September 2002)
  Paul Wolfowitz, the Deputy Secretary of Defense
  Doug Feith, Undersecretary of Defense for Policy
    Stephen Cambone, Director, Program Analysis and Evaluation,
      Office of the Secretary of Defense
    Marshall Billingslea, the Acting Assistant U.S. Secretary of Defense
      for Special Operations/Low-Intensity Conflict

Defense Intelligence Agency
Vice Admiral Lowell Jacoby, the Director
  Caleb Temple, Chief, Counterterrorism Division, Joint Intelligence
    Task Force for Combating Terrorism (JITF-CT)

JOINT CHIEFS OF STAFF
> *General Richard Myers*, the Chairman
> *Jane Dalton*, his General Counsel

DEPARTMENT OF THE ARMY
> *Thomas E. White*, Secretary of the Army,
> *Steve Morello*, his General Counsel
> *Major General Thomas Romig*, Judge Avocate General, U.S. Army

DEPARTMENT OF THE NAVY
> *Gordon England*, Secretary of the Navy
> *Alberto Mora*, his General Counsel

> *Naval Criminal Investigative Service*
> *Dave Brant*, Director
> *Mike Gelles*, Chief Psychologist

DEPARTMENT OF THE AIR FORCE
> *Mary Walker*, General Counsel

SOUTHERN COMMAND
> *General James T. Hill*, Commander
> *Manny Supervielle*, his Staff Judge Advocate

> *Joint Task Force 170 (became Joint Task Force Guantánamo)*
> *Major General Michael E. Dunlavey*, Commanding Officer (until November 8)
> *Major General Geoffrey D. Miller*, Commander (from November 9)
> *Lieutenant Colonel Diane Beaver*, their Staff Judge Advocate
> *Lieutenant Colonel Jerald Phifer*, their Director of Intelligence (J2) (until November 2002)

DEPARTMENT OF JUSTICE

John Ashcroft, the Attorney General
> *Michael Chertoff*, his Assistant Attorney General to the Criminal Division

OFFICE OF LEGAL COUNSEL
  Jay Bybee, Assistant Attorney General
  John Yoo, Deputy Assistant Attorney General

FEDERAL BUREAU OF INVESTIGATION
  Marion (Spike) Bowman, Deputy General Counsel, National Security
    Law Branch.

DEPARTMENT OF STATE
  Colin Powell, the Secretary of State
    William Taft IV, his Legal Adviser

CENTRAL INTELLIGENCE AGENCY
  George Tenet, Director
    John Rizzo, Senior Deputy General Counsel

LIST OF ABBREVIATIONS

BAU	Behavioral Assessment Unit (FBI)
BSCT	Behavioral Consultation Team
CA3	Common Article 3 (Geneva)
CAT	computed axial tomography (scan)
CENTCOM	United States Central Command
CCR	Center for Constitutional Rights
CIA	Central Intelligence Agency
CITF	Criminal Investigation Task Force (DoD)
CJTF-7	Coalition Joint Task Force (Iraq)
CSRT	Combatant Status Review Tribunal
D.C.	Washington, District of Columbia
DHS	Defense Human Intelligence Service (DoD)
DIA	Defense Intelligence Agency (DoD)
DoD	United States Department of Defense
DoJ	Department of Justice
Fay-Jones report	report by Major General George Fay and Lieutenant General Anthony Jones, *Investigation of Intelligence Activities at Abu Ghraib* (August 23 2004)
FBI	Federal Bureau of Intelligence
FBIHQ	Federal Bureau of Intelligence headquarters
FM 34-52	*U.S. Army Field Manual 34-52* (1992)
HUMINT	human intelligence
ICE	Intelligence Control Element (DoD)
ICRC	International Committee of the Red Cross
intel	intelligence
IRA	Irish Republican Army
IV	intravenous drip

J2	Intelligence Directorate (U.S. military)
JAG	judge advocate general
JITF-CT	Joint Intelligence Task Force for Combating Terrorism (DoD)
JTF	Joint Task Force
GTMO *or* Gitmo	Guantánamo
KUBARK	CIA headquarters
MP	military police (DoD)
MRE	meal, ready-to-eat
NATO	North Atlantic Treaty Organization
NCIS	Naval Criminal Investigation Service
NSA	National Security Agency
NYU	New York University
OKW	Oberkommando der Wehrmacht
OLC	Office of Legal Counsel (DoJ)
OSD	Office of the Secretary of Defense
POW	prisoner of war
ROTC	Reserve Officers' Training Corps
SA	Sturmabteilung
Schmidt-Furlow report	report of Brigadier General John Furlow and Lieutenant General Randal Schmidt, Investigation into FBI Allegations of Detainee Abuse at Guantánamo Bay, Cuba Detention Facility (April 1 2005) amended June 9, 2005
Schlesinger report	Final report of the Independent panel to Review DoD Detention Operations, chaired by James R. Schlesinger (August 2004)
SD	Sicherheitsdienst
SECDEF	secretary of defense
SERE	survival, evasion, resistance, escape
SJA	staff judge advocate
SOUTHCOM	United States Southern Command
SS	Schutzstaffel
SSA	supervisory special agent (FBI)
TJAG	The Judge Advocate General
UCMJ	Uniform Code of Military Justice
USD(P)	Under Secretary of Defense for Policy
USMT	United States Military Tribunal
VOCO	vocal command

TORTURE
TEAM

KICK-OFF

1

Only a few pieces of paper can change the course of history. On Tuesday, December 2, 2002 Donald Rumsfeld signed one that did.

It was an ordinary day. The Secretary of Defense wasn't traveling. No immediate decisions were needed on Iraq and Washington awaited Saddam's declaration on weapons of mass destruction. The only notable public event in the Secretary's diary for that day was the President's visit to the Pentagon to sign a Bill to put the Pentagon in funds for the next year. Signings are big, symbolic public events. They offer an opportunity to lavish praise and on this occasion neither man showed restraint. The Secretary of Defense introduced President Bush effusively as our "leader in the global war on terrorism."[1] The President thanked Mr. Rumsfeld warmly, for his candor, and for doing such a fabulous job for the American people. The United States faced unprecedented challenges, Bush told a large and enthusiastic audience, and terror was one of them. The United States would respond to these challenges, and it would do so in the "finest traditions of valor." And then he signed a large increase in the Defense budget.

That same day, elsewhere in the Pentagon, a less public event took place for which there was no comment, no publicity, no fanfare. With a signature and a few scrawled words Donald Rumsfeld cast aside America's international obligations and edged on the tradition of valor to which President Bush had referred. Principles for the conduct of interrogation, dating back more than a century to President Lincoln's famous instruction of 1863 that "military necessity does not admit of cruelty" were discarded. His approval of new and aggressive interrogation techniques would produce devastating consequences.

That these consequences should flow from so innocuous an act was a fact Mr. Rumsfeld did not foresee because he probably never turned his mind to the possibility. He was handed a modest sheaf of papers, on the

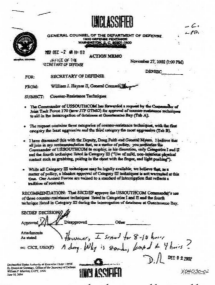

The Haynes memo, signed and annotated by Donald Rumsfeld.

top of which was placed a single sheet, an "Action Memo," headed "Counter-Resistance Techniques." It had been drafted a few days earlier by William J. Haynes II, the General Counsel at the Defense Department. Jim Haynes, trained at Harvard Law School, was Donald Rumsfeld's most senior lawyer, and one of his closest and most trusted advisers. On September 11, 2001 they had spent the entire day together. The Haynes memo was addressed only to Rumsfeld, and copied to just two colleagues. One was General Richard Myers, the Chairman of the Joint Chiefs of Staff and the most senior military official in the United States, a genial and unassuming man known to his friends as Dick. The other was Doug Feith, Under Secretary of Defense for Policy and number three at the Department, after Rumsfeld and Paul Wolfowitz. He was a lightning rod for military discontent and the military did not regard him as genial.

Attached to the memorandum was a paper trail of four short documents.[2] First was a legal opinion written by Lieutenant Colonel Diane Beaver, a Staff Judge Advocate at Guantánamo. Second, a request for approval of the new methods of interrogating detainees from Beaver's boss, reservist Major General Mike Dunlavey, the Army head of interrogation at Guantánamo whose regular job was as a judge in Erie, Pennsylvania. The third document was a memorandum from General Tom Hill, Commander of U.S. Southern Command (SOUTHCOM, as it is known, has responsibility for all U.S. military activities in South America and Central America) and next up in Dunlavey's chain of command; Hill was looking for new and lawful tools of interrogation. Last and most important was a list of eighteen techniques of interrogation, set out in a three-page memorandum from Lieutenant Colonel Jerald Phifer.

These techniques were new to the military, which didn't "do" aggression or cruelty by way of interrogations. They were accompanied by limited instructions: the detainee was to be provided with a chair, the environment should be generally comfortable; if the detainee was uncooperative, the detainee went to Category I, characterized by two techniques, yelling and deception. If Category I produced no results the military interrogator could move to Category II, although additional permission was required from higher up the military chain of command. Category II included twelve techniques, aiming at humiliation and sensory deprivation. Stress positions, like standing, for a maximum of four hours. Falsified documents. Isolation for up to thirty days. Interrogation outside the standard interrogation booth. Deprivation of light and auditory stimuli. Hooding during transportation and questioning. Twenty-hour interrogations. Removal of religious and all other comfort items. Switching away from hot rations to "meals, ready-to-eat" (MREs). Removal of clothing. Forced grooming, such as shaving of facial hair. And the use of individual phobias, like fear of dogs, to induce stress.

Finally, Category III. These methods were to be used for only a very small percentage of detainees—the most uncooperative (said to be less than 3 percent) and exceptionally resistant individuals and required approval by the Commanding General at Guantánamo, with a legal review and information to be sent to the SOUTHCOM Commander in Miami. In this category were four techniques: the use of "mild, non-injurious physical contact," like grabbing, poking and light pushing; the use of scenarios designed to convince the detainee that death or severely painful consequences were imminent for him or his family; exposure to cold weather or water; and, finally, the use of a wet towel and dripping water to induce the misperception of suffocation. This last technique came to be known as water-boarding, described by Vice President Cheney as a "dunk in the water" and a "no-brainer" if it could save lives.[3]

The documents detailing these techniques said nothing about limits on their use over time. Nor did they preclude the use of two or more techniques simultaneously. The Haynes memo recommended "blanket approval" of fifteen of the eighteen techniques, including just one of the four techniques listed in Category III: mild non-injurious physical contact. However, he did not reject the others, nor did he advise that they were excessive or illegal, or contrary to the Geneva Conventions' prohibition on humiliation, cruelty and torture. On the contrary, he advised that "all Category III techniques may be legally available," though "as a matter of policy, a blanket approval of Category III techniques is not warranted at this time." Blanket approval could come later.

Jim Haynes's memo gave no hint that the techniques he was recommending went against long-standing U.S. military practice, and went far beyond what the *U.S. Army Field Manual 34–52*, the military interrogator's bible, allowed. He did not indicate that the techniques were inconsistent with Common Article 3 of the Geneva Conventions, prohibiting cruel or inhumane treatment, and he did not indicate that the application of aggressive interrogation techniques at Guantánamo had already attracted strong objections from some of the interrogators there. By the time Haynes sent his memo to Donald Rumsfeld, the FBI had expressed concerns to Haynes's office, down the corridor from Rumsfeld.

Haynes's memo adopted a format with which the U.S. Secretary of Defense would have been familiar. It gave Rumsfeld three options: approve, disapprove, other. But if the Secretary had looked carefully at the document he would have picked up hints that this was no usual document. It wasn't signed by the Chairman of the Joint Chiefs of Staff, General Richard Myers, and it hadn't been subject to a broader process of consultation. Whether that gave Rumsfeld pause for thought or not, it didn't stop him from signing his name firmly next to the word "Approved," and adding his comment at the bottom of the page: "I stand for 8–10 hours a day. Why is standing limited to 4 hours?"

Signed and approved, the Haynes memo was communicated by secure route to General Hill at SOUTHCOM in Miami. From there it went orally to Major General Geoffrey Miller, the man who replaced Major General Mike Dunlavey as Commander of the Joint Task Force at Guantánamo a month after Dunlavey's request. This was the same Miller who would later achieve notoriety for his role at Abu Ghraib.

When the Haynes memo reached Guantánamo on December 2, Detainee 063 was in an isolated, plywood interrogation booth at Camp

X-Ray, the most secure and secret of the various Guantánamo sites. He was bolted to the floor and secured to a chair, his hands and legs cuffed. The new techniques were to be applied to him, starting with twenty hours of continuous interrogation, every day, and just four hours of sleep. Detainee 063 had been separated from all other detainees and put in isolation on August 8, nearly four months earlier. He was dehydrated and in need of regular hook-ups to an intravenous drip to give him liquid replenishment. His feet were swollen, he was constipated and forced to take enemas. He urinated on himself. He watched a video of the events of 9/11, with the volume turned up loud, very loud. Pictures of 9/11 victims were taped to the walls of the interrogation room, and to his body. The air conditioning system was being turned on and off to vary the temperature. A German shepherd dog named Zeus kept close watch. The interrogators told Detainee 063 that the "onion strategy" would be applied to him. He would be stripped of all control over his life, layer by layer by layer.

On December 2, 2002 a new phase in the aggressive interrogation of Detainee 063 was inaugurated. Over the next six weeks every one of the aggressive interrogation techniques recommended by Jim Haynes and approved by Secretary Rumsfeld was used. Occasionally he would get a treat, like a Hostess cupcake.

Then the interrogation would resume. After the end of the interrogation process he had, as one senior military officer later described it, "black coals for eyes."[4]

2

Detainee 063 was captured in Afghanistan in November 2001, in circumstances that were unclear. In January 2002 he joined the first captives to be transported to Guantánamo, one individual in a group labeled by the Administration as "the worst of the worst."[1] These Guantánamo detainees were so dangerous, said General Myers, that that they would "gnaw hydraulic lines in the back of a C-17 [aircraft] to bring it down."[2] Within days of arriving Detainee 063 was being interrogated by the U.S. military and the FBI. "The faster we can interrogate these people and identify them," said Rumsfeld, "and get what they have in them out of them, in as graceful a way as is possible, we have a better chance of saving some people's lives."[3]

Getting out of Detainee 063 what was in him, assuming it was there at all, proved troublesome. To begin, the interrogation followed established practices for military interrogations, and for law enforcement interrogations. The object of the military interrogations was simple: to get intelligence for use in the war on terror, to protect America from the next attack. The FBI's law enforcement interrogations went on in parallel, but with a different purpose: to obtain evidence to be used in criminal proceedings. Despite the different objectives, both sets of interrogation shared common characteristics premised on a key principle: interrogation only produces results if rapport is created between the interrogator and the detainee, a recognition of the fact that you are more likely to get something meaningful out of somebody if they feel okay around you. It's an application of a broader life principle. For five decades this principle dominated U.S. military interrogation techniques.

Building rapport is the overriding aim of the *U.S. Army Field Manual 34–52*, the rulebook for the military interrogators at Guantánamo. Colloquially referred to as *FM 34–52*, its subtitle was "Intelligence Interrogation."

Published by the U.S. Army Intelligence Centre at Fort Huachuca in Arizona, it was widely available on the Internet. It set out four key propositions. One: any interrogation has to have a specific purpose. Two: it must be based on rapport. Three: every detainee has a breaking point, although it is not usually known until it has been reached. Four: susceptibility to interrogation diminishes with the passage of time. These principles drove Detainee 063's initial interrogations

FM 34–52 was intended to be comprehensive, covering all aspects of human intelligence gathering, known as HUMINT. It applies to all humans. Well, all non-U.S. humans. It doesn't matter whether you are an enemy prisoner of war, or a civilian, or a terrorist, or a man, or a woman, or a Muslim, Jew, Christian, or atheist. It applied even to insurgents, fighters who posed particular difficulties because they did not wear uniforms or other recognizable insignia and didn't follow the rules. FM 34–52 was crystal clear about this. Updated in 1992, FM 34–52 took interrogation into the twenty-first century, building on the experience of the 1991 Gulf War. The goal was to obtain reliable information in a minimum amount of time. Reliability was key. So was legality. For FM 34–52 legality meant operating in accordance with the rules set out in the U.S. military's Uniform Code of Military Justice and international law, in particular the four Geneva Conventions.

Even a casual glance at FM 34–52 reveals the influence of the Geneva Conventions. These international instruments had a long but difficult pedigree, and no country had done more to put them in place or respect them than the United States. The Geneva Conventions were agreed to in 1949 as part of the post–World War Two settlement to create a new rules-based global order. The Bush Administration often referred to them collectively as "Geneva." Geneva aimed to limit the horrors of war by setting minimum standards that everyone had to follow. At its heart lay "Common Article 3," so called because it appeared in each of the four conventions. It reflected the most fundamental of Geneva's rules, requiring anyone who was not taking an active part in hostilities to be treated humanely, in all circumstances. All circumstances meant what it said. Anyone meant anyone. Some acts were considered so heinous that they were expressly prohibited by Common Article 3. They included cruel treatment and torture, as well as "outrages upon personal dignity," in particular.[4] That meant no humiliating and degrading treatment.

The general rule of Common Article 3 was elaborated in the individual conventions. The Third Geneva Convention was specifically addressed to prisoners of war. They had to be treated humanely, at all times (article 13). They had to be protected against acts of violence or intimidation and against insults and public curiosity. They were entitled to respect for their persons and their honor, in all circumstances (article 14). And famously, upon questioning, prisoners of war were bound to give only their name and rank, date of birth, and army, regimental, personal or serial number, or equivalent information (article 17). Any form of torture or cruelty was expressly forbidden (article 88).

There was no doubt that Common Article 3 constrained interrogations. Indeed, any act on a detainee that amounted to torture, inhuman treatment, or that caused great suffering or serious injury to body or health was considered to be so serious that it would be treated as a "grave breach" of Geneva. The person who violates Common Article 3 is an international outlaw, liable to prosecution in many parts of the world. There are no exceptions to the customary rule reflected in Common Article 3, not even necessity or national security.

FM 34–52 reflected a strong and modern commitment by the U.S. military to apply these international rules of law. Until September 11 no one thought *FM 34–52* was quaint or obsolete. It reflected the finest traditions of valor, to borrow President Bush's phrase. It prohibited the use of force, meaning all acts of violence or intimidation, including "physical or mental torture, threats, insults, or exposure to inhuman treatment as a means of or aid to interrogation." These were illegal acts that would not be condoned by the U.S. military. The rationale for the blanket prohibition was simple. Prohibited interrogation techniques weren't necessary. They yielded unreliable results. They damaged subsequent collection efforts. Experience showed that they induced the source to say "what he thinks the interrogator wants to hear."[5] Such acts discredited the United States and undermined the war effort. They risked placing American detainees in enemy hands at a greater risk of abuse. That was what *FM 34–52* said. And, to avoid any doubt, *FM 34–52* made it clear that the barbarity of the enemy did not justify using illegal methods.

These principles governed the interrogation of Detainee 063 for his first few months at Guantánamo. Its strictures were followed. But after June 2002 the tactics changed, most dramatically on November 23. The log of

Detainee 063's interrogation, an incomplete version of which first appeared in *Time* magazine,[6] described a process of aggressive interrogations over a period of fifty-one days, from November 23, 2002 until January 11, 2002. On November 27 Jim Haynes signed off on his memo. That was Day 5. On December 2 Secretary Rumsfeld gave his written approval to the Haynes memo. That was Day 10 of the aggressive interrogation. In unwitting celebration of the dark event that took place thousands of miles away in Washington, the lead interrogator placed a party hat on Detainee 063's head and offered him a birthday cake. He and the other interrogators sang "God Bless America." The interrogation log described what happened in the forty-eight hours immediately after Rumsfeld signed the Haynes memo.

Detainee 063 was woken at 4 A.M. on December 3, after four hours of sleep. The first interrogation session lasted from 4.25 A.M. until 6.15 A.M. There were two themes, one referred to as "circumstantial evidence" and the other as "you are a failure." Their names speak for themselves, but didn't have much effect. According to the log, Detainee 063 was attentive but unresponsive. After a fifteen-minute exercise break, during which he drank water, a second session began. They ran the "you have no control" approach, which lasted for an hour and a half until 8 A.M. Detainee 063 was then offered a meal, which he refused. A third interrogation session began at 8.30 A.M. and ran for an hour. They had moved on to the "telling the truth" approach. At 9.30 A.M. the interrogators gave a class to a group of Military Police recruits in front of Detainee 063. They ran a puppet show satirizing his involvement with Al Qaeda. At 10.40 A.M. he was given a 20-minute nap. He was woken at 11 A.M. and given a short exercise.

A new group of interrogators took over at 11.20 A.M. They attempted to calm Detainee 063, who was described in the log as being "upset." At 12.15 P.M. he refused water. At 12.35 P.M. he was offered lunch, which he also refused. Interrogations continued until 4 P.M., when he was allowed a nap. By then he had drunk nothing for twelve hours, and not eaten for more than twenty. He was woken at 8 P.M. and told he was being taken to Cuba. He was hooded and loaded into an ambulance. The ambulance was driven a few feet. He was taken out and put in a different interrogation booth. Another interrogator took over, dressed in civilian clothes and assisted by a female translator. At 8.40 P.M. Detainee 063 was again hooded and moved to another interrogation booth. This one was bathed in red lighting and decorated with photographs of 9/11 victims and U.S. and coalition flags. Loud music was played for twenty minutes. At 9 P.M. the hood was removed and the U.S. national anthem played. At 9.05 P.M. his head and beard were shaved with electric clippers. He resisted, so had to be restrained. He was photographed. At 9.30 P.M. a new interrogation session began, running the "bad Muslim" theme. At 11.45 P.M. he was again hooded, and at midnight taken to yet another interrogation booth. At 1 A.M. (now December 4) he was offered a meal and water that he initially refused. Five minutes later he changed his mind. He ate one MRE and drank water. According to the log, by this point he had not drunk for 19 hours, or eaten for 29 hours.

At 1.15 A.M. the interrogation resumed. Detainee 063 was told that his family was at risk. The interrogation log recorded that this caused him to feel confused and concerned. Fifteen minutes later he was hooded and taken back to the primary interrogation booth. Loud music was played and a photograph was shown of smoke pouring out of the Twin Towers, from which an image appeared to emerge showing a satanic face. At 3 A.M. he was exercised, and refused water. At 3.20 A.M. the "arrogant Saudi" approach was run. The log said this angered him. At 4 A.M. his cover story—coming to the United States to buy used cars—was mocked. He told his interrogator that he would not talk until properly interrogated. At 5.15 A.M. he complained about a picture of a 9/11 victim taped to his trousers. "I control all," the interrogator told him. At 7 A.M. he was permitted a short period of sleep.

He was woken at 11 A.M., and taken to another interrogation booth. At 12.30 P.M. he ate a single MRE and drank a bottle of water. At 1 P.M. he complained of dizziness. His vital signs were checked. Christina Aguilera's music was played. At 2.10 P.M. his vital signs were checked again. At 3.40 P.M. he refused water. The interrogation session now focused on "circumstantial evidence." At 5.40 P.M. a doctor checked his vital signs. He was becoming dehydrated. The doctor drew blood to check his kidney function. It was normal.

At 6 P.M. a new interrogation shift began. A medic inserted two intravenous (IV) tubes into his body. He complained about the presence and touch of a female, struggling to get out of his seat and the restraints. At 7 P.M. he refused water and food. By 10 P.M. he had been silent for two hours. An hour later he exercised, to reduce the swelling in his hands and feet. It was now December 5. At 12.25 A.M. he complained of tiredness. At 12.51

A.M. his hands were strung loosely above his head to reduce the swelling from an earlier IV. He was told to stand, to improve his circulation. He refused water. By now he had drunk nothing for nearly 13 hours. At 3.30 A.M. he was asked to stand up. He was then told to sit down in order for the interrogators to maintain control. At 4.20 A.M. he was allowed a 30-minute nap, as he was no longer able to stay awake during interrogation. He had not been permitted to sleep for seventeen hours. At 4.50 A.M. the interrogators took him over his cover story again. At 6 A.M. he was told to sit up straight. He did not comply, so the Military Police sat him upright. Then they made him stand and face the American flag while the national anthem was played. He resisted, and they physically sought to control him. At 7 A.M. his request to be allowed to pray was denied. He refused water and food. He said he was on strike. He was put to bed. He slept for four hours. The routine began again.

⎯◆⎯

These paragraphs summarize a two day period described over several pages of the interrogation log. They were Days 11 and 12 of Detainee 063's aggressive interrogation. That log went on to describe a further forty days. The pattern was always the same. Twenty-hour interrogation sessions, followed by four hours of sleep. Over the next six weeks new techniques were applied, taken from the list approved by Rumsfeld. Sleep deprivation appears as a central theme, along with stress positions and constant humiliation, including sexual humiliation. These techniques were supplemented by the use of water. Regular bouts of dehydration. The use of IVs. Loud noise and white noise. Nudity. Female contact. Humiliation with girly magazines. An interrogator even tied a leash to him, led him around the room and forced him to perform a series of dog tricks. He was forced to wear a woman's bra and a thong was placed on his head. And so on.

The log showed that members of the medical profession were involved directly and throughout the interrogation of Detainee 063. So were lawyers. At 9 P.M. on Day 47, for example, and at 6.40 P.M. on Day 50, the interrogation logs were reviewed by the Staff Judge Advocate of the Guantánamo Joint Task Force, whose job was to ensure that the Haynes memo and the rules approved by Rumsfeld were followed. That meant a military lawyer had reviewed and, presumably, signed off on the use of the interrogation techniques on this particular detainee.

FM *34–52,* the U.S. Army Field Manual, aimed to ensure that all interrogations complied with the law. The log of Detainee 063's interrogation described a process authorized by Rumsfeld that went well beyond what *FM 34–52* allowed. The manual of military interrogation takes a broad definition of what is prohibited, describing torture as "the infliction of intense pain to body or mind to extract a confession or information, or for sadistic pleasure." This adopts the definition of the 1984 Torture Convention, to which the United States is a party. *FM 34–52* provides various examples of torture. These are not limited to extreme acts, such as electric shock or the use of chemicals. Physical torture includes "any form of beating" food deprivation, and forcing an individual to stand, sit or kneel in abnormal positions for prolonged periods of time. *FM 34–52* describes abnormal sleep deprivation as a form of mental torture.

By putting his signature to a piece of paper on the morning of December 2, 2002, Donald Rumsfeld gravely changed the life of one man held at Guantánamo. It may or may not have made America a safer place. Worse, it may have opened the door to the migration of abuse to other places. The details of the Haynes memo remained secret for more than two years. They only emerged with revelations of other shocking acts many thousands of miles away, in Iraq.

INTERROGATION LOG OF DETAINEE 063
Day 14, December 6, 2002

1400: Detainee taken to bathroom and walked 10 minutes. Corpsman replaced ankle bandages to prevent chafing from cuffs. . . .

1930: Third shift interrogation team enters the booth. The approaches employed were . . . Invasion of Space by a Female. The detainee became very violent and irate. Detainee attempted to liberate himself from the chair in order to get away from the female. He struggled for approximately forty minutes attempting to move out of the presence of the female.

3

Donald Rumsfeld led the charge for war in Iraq, with the support of his deputy, Paul Wolfowitz, his head of policy, Doug Feith, and his lawyer, Jim Haynes. In part he did so because of Saddam's contempt for human life. "Torture is systematic in Iraq, and the most senior officials in the regime are involved," Rumsfeld said a few months before Saddam was overthrown. "Electric shock, eye gouging, acid baths, lengthy confinement in small metal boxes are only some of the crimes committed by this regime."[1] He spoke those words one day after secretly signing the Haynes memo and approving his own techniques of aggressive interrogation at Guantánamo. Ironically, it was the Iraq War that brought the Haynes memo into the open.

In April 2003 Saddam was removed from power. Paul Bremer was eventually installed as head of the Coalition Provisional Authority, reporting directly to Rumsfeld. One of Bremer's responsibilities was the Abu Ghraib prison, located about twenty miles west of Baghdad, and thousands of miles from Guantánamo. It was known as the Baghdad Central Confinement Facility, the site of horrendous abuses by Saddam's henchmen, including torture and executions.

By the autumn of 2003 Abu Ghraib was being run by the United States as a detention facility. From October, terrible abuses of Iraqi prisoners at Abu Ghraib were taking place, the full extent of which were kept secret from all but the highest authorities in the Pentagon, who failed to appreciate their significance. However on April 28, 2004 CBS's *60 Minutes* broadcast a television program that revealed the nature and scale of the abuse. Photographs taken by U.S. military participants were published, including one, now notorious, showing a prisoner standing on a box with his head covered and wires attached to his fingers and genitals. Another showed Private First Class Lynndie England holding a leash tied to the neck of a naked man on the floor. Yet others showed a terrified detainee cowering before naked dogs; a hooded detainee handcuffed in an awkward position on top of two boxes in a prison hallway; a soldier kneeling on naked detainees; a hooded detainee collapsed over railings to which he is handcuffed; and two soldiers posing over the body of Manadel al-Jamadi, a detainee allegedly beaten to death by the CIA or civilian interrogators in the prison's showers.

The photographs thus appeared to show systematic abuse by American interrogators at Abu Ghraib, and their publication unleashed an immediate and violent reaction. "A photograph is a secret about a secret," the photographer Diane Arbus once said. As Abu Ghraib's secrets were uncovered, the *Wall Street Journal* published an article about a classified Defense Department Working Group report on interrogation methods.[2] Hazy details about secret memos began to emerge; some documents and even legal advice were leaked; and the kernel of a suggestion began to germinate. Was there a connection between the abuses at Abu Ghraib and the Administration's own secret interrogation policies at other places, including Guantánamo?

The U.S. Administration struggled to respond. In May 2004, Paul Wolfowitz appeared before the Senate Armed Services Committee. The lawyers had looked at the interrogation techniques at Guantánamo, he said, and found them to be compliant with Geneva: "extreme care" was taken at Guantánamo, downplaying any connection that might be made between that place and what happened at Abu Ghraib. Guantánamo did not "explain the incredible abuses that took place in Iraq."[3] A few days later a visibly irritated Attorney General, John Ashcroft, appeared before the Senate Judiciary Committee. He was asked repeatedly about secret Pentagon and Justice Department memos on interrogation techniques, but the Committee were denied access to such documents. "The President has a right to receive advice from his Attorney General in confidence and so do other executive agencies of Government,"[4] Ashcroft argued.

A few days later President Bush hosted the annual G8 Summit in Savannah, Georgia. The "spread of freedom . . . is the imperative of our age," he proclaimed. But the media was not about to be quiescent—they were interested in torture, not inanities. Had Bush authorized any kind of interrogation techniques necessary to pursue the war on terror? No, he said, his authorization was that anything the United States did would conform to U.S. law and be consistent with international treaty obligations. "That's the message I gave our people."[5] Had he seen the legal memos, he was asked. "I can't remember but I gave those instructions," he replied, apparently referring to the treaties. The questions persisted. Had the lawyers at the Justice Department and the Pentagon worked out a way for U.S. officials to torture detainees without running foul of the law? Was torture ever justified? The President was evasive and clearly getting irritated. "Look, I'm going to say it one more time. If I—maybe—maybe I can be more clear. The instructions went out to our people to adhere to law. That ought to comfort you. We're a nation of law. We adhere to laws. We have laws on the books. You might look at those laws, and that might provide comfort for you. And those were the instructions out of—from me to the government."

The questioners were not comforted. The debate grew and the administration was now under intense pressure. Jobs were on the line, including Rumsfeld's. Four days later, the Administration did something unexpected: it declassified and released a number of documents relating to interrogation, including the Haynes memo and the four accompanying documents,[6] in the belief that this would reflect the thorough process of deliberation that, it was claimed, took place, and demonstrate a commitment to the rule of law.

At three o'clock on Tuesday, June 22, 2004, the President's legal adviser, White House Counsel Alberto Gonzales, purposefully entered a large room at the Eisenhower Executive Office building next to the White House. He was accompanied by Jim Haynes, Rumsfeld's General Counsel, a Harvard-trained lawyer who would sort this out. Haynes's deputy, Dan Dell'Orto, also joined them. Gonzales and Haynes were members of the self-styled "War Council," a tight-knit group of senior Administration lawyers that also included David Addington, who was Vice President Dick Cheney's lawyer, John Yoo from the Office of the Legal Counsel in the Justice Department, and Tim Flanigan, who was Gonzales's deputy.[7]

The role of the "War Council" was later described by Jack Goldsmith—who served as Haynes's Special Counsel from September 2002 until mid-2003—as being to "plot legal strategy in the war on terrorism." Meetings were held every few weeks in Gonzales's office at the White House, or in Haynes's office at the Department of Defense, prior to dealing with lawyers from the State Department, the National Security Council, and the Joint Chiefs of Staff. Sometimes the interagency process was excluded altogether.[8]

(top, left) Alberto Gonzales, Counsel to President George W. Bush

(top, right) William J. Haynes II, General Counsel to U.S. Secretary of Defense

(left) David Addington, General Counsel to Vice President Cheney

Alberto Gonzales was an American success story. From a humble Mexican immigrant background, he graduated from Harvard Law School. After a few years of private practice Texas Governor George W. Bush appointed him first as his General Counsel, then Texas Secretary of State, and then to the bench and the Texas Supreme Court. By 2001 his reliability made him the logical choice for White House Counsel: his role in public life depended on Bush—and everyone in the room knew it. For an hour and forty minutes Gonzales, Haynes and Dell'Orto briefed the press on the newly released documents. Scott Lindlaw of the Associated Press was amazed; he'd covered President Bush's reign at the White House from day one and had never seen anything like this. "Is it fair to assume you think you have an extraordinary public relations problem on your hands, is that why you're doing this?" he asked Gonzales.

Gonzales's reply was nuanced; everything he said was scripted.[9] He had to balance two objectives that weren't necessarily compatible: the Administration believed that releasing information would benefit the United States's enemies, but the suggestion that the United States allowed torture was also harmful. Meanwhile the deliberations between Gonzales, Haynes and Dell'Orto were clearly visible. Just two weeks earlier Attorney General John Ashcroft had refused the Senate Judiciary Committee's request for documents and now some had been released. Gonzales's response proceeded: the United States did not do torture; it acted with deliberation; everything was vetted; none of the approved interrogation techniques amounted to torture; yes, lawyers were asked to stargaze but the decisions taken were reasonable, restrained and lawful. Finally, there was no connection between Administration policy and Abu Ghraib.

Gonzales was nothing if not an advocate. Context is everything, as he and any courtroom lawyer knew—so he provided context. Al-Qaeda was a different kind of enemy, deadly and shadowy; it targeted civilians, and it didn't follow Geneva or any other international rules. The nature and scale of the threat was qualitatively different and so the Administration had decided to move away from a law-enforcement approach toward a strategy that marshaled "other elements." This was war. With this shift the Administration's lawyers faced new questions. What was the legal status of individuals caught in this war? How should they be treated and questioned? What were the rules? Curiously, Gonzales didn't explain why the Administration now believed that aggressive interrogation worked, or why FM 34–52 had been abandoned.

The newly released documents were not an easy sell. Gonzales divided them into two groups. The first group, which included the Haynes memo, reflected "actual decisions" taken by the President and senior officials. Two documents were crucial: the Haynes memo and a decision taken a few months earlier by the President, on February 7, 2002, documented in Tab A. This key decision by President Bush was that *none* of the detainees at Guantánamo, whether Taliban or al-Qaeda, could rely on any of the protections granted by Geneva, not even Common Article 3. This effectively created a legal black hole at Guantánamo.

Government lawyers generated the second set of documents—legal opinions intended only to explore "the limits of the legal landscape." And Gonzales went out of his way to downplay them: the opinions included "irrelevant and unnecessary" discussion that circulated only among lawyers and a few policymakers and so they didn't make it into the hands of soldiers in the field or to the President. Whilst interesting for lawyers, they could be put to one side. "They do not reflect the policies that the administration ultimately adopted," he said, referring to two opinions issued on August 1, 2002, both requested by him. One of these was written by Deputy Assistant Attorney General John Yoo of the Justice Department's Office of Legal Counsel and concluded that various techniques used to interrogate members of al-Qaeda did not violate the 1984 Torture Convention. The other had Assistant Attorney General Jay Bybee's name on it, although it was known his colleague John Yoo had co-written it. It concluded that physical torture occurred only when the pain was "equivalent in intensity to the pain accompanying serious physical injury, such as organ failure, impairment of bodily functions, or even death." Mental torture required "suffering not just at the moment of infliction but . . . lasting psychological harm, such as seen in mental disorder like post-traumatic stress disorder." The memo concluded that torture of suspected terrorists for interrogation would not be unlawful if it could be justified on grounds of necessity or self-defense.

Parts of these legal opinions had already been leaked. Gonzales knew they were dangerous for the Administration and had to be neutralized. But this was a job for Jim Haynes. Haynes had joined Rumsfeld as General Counsel in May 2001. He was a protégé and close friend of David Addington, Vice President Cheney's lawyer, with whom he worked closely in the previous Bush Administration, as General Counsel of the Army to Addington's General Counsel to Secretary of Defense Cheney. Like Addington he avoided publicity, and all the more since President Bush had recently nominated him for appointment as a judge on the 4th Circuit of the U.S. Court of Appeals. And like Addington, he left few tracks and gave almost no interviews. His presence at the press conference was therefore significant. The full authority of his office was brought in to support the Administration's narrative, emphasizing the vital need to get information necessary to protect the American people in a way that was lawful. Context was everything. Asked whether stress techniques and prolonged isolation constituted torture under American laws and treaties, Haynes did not rule out the possibility: "any one technique improperly applied could, you know, produce all sorts of undesirable consequences, including perhaps torture." But, he added, "the United States is not permitted to go near that."

Haynes reminded those present that Guantánamo had been set up to protect the American people and their allies from those who were trying to kill them; it was not about punishing criminals. Some people thought the approach wrong, he acknowledged, and wanted the detainees to be charged with a crime, or treated as prisoners of war, or released. He disagreed, however: this conflict was unique. Americans were being killed on a scale that amounted to warfare and therefore "other options" were needed, including aggressive interrogation. Like Gonzales, he said nothing about the utility of such techniques, or the consequences of discarding decades of military restraint, or the interrogation log of Detainee 063, which was not yet public. Haynes was also asked about the lawyers. He explained that their role in the development of interrogation policy was limited; he was not saying that a lawyer should step back and be austere and discuss only the law, but that a lawyer "must make the distinction between what the law is and what the policy is, and in certain cases, make recommendations—make clear what is what." His memo did just that.

The third lawyer at the briefing was Dan Dell'Orto, Haynes's deputy. Unlike the two others he was not a political appointee, having served previously in the Clinton Administration. He talked about Guantánamo as a strategic intelligence center, set up after September 11, 2001. The governing interrogation rules were set out in U.S. Army Field Manual 34–52, updated in 1992. They were designed for the interrogation of enemy prisoners of war who were lawful combatants, not the people picked up in Afghanistan who fought without following the rules of war. Those people were not in uniform and they didn't come with unit rosters, ID tags or anything to indicate where they fitted into al-Qaeda or the Taliban. It was therefore not possible to glean who they were or what information they had. (Dell'Orto's limited and erroneous interpretation of FM 34–52 went unchallenged by any journalist present.)

Dell'Orto went on to describe how the 10,000 individuals captured in Afghanistan had been reduced to the "select few" taken to Guantánamo, for "strategic intelligence-gathering." The first detainees were interrogated under FM 34–52, but by the summer of 2002 it was clear that some had been trained to resist these techniques. The United States had found al-Qaeda's own training manual, known as the "Manchester Manual," which included a chapter on resisting interrogation. (The manual was so named because it was said to have been found by the British police in Manchester, on the computer of an individual said to be an al-Qaeda member.)

By then "key people" had been identified at Guantánamo, including "a guy named al-Qahtani," who resisted traditional interrogation techniques. "And so it is concluded at Guantánamo," Dell'Orto said, "that it may be time

to inquire as to whether there may be more flexibility in the types of techniques we use on him." These innocuous words were significant: Dell'Orto
was pinning responsibility for the demand for "flexibility" squarely on the
people at Guantánamo; they were not imposed from the top. On October 11,
2002, Guantánamo generated a request that additional techniques beyond
those in FM 34-52 be approved for use against high-value detainees, most
specifically al-Qahtani. The request included a "multi-page, single-spaced
legal review supporting those techniques." On October 25 the Commander
of U.S. Southern Command, General Hill, forwarded the request to the Joint
Staff for review at the Pentagon, "during November." On December 2, 2002
Rumsfeld approved "all but three of the requested techniques": the most severe of those approved was "mild, non-injurious physical contact—poking,
grabbing, lightly shoving," which suggested how innocuous it all was.

The underlying message was spelled out: first, Rumsfeld had merely
responded to a request from Guantánamo and in doing so had acted reac-
tively and reasonably; second, the request came with a supporting "multi-
page, single-spaced legal review" written at Guantánamo; third, the request
was supported by General Hill, the Commander of Southern Command in
Miami—so the upper echelons of the military were on board; fourth, the
Pentagon wasn't involved until November. Dell'Orto was silent about anything that happened before October 11. And finally, the new techniques
authorized nothing more serious than poking, grabbing and light shoving.
Dell'Orto provided further reassurance: the request from Guantánamo
had included a detailed interrogation plan that outlined the military necessity for applying the new techniques of interrogation to al-Qahtani, the
way the techniques were to be employed, and the safeguards that would be
employed. That plan remained secret.

The facts were simple and compelling: they "set the record straight,"
said Gonzales, demonstrating a "thorough, deliberative process" and the
"great degree of care" that was inconsistent with torture. The abuses at
Abu Ghraib were unauthorized and unconnected to actual policies; they
had "nothing to do with the policies contained in these memos." The clar-
ity of the presentation was striking: Gonzales dealt with the documents,
Haynes dealt with the law, and Dell'Orto dealt with the facts. And the gaps
were not immediately apparent.

That narrative remained constant. Two years later, in the summer of
2006, Jim Haynes appeared before Senate Judiciary Committee, hoping to be
confirmed as a judge on the 4th Circuit. His opening statement was a reprise
of the message delivered in the aftermath of Abu Ghraib. He'd endeavored to

develop appropriate guidelines for questioning terrorists who held information critical to protecting the United States. Detainee 063 had frustrated the interrogators, causing Haynes and many others to struggle over the question of interrogation techniques.[11] Repeatedly he implied that his involvement did not begin until November 2002, no earlier. From the beginning and at all times the rules had been clear: "even the terrorists must be treated humanely and we must operate within the law as best we see it." He had simply responded to a request from "an aggressive Major General" at Guantánamo,[12] which had been accompanied by "a concurring legal opinion of his Judge Advocate." This now put Mike Dunlavey and Diane Beaver center stage in the decision-making process. Eventually, he had joined General Myers, Doug Feith and Paul Wolfowitz in recommending that some of the requested techniques be approved and that "the more extreme ones be rejected." But again, the whole thing had come from the bottom up. It was not imposed by Donald Rumsfeld or anyone else at the Pentagon.

It was clear that every word spoken by Haynes was carefully parsed—there was no room for spontaneity. His speech was mechanical and strained, cautious and evasive. Unspecified concerns had come to his attention after the memo had been signed. Without specifying dates, he said that he had alerted Rumsfeld and the senior leadership and sought assurances that the interrogations were being properly conducted.[13] In early January 2003 he had asked Rumsfeld to rescind.[14] He referred to onerous duties and he took his responsibility for his part in them. Except that it didn't really look as though he did. As the session went on, Haynes's performance became ever more evasive. He swatted away questions about who else had given legal advice, but looked tense. He was equally slippery on the eighteen techniques of interrogation: he didn't recommend any techniques that were "cruel, inhuman or degrading." But he was not convincing.

This was certainly a less confident performance than in June 2004. Yet on both occasions there were points that nagged away. Lawyers are advocates, trained to present stories: their job is to make the complex appear uncomplicated. In June 2004 Haynes, Gonzales and Dell'Orto sought to persuade, and mostly they succeeded. Yet their accounts exposed bigger questions. The Geneva Conventions were not being applied to any detainees at Guantánamo and the U.S. military's long-established constraints on cruelty and torture, dating back to President Lincoln in 1863, were being circumvented. For a start, there was the President's decision on February 7, 2002, on the applicability of Geneva to the detainees at Guantánamo. Was it connected to Rumsfeld's later decision on the interrogation techniques? There were clear gaps in the narrative. And then there were the legal opinions of Jay Bybee and John Yoo in August 2002. Gonzales said they merely defined the outer limits of the legal landscape and did not reflect the policies actually implemented. Was there really no connection between legal advice that had set the bar to torture so very high, and the decision just a few weeks later to discard the constraints on interrogation imposed by *FM 34–52*?

And there was the Haynes memo itself, with the four short attachments: the list of new interrogation techniques; Dunlavey's request; Beaver's legal advice, the "multi-page, single-spaced legal review"; and the cautious request from General Hill. Did Haynes really advise the Secretary to sign off on the basis of legal advice from Diane Beaver, the relatively inexperienced lawyer at Guantánamo?

Like everyone else, I first saw these documents in June 2004. For a year or two they festered; something wasn't right about this document trail. The lawyers had too big a role in the story and, moreover, they were all civilian lawyers who were political appointees and close to the President, not military lawyers. By the time Haynes faced the Senate Judiciary Committee two years later, in July 2006, gaps in the story were too large to ignore. In March 2006, *Time* magazine published the interrogation log of Detainee 063 on its website. Some of the Abu Ghraib images bore a resemblance to what Detainee 063 had been through: humiliation, stress, hooding, nudity, female interrogators, shackles, dogs. Was this just a coincidence? A reflection of the limits of the human imagination? Or was there another, more sinister, reason for the similarities?

In the autumn of 2006 I caught a cold, and spent a day in bed. I chanced across an old Oscar-winning movie that I hadn't seen for a very long time.

INTERROGATION LOG OF DETAINEE 063
Day 15, December 7 2002

001: Detainee made to stand for the National Anthem. . . . Detainee taken to porch where he can see foraging banana rats. . . .

[Military Police] 0120: Issues arise between MPs [Military Police] and dog handler. . . .

0350: Vitals show dehydration is beginning. Detainee was given an IV [intravenous drip] by corpsman. Detainee was told that we would not allow him to die. . . .

1100: Schedule is given to MPs to . . . keep music playing to prevent detainee from sleeping . . . detainee's pulse is unusually slow. . . . Heartbeat is regular but very slow—35 bpm. Decision is made to take detainee to GTMO hospital to perform a CT scan of the detainee's brain to see if there are any irregularities. . . .

2330: Doctors review scan and do not find any conclusive evidence of any conditions.

4

I first watched *Judgment at Nuremberg* (1961) many years ago. In 2006, as the credits came up on the screen I had a dim recollection of the impression it had made at that first viewing, not just because of the quality of the performances but also because the story was so compelling: how ordinary, decent people sometimes cross lines, and how lawyers educated at the finest law schools can give warped legal advice. How legal advice can lead to abuse.

The film tells the story of the prosecution at Nuremberg of a group of lawyers for complicity in crimes committed by the German state. Spencer Tracy stars as the American Chief Justice of the tribunal. Burt Lancaster is lead defendant Dr. Ernst Janning, a former Nazi judge. There are memorable cameo appearances from Marlene Dietrich, as Spencer Tracy's near love interest, and Montgomery Clift as a lead prosecution witness, a banker who was sterilized under Nazi social laws. *Judgment at Nuremberg* was the fictionalized account of real cases that the United States had brought against sixteen senior lawyers in the Nazi regime. The aim of those cases—with the official title of *United States v. Josef Altstötter and others* (1947), better known as the "Justice Cases"—was to make an example of one group of professionals who created the legal framework for atrocities to occur. The lawyers had designed the laws, applied them, and enforced them. In real life, Brigadier General Telford Taylor was the driving force behind the cases, wanting to make an example of the lawyers. Chief Prosecutor at Nuremberg, he later became a leading American constitutional lawyer, teaching at Columbia Law School.

The scale of the atrocity described in the Justice Cases was staggering and cannot be compared with what apparently happened at Guantánamo or Abu Ghraib. I felt uncomfortable even making that kind of comparison, but what struck me as a point of connection was the underlying issue of principle: the idea that lawyers, as the guardians of constitutionality and legality, have a special responsibility to ensure that rules of law are protected. Telford Taylor wanted to emphasize that special responsibility (a theme that is alluded to in Marcel Ophüls's classic 1976 film, *The Memory of Justice,* which should be reqired viewing but has never been commercially released). The charge, as prosecutor Charles LaFollette put it in his opening statement on behalf of Taylor in the real case, was that men who had been leaders of the German legal system had "consciously and deliberately suppressed the law" and contributed to crimes, including torture, that "were committed in the guise of legal process." "Men of law," the prosecutor told the Nuremburg judges, "can no more escape . . . responsibility by virtue of their judicial robes than the general by his uniform."[1] In his closing arguments prosecutor LaFollette summarized the various bases for individual responsibility. One of them was that the defendants "administered legislation which they must be held to have known was in violation of international law."[2] Those words rang a bell.

In the Justice Cases, Taylor and LaFollette affirmed the principle of complicity, and its application to lawyers. In the fictionalized film the principle is taken a step further. "How easily it can happen," says the Spencer Tracy character of the judge, announcing the tribunal's guilty verdict for Ernst Janning. "There are those in our country too who speak of the 'protection of country,' of survival," he says by way of warning. "A decision must be made in the life of every nation at the very moment when the grasp of the enemy is at its throat. Then, it seems that the only way to survive is to use the means of the enemy, to rest survival upon what is expedient, to look the other way."[3]

Spencer Tracy's words bore some resemblance to the arguments that Gonzales and Haynes had made in June 2004 to justify the aggressive new techniques of interrogation. I went back to the transcript to remind myself precisely what they had said. The United States faced a "unique circumstance," said Jim Haynes. The new techniques needed to be seen against the context of "the extraordinary war we are in," involving a new kind of enemy whose "training manual spends an extraordinary amount of time talking about how to resist interrogation." The United States needed "to know what's coming to protect the American people." It had to consider the values it held dear and the standards it wanted to uphold. And it had to consider "the type of information that we were seeking to derive and try to get that." Necessity justifies all. Anything goes in the quest for national security.

I did a bit more ferreting around. I wanted to know more about the lawyers who had contributed to the decision to justify new interrogation techniques at Guantánamo that were so plainly inconsistent with international rules. The starting point seemed to be President Bush's decision on Geneva in February 2002, which was a major policy decision. Doug Feith was Rumsfeld's Undersecretary of Defense for Policy at the Pentagon—and also a lawyer. I thought I would start with him.

INTERROGATION LOG OF DETAINEE 063
Day 18, December 10 2002

0400: Lead established control over detainee by instructing him not to speak and enforcing by playing loud music and yelling. . . .

1930: Medical Representative weighed detainee and logged detainee's weight at 119 pounds. . . .

2230: Detainee urinated on himself as he was being taken to latrine.

THE PATH

(left) Doug Feith, Undersecretary of Defense for Policy

(below) Doug Feith and Jim Haynes at U.S. Department of Defense press briefing, March 21 2002

5

It is always good to begin with the actual documents. In his memo Jim Haynes wrote that he consulted three people; one was Doug Feith. Once written, the memo was then copied to two people: again, Feith was one.

⚬

Back in 2002 Doug Feith was number three in the Pentagon. As Undersecretary of Defense for Policy his job was to provide the U.S. Secretary of Defense with policy advice that was "responsive, forward-thinking, and insightful." It was difficult to think of many policy decisions that the greatest military power in the world might consider more carefully than one limiting the application of the Geneva Conventions.

When I met Feith he had left Bush's Administration, having served for four years until August 2005. He had been intimately involved in the big decisions, and had achieved some notoriety for his role in preparing the intelligence in the run-up to the Iraq War. He was a high-profile public figure and there was no shortage of interviews, quotes, photos and profiles. He regularly expressed strong political views, especially in support of Israel. In the media he was colorful and controversial. He also had a clearly defined sense of his place in the historical moment immediately following September 11. "I want to be in the class of people who did the right thing, the sensible thing, and not necessarily the fashionable thing, the thing that met the aesthetic of the moment," he told the *New Yorker* magazine.[1]

Some observers have referred to his acute intelligence. Rumsfeld described him as an "intellectual engine"[2] and at Feith's farewell event, he invoked the words of President Theodore Roosevelt. "Aggressive fighting for the right is the noblest sport the world affords." However, Rumsfeld said nothing on that occasion about Feith's role in the new interrogation rules for Guantánamo. And not everyone had always been so complimentary. General Tommy Franks led the wars in Afghanistan and Iraq and it was he who pushed for detainees to be sent from Afghanistan to Guantánamo, working closely with Feith. He reportedly described Feith as "the fucking stupidest guy on the face of the earth."[3]

⊷⊶

I first came across Feith's name in the mid-1980s when he served in Ronald Reagan's Administration. He'd published an article entitled "Law in the Service of Terror" in the inaugural issue of a conservative publication, *The National Interest*.[4] His piece was a passionate, no-holds-barred diatribe against certain provisions of a 1977 Protocol to supplement the rules of the 1949 Geneva Conventions, on the treatment of POWs. The object of Feith's ire was the new rules that gave legal protection to fighters who "cannot" distinguish themselves from the civilian population "owing to the nature of the hostilities" (this was a reference to guerrilla warfare and included the wars of national liberation that were plentiful in the 1970s). Feith believed that the Protocol was "a masterstroke of amoral draftsmanship": it was malign and perverse, a sinister prostitution of the law and would cause untold harm to the victims of war and terrorism. Feith objected to rules of international law that gave rights and legitimacy—any legitimacy—to terrorists. He believed in incentives. If everybody had rights under Geneva, irrespective of whether they followed the rules, then any incentive to follow them would fall away. I remembered the piece because it was unusually colorful for a dry and academic subject.

After leaving the Pentagon in 2005 Feith was appointed to the School of Foreign Service at Georgetown University. This generated controversy, with some faculty members objecting to his stance on interrogations and Geneva. He rejected these accusations as "flatly false" and "outrageous," unfounded charges that were frequently repeated to his detriment.[5] My visit to his office in the University's Intercultural Center provided an opportunity for clarification. His new surroundings on the eighth floor were not glamorous—the elevators only reached the floor below. Feith was well hidden away, but eventually I found him perched at the top of the building, out of harm's way, occupying the kind of small book-lined space usually reserved for distinguished short-term visitors from abroad. Many of the books on his shelves dealt with international law, reflecting a long-term interest. He greeted me with a smile, an impish face under a large mop of graying hair belying his age, early fifties.

Feith had phenomenal energy: he was like one of those bunnies running on Duracell batteries and it was difficult to get a word in edgeways. He had a clear agenda and a strong commitment to international law and the Geneva Conventions, as well as his incentive argument. By the time we reached the issues I was interested in, Feith had provided me with a detailed account of his historical battles on the Protocol to the Geneva Conventions and other great international legal wrongs, like the Anti-Ballistic Missile Treaty. Happily, our agendas converged on Geneva. He was keen to talk about his role as the architect of President Bush's decision of February 7, 2002. He didn't buy the argument that the decision had had the effect of casting the detainees into a great legal black hole. On the contrary, the President's decision was actually a strike for the Geneva Conventions and for international law. "This was something I played a major role in," he said with pride.

I had already learned from another former Pentagon official that the Geneva decision didn't come out of the blue. In December 2001 the U.S. Central Command started capturing Taliban and al-Qaeda personnel in Afghanistan. CENTCOM proceeded on the basis that Geneva applied, an approach that governed the initial treatment of detainees like John Walker Lindh (the U.S. national who was Detainee 001) and David Hicks (the Australian who was 002). There were objections, however, to the application of Geneva, from Rumsfeld and Haynes, as well as from the Vice President and his counsel, David Addington and Alberto Gonzales. The "War Council" was flexing its muscles. Even at this early stage, the most senior lawyer at the Defense Department was involved in decisions on individual detainees. Lindh was being held at Mazar-e-Sharif, and the American Admiral in charge told the JAG officer that the Secretary of Defense's counsel, Jim Haynes, had authorized him "to 'take the gloves off' and ask whatever he wanted."[6]

The issue of Geneva's applicability went to the Office of Legal Counsel at the Justice Department, where John Yoo and Robert Delahunty prepared an opinion for Jim Haynes. Their draft memo of January 9, 2002 concluded that Geneva didn't apply to al-Qaeda or Taliban detainees.[7] On January 19, with Haynes's support, Rumsfeld directed a decision to General Myers determining that neither the Taliban nor al-Qaeda were entitled to POW status, but that they should be treated humanely and, to the extent appropriate to military necessity, in a manner consistent with

Geneva.[8] Myers forwarded the decision to Guantánamo. The military service lawyers—the TJAGs—were not consulted. "Don't bring the TJAGs into the process, they aren't reliable," David Addington was overheard to say, according to General Romig, the former Army TJAG. When they did find out about the decision they were not impressed. "A ridiculous decision," General Romig told me.

Rumsfeld's decision encountered strong opposition from Colin Powell and his lawyer, Will Taft, at the State Department. On January 25, Alberto Gonzales put his name to a memo to President Bush that supported Haynes and Rumsfeld over Powell and Taft, motivated in large part by fear of war crimes prosecutions. This infamous memo described the war against terrorism as "a new kind of war" and a "new paradigm" that showed Geneva's "strict limitations on questioning of enemy prisoners" to be "obsolete" and even "quaint."[9] A White House lawyer with direct knowledge told the *Washington Post* that the memo was actually written by Vice President Cheney's lawyer, David Addington, not by Gonzales.[10] A former White House official told me that he doubted whether Gonzales fully understood the complexities of the issues. He did recognize, however, that without Geneva in the frame the threat of domestic criminal proceedings in the United States under the War Crimes Act would be substantially reduced.[11]

Feith told me that Powell had an ally in General Myers, the Chairman of the Joint Chiefs of Staff. In late January 2002 Feith and Myers went to meet Rumsfeld to talk about Geneva. Before they got to Rumsfeld's office, Myers turned to him. With fire in his eyes he said: "We have to support the Geneva Conventions . . . if Rumsfeld doesn't go along with this, I'm gonna contradict them in front of the President." Feith was amazed. It was an unusually tough statement, and the reference to the Secretary as "Rumsfeld" was uncharacteristic. As they approached Rumsfeld's office he was at the door, not wanting to let them into the room as he had other matters to attend to. Myers was grilled by Rumsfeld, who asked questions but didn't adopt any position. Rumsfeld was "more of a lawyer than most lawyers when it comes to precision and questions," a stickler for the law who constantly invoked the Constitution and statutes, Feith reported.

As Rumsfeld fired his bullets at Myers, Feith described how he jumped protectively in front of Myers. He paused and looked me straight in the eye, "I gave a little speech—I remember—I often don't remember what I said in meetings—but this I remembered. This was an interesting moment." This was how he put it:

"There is no country in the world that has a larger interest in promoting respect for the Geneva Conventions as law than the United States, and there is no institution in the U.S. government that has a stronger interest than the Pentagon." And then I said something else that was kind of interesting to them: "Obeying the Geneva Conventions is not optional. The U.S. Constitution says there are two things that are the supreme law of the land—statutes and treaties." He said, "Yeah." And I said, "The Geneva Conventions are a treaty in force. It is as much part of the supreme law of the United States as a statute." You could see that that put a completely different color on it. In other words, to say to Rumsfeld, "This is the law"—that ends the conversation. Rumsfeld obeys the laws. Myers then chimed in and added his point. He [Myers] said, "I agree completely with what Doug said and furthermore it is our military culture." And then he said: "We train our people to obey the Geneva Conventions, it's not even a matter of whether it is reciprocated—it's a matter of who we are."

I was impressed, but how had they gone from that discussion to the decision that none of the detainees had any rights under the rules reflected in Geneva? Feith seemed surprised by my question and went on to explain. Rumsfeld had asked him to turn his little speech into a brief for President Bush. That too had never happened before. Feith became increasingly animated as he told me the story. In his view, Geneva didn't apply at all to Al Qaeda fighters, because they weren't part of a state and so couldn't claim rights under a treaty that was only binding on states. Geneva did apply to the Taliban, but by Geneva's own terms Taliban fighters weren't entitled to POW status because they hadn't worn uniforms or insignia. "I said we should not be worming out, wiggling out, of the applicability of the Geneva Conventions to the conflict," he explained. "So the argument that I made in this memo was that . . . we needed to say that the Geneva Conventions applied as a matter of law to the conflict with the Taliban," but "what I thought was . . . also important, is the Taliban fighters are not entitled to POW status under the Geneva Conventions." He referred again to the incentive system that was built into the Geneva Conventions, providing the greatest protection to non-combatants and the least protection to "fighters who don't obey the rules." "If we promiscuously hand out POW status to fighters who don't obey the rules," Feith offered, "you are undermining the incentive system that was wisely built into the Geneva Conventions." This was at least arguable, I thought. But what should have been left was the safety net provided by the principles reflected in Common Article 3, including the prohibition on abusive interrogation. But that too went: none of the detainees could rely on Common Article 3 since its provisions only applied to "armed conflicts not of an international character." To reach this conclusion, which also removed the protections of customary law, required a departure from long-standing practice that treated the rules reflected in Common Article 3 as a minimum that applied to everyone, in all conflicts. Feith might have looked to the official commentary to Geneva ("The scope of the Article must be as wide as possible") and numerous judgments of the World Court and international criminal tribunals ("There is no doubt that, in the event of an international armed conflict, these rules also constitute a minimum yardstick"). But he didn't. The upshot was that no one at Guantánamo was entitled to protection under any of the rules re-flected in Geneva. Feith's logic was that to allow any detainees to rely on Geneva's protections would have been to undermine their very objective. "That's what the President decided," Feith concluded, "and so as far as I was concerned, that was a success and my memo specifically addressed those . . . points and the President agreed with us."

His memo caused the other approaches to the Geneva decision to be set aside by the President, including that put forward by Colin Powell's lawyer at the State Department, William Taft IV, the great grandson of William Howard Taft, the twenty-seventh President of the United States. Taft believed that the Conventions applied to the conflict in Afghanistan, and that their provisions were applicable to all the persons involved in that conflict, including al-Qaeda and the Taliban. "[T]his conclusion is appro-priate," wrote Taft, "for policy reasons because it emphasizes that even in a new sort of conflict the United States bases its conduct on its international treaty obligations and the rule of law, not just its policy preferences."[12] The lawyers for the Joint Chiefs of Staff also had concerns. They wanted a statement emphasizing the importance the United States attached to Geneva, and a statement that the United States would treat all detainees as if the Geneva Conventions applied to them.

But these were minority views. The Vice President's lawyer, David Addington, wanted Geneva out of the picture. So did Alberto Gonzales. So did Jim Haynes. The detainees should *not* be able to rely on Geneva, and President Bush bought it, hook, line, and sinker. On February 7, 2002, then, he decided that Geneva didn't apply to the conflict with al-Qaeda. As regards the conflict with the Taliban, Bush stated that although Geneva was applicable as a matter of law, the Taliban fighters were not entitled to prisoner of war status under the Geneva Conventions because they hadn't followed the Geneva rules. The United States could not hand out POW status to fighters who didn't obey the rules, that would undermine the incentive system that was wisely built into the Geneva Conventions. As regards Common Article 3, Bush decided that it didn't apply to any suspected terrorists, whether Taliban or al-Qaeda. The upshot was that no one at Guantánamo could rely on Geneva. The President decided that detainees would be treated "humanely," but military necessity would trump the principles of Geneva. "All the President said," Feith mused, was "'humane treatment' and I thought that was OK, a perfectly fine phrase, that needs to be fleshed out, but it's a fine phrase."

Feith referred me back to his 1985 article, which argued that those who didn't follow the rules should not be able to take refuge in the Convention. Now this incentive argument had been applied in real life to the Taliban. Feith was bowled over by the success of the argument. "This year I was really a player, this was a moment." I wanted to ask him—but didn't—whether his own exposure to possible war crimes complicity would have been a price worth paying for that moment.

Feith's little speech thus became a memo, the memo became a policy decision, the policy decision became new interrogation rules, and the new interrogation rules became torture. How linear, I thought, as Feith unwittingly drew the line that connected the interrogation of Detainee 063 at Guantánamo straight to his own computer. But I was still puzzling over the rationale of an argument that allowed the refusal of rights under Geneva to be presented as safeguarding international law.

I was also curious about the connection between the decision on Geneva and the new interrogation rules approved by Rumsfeld at the end of 2002. Alberto Gonzales didn't deal with that issue when he released all the documents during his Abu Ghraib moment. I observed to Feith that his memo to the President and the Geneva decision meant that its constraints on interrogation didn't apply to anyone at Guantánamo. "Oh yes, sure," he shot back. So that was the intention, I asked. "Absolutely," he replied, without any hesitation. Under the Geneva Conventions no one there was entitled to any protection. "That's the point." So either you were a detainee to whom Geneva didn't apply, or you were a detainee to whom Geneva applied but whose rights you couldn't invoke. What was the difference for the purpose of interrogation, I asked? Triumphantly Feith answered: "It turns out, none. But that's the point."

And that indeed was the point, the crucial point. A more cautious man would have held back on that decisive piece of information. None of the detainees had any rights under the Geneva Conventions. Common Article 3 prohibited torture and "outrages upon personal dignity," but provided no protections for anyone at Guantánamo, whether Taliban or al-Qaeda. Nor could any of the provisions in the third Geneva Conventions, dealing specifically with prisoners of war, be invoked. "That's the point," Doug Feith said. The same logic would apply to the rules of customary law, which were equally inconvenient, and which the State Department lawyers pushed but which Haynes also rejected.[13]

***

So all constraints on military interrogation were gone. The slate was clean, the page on which the old interrogation rules were written was now blank. But what did that mean on the ground at Guantánamo? A few days after the President made this decision Donald Rumsfeld appointed the head of military interrogations at Guantánamo. He met Major General Michael E. Dunlavey, as did Doug Feith and Jim Haynes, and they all agreed Dunlavey was the right man for the post. His name was familiar to me. The request on October 11, 2002 for aggressive new techniques of interrogation that led to the Haynes memo came from Dunlavey. He would be a good person to see next.

INTERROGATION LOG OF DETAINEE 063
Day 19, December 11 2002

0320: Detainee was agitated at music being played in his presence and attempted to voice his opinion. He was ignored and moved excessively during this time while seated in the chair with his hands clenched in a fist. . . .

1115: Interrogators held an exorcism to purge the evil Jinns that he claimed were controlling his emotions.

6

From February to November 2002 Major General Michael E. Dunlavey's official title was Commanding Officer of Joint Task Force 170 at Guantánamo Bay. JTF–170 ran military interrogations. Alongside it, JTF–160 was responsible for the administration of the facility, commanded by Brigadier General Rick Baccus. By Jim Haynes's account of June 2004, Dunlavey's memo of October 11 set the ball rolling. A couple of years later Haynes described him to the U.S. Senators as "an aggressive Major General."[1] A document changes with each reading, even if it is only a few sentences long. Dunlavey's short memo of October 11 had a particular quality that was difficult to discern. It communicated a clear but unstated message, with no hint of reservation. It propelled a momentous request into the heart of the Pentagon without raising a single policy concern about the consequences of ditching *Field Manual 34–52*.

Dunlavey's memo set out the key facts, as he saw them. The usefulness of the existing techniques had been exhausted. The interrogators were at a dead end. Some detainees had more information. The unstated message was that these new techniques should be approved because they would work. This memo was written by someone who knew the request would be approved, which suggested prior contact with decision-makers in the Pentagon. Such a request would not have been made if its author entertained doubts as to its prospects.

⟶⟷⟵

So who was Michael Dunlavey and how did he get to Guantánamo? He was a lawyer, an army reservist and, after Guantánamo, a judge at the Court of Common Pleas in Erie, Pennsylvania. My initial research revealed no photograph and few news items. On March 28, 2002 the *Erie Times-News* ran a

*Major General Michael E. Dunlavey,
Commanding Officer, Joint Task Force
170*

story about his role at Guantánamo. His secret job was "secret no more."[2] He'd been chosen by Rumsfeld because of his "unique" background: thirty years of intelligence experience. He had arrived in Guantánamo on March 1, 2002 from the National Security Agency. His task was "to establish the standards for interrogation." Since Geneva no longer applied, the blank pages needed to be filled. He was quoted as saying that among the detainees they were looking for people who were in it with their heart and soul, whose goal was "the destruction of our culture as we know it, our way of life."

The media trail went quiet until early October 2002. The interrogations were producing limited information and the interrogators were having trouble getting information out of the detainees. General Baccus, who was in charge of JTF–160, was undermining the interrogations by being "too nice" to the detainees. The *Washington Times* reported that Baccus had promised the detainees would be "treated humanly"[3]—it was not clear whether that was a typo—and had placed Red Cross posters around the camp, reminding prisoners they needed only to cooperate as required by the Geneva Conventions, by providing name, rank and serial number. According to this press report the "too-kind treatment" upset Dunlavey.

The *New York Post* reported that Brigadier General Baccus was relieved from his duties on October 9, 2002, just two days before Dunlavey wrote his memo. Was this a coincidence? The paper reported that Baccus's departure wasn't planned and that the command of the prison guards (JTF–160) and the interrogations (JTF–170) would be merged and temporarily run by Dunlavey. In November 2002, within a month of sending of his memo, Dunlavey was replaced by Major General Geoffrey Miller and left Guantánamo.

Dunlavey went on to serve as Associate Director of the Terrorist Threat Integration Center, created by President Bush. By March 2004 he was back in his courtroom in Erie. In June that year Alberto Gonzales released the October 11, 2002 memo and a local newspaper devoted much of its front page to the story.[4] "Judge Dunlavey crossed the line," ran an editorial, "disgust is the only appropriate reaction." But a counter-view was put forcefully and Dunlavey was thanked for "putting the well-being and safety of this country before the comfort of captured terrorists." Many letters were published. "Why isn't Judge Dunlavey getting charged," a Vietnam vet asked. Should the American justice system be traded for Taliban clerics? Would it be better to have "the Arab sheikdom practices of amputation or decapitation, or perhaps Oriental jurisprudence administered from the muzzle of an AK–47?"[5]

The town of Erie was galvanized, and in October 2004 Dunlavey was sued, along with Rumsfeld and numerous others, in a civil suit in Washington, D.C.[6] The case was brought by four former Guantánamo detainees— all British—alleging violations of laws prohibiting torture and other abuses. In March 2005 Dunlavey was investigated by U.S. Air Force Lieutenant General Randall M. Schmidt, who had been appointed to run a probe by U.S. Southern Command into FBI allegations of abuse at Guantánamo.[7] In 2006 all abuse claims against Dunlavey were dismissed by the D.C. Federal Court, with one exception: the claim that the detainees were forced to shave their beards and that camp guards had placed a Koran in the toilet.[8]

⎯⚬⎯

Over two years of argument and counter-argument Dunlavey maintained complete silence. He continued to sit as a judge, no easy matter in a relatively small town like Erie. And in October 2006 I wrote to him: "I am an English barrister and Professor of Law at University College London, having previously taught at NYU Law School," I began. "I am engaged in a research and writing project on legal aspects of the global war on terror, including the role of lawyers and judges." I did not put quotation marks around the words "global war on terror," as this might have marked me out as a skeptic, in the United States. I asked whether I might come and interview him and after several days I phoned his chambers to check that the fax had arrived. His secretary Brenda was helpful and friendly. The fax had arrived, but she was not sure where it had gone. Did I want to speak with Judge Dunlavey? I did. After a few exploratory questions to ascertain my *bona fides*—that I was a lawyer and not a journalist—he agreed to meet.

I'd assumed that Erie was somewhere near Philadelphia, close to New York City. It was not. Pennsylvania is large, extending far to the west and north of New York City; one part touches Canada, on Lake Erie, which was where Dunlavey lived. I booked a flight to Buffalo in upstate New York, and rented a car to drive the hundred or so miles to Erie.

But the day before I left for Buffalo an email arrived from Brenda. "Judge Dunlavey is unable to keep his appointment with you tomorrow. If you would like to call he will be able to explain." I wondered whether a last-minute Google search had alerted him to my writing. I called him. It was not clear what had caused him to cancel; he wanted to talk, but was fearful. However, the non-refundable air ticket clinched it and we agreed to meet at 2.30 the following day, for an hour. It was a long way to go for a short conversation that might lead nowhere. My hope was that once we met face to face we might build some rapport.

The following morning I was on the way to JFK airport in New York to catch the flight to Buffalo. My assistant phoned from London and left a message on my mobile. Judge Dunlavey's office had called, he was going to have to cancel the meeting. Either he had bailed out again or the message was left the previous day and had been superseded by our phone conversation. I hesitated, and decided it would be better not to know. I would press on to Erie and turn up at his chambers.

A few hours later I was in a rental car on the road between Buffalo and Erie. It was a spectacular late autumn day, and I followed Interstate 90 along the southern side of Lake Erie. Between the road and the lake were miles and miles of vineyard, which seemed surprising so far north. The towns of upstate New York had names associated with solidity and middle America: Lackawanna, home of the Seneca Indians, later a great steel-making town (also a place where an alleged al-Qaeda cell would emerge).[9] Gowanda, an Indian term that meant "beautiful place among the hills," Fredonia, the first home of the Grange movement (Order of Patrons of Husbandry), a national movement of local farmers who were organized into granges to work for political and economic advantages. And then across the state line into Pennsylvania. Erie was the first town I came to, with its Greek-style County Court House in the historic downtown.

Judge Dunlavey was in his courtroom hearing a juvenile delinquency case. Waiting in the conference room I recalled the letters in the *Erie Times-News,* complaining that he was too "short-fused" to hear family cases. "We are not Afghan prisoners," wrote a correspondent, "we are Erie citizens expecting our elected judges to listen and be fair, not short and dismissing us without allowing all the facts to be presented." I thought of Jim Haynes's comment to the Senate Judiciary Committee earlier that summer, which had described Dunlavey as "the aggressive Major General." In the judge's room there were family photos and much military memorabilia as well as law books and, on his desk, a well-thumbed copy of my own book *Lawless World*. In his early sixties, Dunlavey was a neat man with a good head of dark hair and a decent, ruddy complexion. He wore a dark blue suit with an American flag pin in the lapel, and a light blue tie. His bearing was upright, military or judicial, or a bit of both, but his eyes were tired, his face tense. He seemed weary, and wary.

It took time for the conversation to hit its stride. We started with soccer. He'd always been a big fan and had spent the previous summer watching the World Cup games in Germany on TV. Later on I told him I'd been to a couple of games, including one in Nuremberg, where I'd visited the courtroom of the famous tribunal. He was interested and it helped break the ice. I mentioned the Justice Cases and Josef Altstötter, but he didn't pick up the connections. He wanted to know that I would tell his story straight; I wanted to know that I'd get the story. Whether I did or not seemed unclear, as anything I picked up seemed only part of the truth. But at this first meeting we spent eight hours together, finishing with a meal at his club next door to the courthouse. This was the story he shared with me.

He served on active duty in the U.S. Army from 1967, including a tour in Vietnam. Then he had got a law degree and worked as a lawyer until 1999, when he was elected to the bench. Throughout this period he served in the military reserves, reaching the rank of two-star Major General (in the reserves there was no higher rank). His field was intelligence. He was well traveled, including in Central America but declined to go into detail. He seemed familiar with countries like Honduras that I knew well. On September 11 he was at Fort Huachuca in Arizona, the headquarters of the U.S. Army Intelligence Center, attending a retirement ceremony for a friend.

As a reservist he was assigned to the National Security Agency and within five days of the attacks he was back at the NSA, in uniform. For three months he remained in Washington, in 24/7 operational mode. The NSA collected and disseminated intelligence on a new enemy that was, in his view, dedicated to the destruction of the Judeo-Christian system. It was a monumental struggle, and the stakes could not be higher. In February 2002 he had received a faxed staff order directing that an independent joint task force was being established, and summoning him to meet with the Secretary of Defense. He was picked to be the first head of interrogation at Guantánamo. Why him? "They picked me because of my experience. My experience in intelligence. I am a soldier, a combat veteran. I have experience of law. So I am a combat soldier, an intelligence officer and a lawyer." This was a refrain to which he returned several times: it seemed to reassure him.

Dunlavey was told that he was the only person who met the criteria that Rumsfeld wanted. He met the Secretary of Defense a few days after President Bush had decided that none of the Guantánamo detainees had any rights under Geneva. Rumsfeld was intense, intelligent, focused. "When he wanted something he got it done." This meeting took place around February 20 and the two men spent an hour together. "He evaluated me. He wanted to know who I was. He was very focused on the need to get intelligence. He wanted to make sure that the moment was not lost. Are they al-Qaeda? Are they Taliban? Are they foreign fighters?" Rumsfeld told Dunlavey to report directly to him, on a weekly basis, bypassing SOUTHCOM and the usual chain of command. Dunlavey then met Wolfowitz, Rumsfeld's deputy, and Doug Feith. He also spent time with a quiet Jim Haynes, who had few questions for him, and saw General Myers and his deputy, General Pace.

Dunlavey was surprised to be chosen, because he was Army and Rumsfeld didn't like the Army. But others weren't surprised. "Dunlavey was a tyrant and a strong Republican," one former JAG told me; that is why he was chosen. I asked about the mission Rumsfeld gave him. He paused. "He wanted me to maximize the information. He wanted me to identify who was there and get the intelligence, to prevent the next 9/11." There was no ambiguity here. Rumsfeld personally selected the man who would run military interrogations at Guantánamo and deliver what Rumsfeld wanted. "I didn't need to raise the Geneva Conventions," Dunlavey told me. "There was no question in my mind that they were trying to decide how to handle these guys. Mr. Rumsfeld wanted to know who they were and what they knew. He wanted me to 'maximize the intelligence production.' No one ever said to me 'the gloves are off.' But I didn't need to talk about the Geneva Conventions, it was clear that they didn't apply. The President said they should be treated humanely. But Geneva didn't apply."

Soon after, Dunlavey arrived at Guantánamo. Resources were minimal. "I had six people, a table and a computer." The United States hadn't been in a major war for thirty-five years and had virtually no experience of dealing with terrorists. As Commander of JTF–170 he was responsible for military interrogations, working alongside the FBI and the CIA. JTF–160 took care of housing the detainees, commanded by Brigadier General James Baccus of the National Guard in Rhode Island. Both Dunlavey and Baccus reported to SOUTHCOM in Miami.

Dunlavey wasn't happy that Guantánamo operations were divided into two units: it wasn't logical and caused a disunity of command. Two units meant two sets of lawyers and JTF–160 and JTF–170 each had their own Judge Advocate General. Dunlavey had little time for Baccus: "He wasn't up to the job in any shape or form." He referred to him as General Buttkiss and was not too complimentary. Baccus relied on a lawyer from Texas, a man who "skulked in the background and couldn't abandon his philosophy of public defender."

The detainees they were handling had been pre-screened in Afghanistan, but their information cards were generally incomplete, often missing vital details like place of capture. That made the interrogations more difficult, because if you don't know where or how they'd been captured you have no starting point. When Dunlavey arrived at Guantánamo, the interrogations had already begun, generally conducted by the military, while the FBI did their own separate interrogations for law enforcement purposes. The facilities weren't ideal, the holding cells weren't what Dunlavey wanted or asked for ("What I got were exact copies of prisons in Oman"). Meanwhile, "planeloads" of detainees were being delivered up on a daily basis. Many posed no threat, men who had been in the wrong place at the wrong time; some were very elderly while others posed a serious threat. Some of the detainees followed the "Manchester Manual." As regards the medical staff, Dunlavey wasn't too impressed with some of the psychologists. Mike Gelles of the Naval Criminal Investigation Service (NCIS), was one of them, said Dunlavey, but he had no understanding of the people they were holding.

By May Dunlavey had concluded that half the detainees had no intelligence value at all. He reported this to Rumsfeld, who told him to take his problems to Feith, who would pass them on. In Feith he met solid resistance to the idea of returning any detainees, so it was on with the interrogations, even if the usual techniques wouldn't work. *FM 34–52* was based on building a rapport. "That won't happen if the detainee knows the route you are taking. You can't interrogate them in the ordinary way. That's the problem I had." Although he emphasized the importance of building rapport, later on he could not explain how the new techniques could work in that way.

Three months after Dunlavey's arrival at Guantánamo, the focus of attention shifted to Detainee 063, whose real name was Mohammed al-Qahtani, a Saudi Arabian who had been refused entry to the Orlando airport in Florida in August 2001. He had been fingerprinted at the Orlando airport and the prints matched. He was captured in Afghanistan later that year. There was also some video footage of him at the Orlando airport from the

Immigration and Naturalization Service. Dunlavey had no doubts about his identity or the threat he posed: they thought al-Qahtani was the twentieth hijacker on September 11. (How many "twentieth hijackers" are there, I asked, alluding to Zacarias Moussaoui, who'd recently been convicted. Dunlavey smiled.) The discovery of al-Qahtani was the catalyst for introducing the new interrogation techniques. "This guy may have been the key to the survival of the United States," Mike Dunlavey told me, categorically: he was not a man who entertained doubts.

By August, Dunlavey was clear that the rule book *FM 34–52* was too restricting for someone like al-Qahtani, who was trained to resist interrogation. On August 8 al-Qahtani was placed in an "isolation facility" to separate him from the general detainee population.[10] By then, Dunlavey was under huge pressure to find out what he knew and where he was in the chain of command. This pressure came from Washington, from the top, and the urgent need for more information caused him to renew his efforts. "Somewhere along the line I got the message: 'are you doing everything humanly possible to get this information?'" Around this time he even got a famous Rumsfeld "snowflake," a memo from the Secretary himself that was intended to prod the recipient into early action. It suggested new approaches to interrogation. His weekly reports to SOUTHCOM and the Pentagon must have added to the pressure, I inquired. They were now talking to SOUTHCOM every day, in particular to Lieutenant General Ron Burgess, the head of intelligence (J2). The pressure to get information from al-Qahtani was real. "I've got a short fuse on this to get it up the chain," Dunlavey said, "I was on a timeline." Dunlavey looked at me attentively as he spoke; maybe he wanted to tell me that I was wrong to suggest he was under pressure—but he didn't. "Here's what I wanted to know," he said, "who he really was; how did he get recruited; where did he train; who gave him visas."

That pressure on Dunlavey led directly to the new techniques, which, within Guantánamo, Dunlavey was responsible for overseeing. When I met with him four years later, he remained adamant that the techniques were needed. So how did they go about that task? "There were lots of suggestions in August about what to do. There were many 'brilliant ideas,' but the difficulty was that military interrogators were trained to interrogate militarily. All this stuff was being thrown at me. The Criminal Investigation Task Force [CITF] hadn't cracked it. The FBI hadn't cracked it. The opinion was that with more effective techniques we could make this work."

So where did the initiative for change come from? When Gonzales and Haynes spoke at their press conference on June 22, 2004 the suggestion was that this was a bottom-up effort. Haynes implied that the "aggressive Major General" was the source of the initiative for new interrogation rules and the Pentagon documents contributed to that impression. By now I'd got to know Dunlavey reasonably well. He was cautious, he acted on instructions. I'd planted a seed in his mind, what he called a "conspiracy theory." Yes, he had been in regular contact with Rumsfeld, he had been up to D.C. to see him, and they had spoken by phone. He had also dealt with Doug Feith and with Jim Haynes. Dunlavey saw himself as Rumsfeld's man on the ground. "We knew we had to go further," he said, "but we wanted to make sure it was legal."

At Guantánamo the final list of new interrogation methods was put together by Lieutenant Colonel Jerald Phifer, Dunlavey's J2 intelligence officer. Where had the new techniques come from? On this subject he was uneasy, he knew it was a dangerous topic and his answer could tilt responsibility in his direction or elsewhere. There were meetings at Guantánamo in September 2002 involving twenty or thirty people, who brainstormed ideas: it was a collective effort. Everyone on the camp was talking it through, although the CIA didn't participate in all the brainstorming sessions. I appreciated the confirmation that the CIA was present and, presumably, aware of the parallel efforts that were underway in Washington to develop new CIA interrogation practices for its detainees. "Ideas were gone over and over and over again. We were getting suggestions from all over the map. The FBI had some real concerns, especially about the admissibility of the evidence in any criminal proceedings. Copies of the materials were sent to all the participants."

The FBI were "rotating people in and out of there like it was a turnstile at Wal-Mart," Dunlavey said. They didn't want to be involved in aggressive interrogations nor did the NCIS (Naval Criminal Investigative Services) that was part of the Criminal Investigative Task Force (CITF). There were obviously competing views about what was right. Unprompted, Dunlavey offered the suggestion that some ideas might have come from the Defense Human Intelligence Service (DHS), which was established in 1995 under the Department of Defense's Defense Intelligence Agency (DIA) to consolidate the gathering of human intelligence within the armed services. Ultimately, the DHS was under the Secretary of Defense. "I am suddenly getting these suggestions from DHS," claimed Dunlavey, "they were interested in what was going on." He didn't know if the DHS person was reporting directly to the Pentagon, but it would certainly have been odd if they weren't.

I asked Dunlavey whether he'd ever heard of the Defense Intelligence Agency's Humint Augmentation Teams, or its Strategic Support Branch. He said he hadn't. I had picked up a reference to them in some news articles in the United States, which suggested the existence of a new Pentagon espionage arm said to indicate Rumsfeld's desire to end his dependence on the CIA for intelligence gathering.[11] Mention was made of Humint Augmentation Teams working in Afghanistan and Iraq, but Guantánamo wasn't mentioned. Later I met Vice-Admiral Lowell Jacoby, who became Director of the DIA in 2002. He confirmed that Humint Augmentation Teams were present at Guantánamo. The DIA provided military and civilian personnel at Guantánamo, Jacoby said, working under Rumsfeld's policy guidance. "Our people going forward as augmenters needed detailed guidance and protection," he added, confirming that the DIA had its own trained interrogators. "They were special people, embedded in military units, largely people who were trained to be interrogation supervisors. There were guys in Gitmo, assigned to operational units." Were they augmenters? I asked. "We were force providers," Jacoby explained.

Because of the pace of operations, the DIA had decided it needed something more focused. "We decided to have a group of people whose only assigned responsibility was to augment operations," Jacoby said. "They were more highly trained, they had a more specific role. At one point they were called Humint Augmentation Teams, later they were called the Strategic Support Branch." They were "a combination of people who had human interrogation skills, a higher level of experience, with knowledge of the region and the language." "They were primarily civilians," he added, "because what we wanted to do was keep these people for the longer term, and they were doing interrogation of willing and unwilling detainees." Vice-Admiral Jacoby smiled knowingly when I suggested they were covert. "We were just managing our assets," he said, "but they weren't covert operations, although they could also augment the special ops people."

If they were overt, Mike Dunlavey certainly didn't let on to me. He seemed to know more than he was willing to say about where the ideas for the eighteen techniques originated. Although he wasn't going into detail, his clipped answers indicated that Washington was closely involved, at the highest levels. I suggested that the idea that these new techniques trickled up from the people on the ground at Guantánamo was counter-intuitive. He was silent on detail, but there was no denial. Was the very top involved? Again Dunlavey was silent. Was there pressure? "It must have been all the way to the White House," he said. "It's possible," he later explained mischievously, "that someone was sent to my Task Force and came up with these great ideas."

The link between the formulation of the eighteen techniques at Guantánamo and Washington was clear. There was a steady stream of prominent visitors from Washington, regular phone calls, videoconferences. "There were backchannels, unconnected communications," involving a military intelligence person and a non-military intelligence person, who was passing information outside. Dunlavey couldn't remember his name. He told me that the most senior Washington lawyers visited Guantánamo, including David Addington, the Vice President's lawyer, with Gonzales and Haynes, at the end of September, before he signed off on his memo. Jane Dalton, General Myers's main lawyer at the Joint Staff in D.C., was not part of the team on that trip, although she saw Dunlavey on one visit to Guantánamo. Interrogation was on the agenda for discussion along with the military commissions before which some detainees would be tried. "They wanted to know what we were doing to get to this guy," said Dunlavey of al-Qahtani, "and Addington was interested in how we were managing it." I asked about Addington, who was Cheney's General Counsel at the Pentagon in 1992. "As soon as we saw each other we knew each other," he said, but revealed no more.

What did Dunlavey talk about with the visiting lawyers, in September? "They brought ideas with them which had been given from sources in D.C. They came down to observe and talk. Haynes came down twice to get a feel for the place. Military deputies came down. Haynes did his job and did it well, and because of that he will not be confirmed as a judge." And throughout this whole period, Dunlavey said, Rumsfeld was "directly and regularly involved." All this was well before he sent his memo to General Hill on October 11, the Commander of U.S. SOUTHCOM.

We talked about the program that trains American soldiers how to respond to interrogation, known as SERE (Survival, Evasion, Resistance, and Escape). Had SERE been reverse-engineered to provide some of the eighteen techniques? This was a delicate issue, since it would suggest that the new techniques drew on those used by the enemy. At our first meeting, Dunlavey did not deny this was a possibility, but would not be drawn. On our second meeting, a few months later, he confirmed the reliance on SERE techniques. "Somebody had a suggestion, let's send our guys up to Fort Bragg, see what they do." There was an implication that the new ideas were based on techniques used by the Israeli military although he denied that Israel had anything to do with the preparation of the documents. It was the only time I saw him look genuinely surprised.

I also asked about General Myers and Doug Feith. "Doug Feith? I do not know how he got to where he is. He was in charge of policy. He was the person who was supposed to give authority. In February 2002 I had dealings with him. What's my view? On policy standards, you have to develop them. By phone I met with him. Then I went up. Perhaps I wasn't very diplomatic. On everything, the Joint Chiefs of Staff was my conduit, and I dealt with Myers directly." Dunlavey liked Rumsfeld but not Feith. At the end of the day the decision was Dunlavey's: he was head of interrogation. And, as he constantly reminded me, the timing was significant. The choice of new interrogation techniques coincided with the anniversary of 9/11. The atmosphere was feverish. "It was the anniversary . . . there was tremendous pressure to be seen to be getting something done." Yet I sensed paranoia, coupled with the self-consciousness that came to a man who was entrusted with a great mission. "You should be careful what you write," he said to me. "I've had a couple of death threats." This was not the only time he alluded to his physical well-being. Once when we were eating at his club he put his hands on the table and said: "Look at these, see anything different?" Faced with my silence he looked at me and said: "Broken."

The new techniques were more or less finalized by the end of September 2002. Dunlavey needed them to be approved by Diane Beaver, his Staff Judge Advocate. "We had talked and talked, brainstormed, then we drew up a list," he said. "Jerald Phifer signed off on them, put them in the order, then he gave them to Diane Beaver." Dunlavey was clear that he wanted—and needed—a legal opinion, and where others would have been happy with oral advice, he wanted it in writing. Rumsfeld had told him that everything he did "would be under a microscope." But Dunlavey was a lawyer, so why did he need a legal opinion? "I wanted legal sign-off, I wanted accountability, I wanted top cover." He looked over at photographs of his grandchildren playing soccer, then at a cabinet that contained Guantánamo memorabilia. "I wanted top cover."

So the list of techniques went to Staff Judge Advocate Diane Beaver, although Dunlavey appreciated the difficulties she was in, not least because she had no background in international law. He told her that someone up the legal chain of command would sign off. "Give it our best shot," he directed. I expressed surprise. Apart from Diane Beaver's legal input, no one else seemed to have provided any detailed legal advice on the new techniques. The documents that were released by Gonzalez and Haynes suggested that there was no written legal advice from General Hill's lawyers at SOUTHCOM, or from the General Counsel to the Joint Chiefs of Staff. It seemed strange that on so important a decision the legal advice of a relatively junior lawyer, with limited experience of these issues, could be definitive. Why did Haynes not require anything more? This question kept coming up.

Dunlavey couldn't enlighten me, or wouldn't. He sent his request to General Hill at SOUTHCOM, who then sent it up to General Myers at the Joint Chiefs of Staff in D.C. He wasn't certain whether General Hill had obtained any other legal opinion, but thought that he might have received oral advice from his own lawyers. Dunlavey seemed to have no information about Haynes's involvement with the legal issues once it got up to the top level, and he did not know anything about other legal advices that may have been prepared by Bybee and Yoo at the Justice Department in Washington in August 2002, on the definition of torture or inhumane and degrading treatment under U.S. and international law. He only found out about these when they were released with his memo on June 22, 2004. Nor were they mentioned when Haynes, accompanied by Gonzales and Addington, visited Guantánamo at the end of September.

At that point, a decision was taken to replace Mike Dunlavey. Major General Miller took over, and Dunlavey left Guantánamo before the new techniques were used on Detainee 063. Despite the adverse publicity and even the lawsuit against him, Dunlavey stood by the techniques. "Those techniques should be available tools," he said, "even if they don't work normally." Despite his sense of pride for his contribution and his troops, I wondered whether that told the full story. "I share your concerns, I know where you are coming from, but when it comes down to it, when it is about protecting rights, we have to come up and develop a way of dealing with terrorists who use the judicial system against us." As far as he was concerned, those techniques were not torture, or even inhuman or degrading treatment. If he'd been presented with a European Court of Human Rights judgment saying that they were torture then he might have paused. But he was not, although part of Diane Beaver's legal advice had referred explicitly to the judgment of the European Court in the case brought by Ireland against the United Kingdom in the 1970s. The Court had ruled that forcing detainees to stand for long hours, placing black hoods over their heads, subjecting them to loud noise and depriving them of sleep constituted cruel, inhuman or degrading treatment. Diane Beaver's advice recommended limitations, and Dunlavey had concurred in her analysis, but these comments were not included in Haynes's recommendation to Rumsfeld. He did not know why they had been removed. "I stand by my letter to Hill." He knew the ramifications. "I may be a small-town lawyer, but I'm not a stupid man."

I asked him about *FM34–52*, about building rapport, about the Army's long-held view that coercion produced unreliable material. But his view did not change. The detainees at Guantánamo were not innocent lambs; they were brutal, insulting, vicious. He took responsibility for the techniques. "The real question was, would I have used them? Probably not. Phobias of dogs? The thought of using that is real difficult." I reminded him that the interrogation log of Detainee 063 indicated the presence of dogs. He was silent.

At our first meeting one hour had turned into eight. On display in his room was a photograph of a close friend killed in Vietnam, his dog tags hanging from the frame; a cabinet filled with Guantánamo memorabilia; a photograph of Dunlavey there, standing in front of a plane taking off. On that plane, Dunlavey told me with pride, was one of the good people who were released, a man who claimed to be more than 100 years old, who had "hugged and kissed" him when he left. Then he went to a drawer and took out a couple of photographs of himself as a younger man—more hopeful photos taken before Guantánamo. They showed that the last few years had taken a toll. "I look forward to continuing to share our values," he wrote on one before handing it over to me. Sitting in Erie, it looked to me as if he had been hung out to dry. Now they wouldn't even let him go back to Gitmo to visit, he said.

As we parted I shared a final thought. How much warning was he given when his memo was made public, in June 2004? The question was painful, judging by his crumpled face and deep silence. I almost regretted the question. He was given no warning. Like everyone else in town he read about it on the front page of the *Erie Times-News*. "Dunlavey accused of torture" was the headline he described. He had called his priest, then SOUTHCOM. There was no warning, no support network. Jim Haynes didn't call him. No one called.

As we left his chambers I passed a framed document that hung proudly on a cluttered wall. It was a certificate, confirming Dunlavey's membership of the Guantánamo Bay Bar Association, an organization "dedicated to justice . . . on a Caribbean island outside the venue of any Cuban or U.S. Federal court." The document was signed by Diane Beaver, his lawyer. I asked whether it was just a coincidence that so many lawyers had been involved in interrogations that had generated so much global criticism. Dunlavey felt that he had let her down, that she had taken too much media attention for her legal advice. He wanted to apologize for not having protected her better. "She was a soldier's soldier, she was not an international lawyer." If you could find her, he remarked ruefully, she would be good to speak with.

INTERROGATION LOG OF DETAINEE 063
Day 20, 12 December 2002

0001: Detainee was subjected to white noise (music) waiting for his IVs to be completed. . . .

0150: SSG M showed the bottom of his boot to detainee . . . He went into a fit of rage. . . . He began to move his arms and legs in his chair as if to want to break away from the shackles and attack. . . .

0515:Interrogators compared lifestyle difference between Camp Delta and Camp X-Ray . . . Camp X-Ray—live in wooden box with no communications and constantly reminded of his low level of self-worth; unable to laugh and only be laughed at; unable to write or receive letters; unable to read; unable to choose when he sleeps, drinks or go to the bathroom; unable to move around freely; unable to practice his religion when he wants to; unable to feel like a human being; the only feeling he knows at Camp X-Ray is the hate he brought with him.

7

As an Army lawyer Diane Beaver knew that the U.S. military did not "do" cruelty or torture. A long and distinguished record of treating detainees decently went back as far as 1863, when President Lincoln promulgated general orders prohibiting ill-treatment. "Military necessity does not admit of cruelty," he instructed his troops, "nor of torture to extort confessions."[1] The rule was confirmed in 1949, when the United States signed the Geneva Conventions, including, without reservation, Common Article 3's ban on cruel treatment, torture and outrages on personal dignity. The rule was confirmed again in 1977, when the United States signed Protocol I to the Geneva Conventions. Although the United States has not ratified that treaty, the U.S. Army's Operational Law Handbook recognized that Article 75, which confirmed and strengthened Common Article 3, applied to the United States as a matter of customary law[2] and these rules were endorsed by the Army's Field Manual FM 34–52. Those were the rules for nearly 140 years—until December 2002 and Detainee 063.

This is not to say that other parts of the U.S. government haven't ever used cruelty or torture.[3] In 1997 two infamous CIA documents were declassified. The first was the CIA's 1963 KUBARK manual on counter-intelligence interrogation, with directions on sensory deprivation, threats and fear, and pain.[4] Twenty years later another secret manual—the *Human Resource Exploitation Training Manual*—was compiled by the CIA from sections of the original KUBARK guidelines. This manual was used until 1987 in Latin American countries as an instructional tool, by CIA and Green Beret trainers. It included "coercive questioning" and psychological and physical techniques. Significantly, the 1983 manual also drew on U.S. military intelligence field manuals written in the mid-1960s as part of the Army's Foreign Intelligence Assistance Program, co-denamed "Project X." That program developed training packages for

Latin American countries on counter-insurgency techniques learned in Vietnam.

The events of the 1980s showed that even the U.S. military violated its own strict rules against coercion. In March 1992 the U.S. Secretary of Defense Dick Cheney received a report on intelligence training resources that contained improper material. Seven Spanish-language manuals prepared with the involvement of SOUTHCOM and the U.S. Army School of the Americas had been distributed in Latin America between 1987 and 1991, and several included materials that violated legal and policy prohibitions, including the handling of human intelligence sources by techniques such as fear, bounties, beatings, false imprisonment, executions and the use of truth serums. The investigation found that the "offensive and objectionable material" undermined U.S. credibility, although it found no evidence of a deliberate and orchestrated attempt to violate DoD or Army policies. The material had come, in part, from Project X, having been retained in the files of the Army Intelligence School at Fort Huachuca in Arizona, where Mike Dunlavey happened to be on September 11.

The 1992 report to Dick Cheney made various recommendations to prevent any recurrence of violations of U.S. and DoD policies prohibiting aggressive interrogation. It recommended that the DoD General Counsel should retain "one copy of each of the seven manuals" and that all other copies and associated instructional manuals should be destroyed. Cheney approved these corrective actions. Under his signature was a handwritten note from his General Counsel. "I concur," he wrote, adding that the Senate's intelligence and armed services committees would be briefed "to let them know we are correcting it."[5] In 1983, when the CIA produced its *Human Resource Exploitation Training Manual*, David Addington happened to be an Assistant General Counsel at the CIA. In 1992 the General Counsel to Cheney was the same David Addington, who visited Dunlavey at Guantánamo.

By that time, however, there had also been a change in the public consciousness. Some elements of popular culture seemed to endorse torture as a technique that worked. On November 6, 2001 Fox Television broadcast the first episode of *24*, a series based on the efforts of a fictionalized counter-terrorism unit in Los Angeles. Just about every episode had a torture scene in which aggressive techniques of interrogation were used to obtain information. The second season of *24* started to air on October 29, 2002, a month after the Guantánamo visit and just as Mike Dunlavey's request for new interrogation techniques reached the Pentagon and Jim Haynes's desk.

Around this time leading academic figures were also talking about the need for new interrogation techniques. On November 8, 2001, a couple of days after the first episode of *24* was broadcast, Harvard Law School professor Alan Dershowitz wrote an article that appeared to sanction torture in limited circumstances. "I have no doubt that if an actual ticking-bomb situation were to arise, our law enforcement authorities would torture."[6] The only real question for Dershowitz was whether such torture should take place outside the law or within it, and put that way there could be only one answer: "If we are to have torture, it should be authorized by the law." However, there should at the same time be accountability and transparency, and in each case a judge should issue a "torture warrant."

Over the next year these views—and Dershowitz himself—were never out of the public eye. In February 2002, just as Rumsfeld was appointing Dunlavey to run military interrogations at Guantánamo, Dershowitz told MSNBC that he'd like to see the criteria for authorized torture to be "set out in advance."[7] In April, after al-Qaeda leader Abu Zubaydah was captured in Pakistan, Dershowitz proclaimed that although this was not a ticking-bomb scenario, most countries in the world would torture him, including the French. "Should we amend the Constitution," he asked, "should we get out of the Geneva Conventions?" The American way, the democratic way, the constitutional way was obvious: "we have to issue torture warrants."[8] In August, as Dunlavey oversaw efforts at Guantánamo to conjure up new interrogation techniques, Dershowitz published a book setting out his proposals for the judicial overseeing of torture warrants in the ticking-bomb scenario.[9] And in September Dershowitz told Mike Wallace on CBS's *60 Minutes* that if torture was debatable on September 10, it was not on September 12: "Experiences change our conception of rights."[10] Another guest on that program that evening was Paul Aussaresses, the retired French general who defended the use of torture on suspected terrorists in Algeria in the 1950s. The best method, he said, was pouring water on a towel draped over the prisoner's face. "He could not breathe," said Aussaresses, "and when he could breathe no more he would talk." Aussaresses, Dershowitz and Mike Wallace would not have known that this very technique was being discussed in the Pentagon and at Guantánamo.

This, then, was the changed environment in which Mike Dunlavey was encouraged to search out new interrogation techniques: an environment in which popular TV shows proclaimed that torture worked and leading academics at Harvard posited theories based on the same assumption. Jim Haynes appreciated this. "I know there's some very good work going on in academia," he observed, "'highly coercive interrogations' is the phrase I've heard up at Harvard."[11] It was an atmosphere in which no one asked about the incidental consequences of changing direction in which Diane Beaver, the lawyer at Guantánamo, was asked to provide legal advice justifying the new interrogation techniques.

INTERROGATION LOG OF DETAINEE 063
Day 21, December 13 2002

0001: Control put a sign on detainee that had the Arabic word for coward written on it. . . .

0120: On occasion when the detainee began to drift off into sleep, lead dripped a couple of drops of water on detainee's head to keep him awake. Detainee jerked violently in his chair each time. . . .

1115: In order to escalate detainee's emotions, a mask was made from an MRE box with a smiley face on it and placed on the detainee's head for a few moments. A latex glove was inflated and labeled the "sissy slap" glove. The glove was touched to the detainee's face periodically after explaining the terminology to him.

8

Diane Beaver was Mike Dunlavey's Staff Judge Advocate at Guantánamo—the lawyer who was asked to sign off on the new interrogation
techniques and did. She was the unnamed author of the "multi-page, single-spaced legal review supporting those techniques," the person on whom
Gonzales and Haynes relied to justify the eighteen techniques.

Finding her was no easy matter. Compared with Feith, and even
Dunlavey, she was anonymous: on the web she was her legal advice and
nothing more. Eventually I located her, with help from a friend at the State
Department. Kate had worked with her, preparing the U.S. government's

Lieutenant Colonel Diane Beaver, Staff Judge Advocate, JTF-GITMO

response to various UN inquiries on Guantánamo. I first spoke to Diane Beaver in November 2005; it was a short conversation and we were both tentative. She seemed coiled up, angry, hard-done by, discarded; she hadn't spoken to anyone, and didn't think she would. She was loyal, a solid military person. But, like Dunlavey, it was apparent she wanted to talk. What she didn't tell me, but I learned later, was that at the time of our first conversation she was working for Jim Haynes at the Pentagon, including help with his judicial confirmation hearings before the U.S. Senate.

Several months passed before we met. By then, like Dunlavey, she was being sued in American courts, although the cases were later dropped. We met in a dreary food court in the basement of a nondescript shopping mall in downtown Washington, D.C., where no one would recognize her, or see us; it was early morning on a wet and miserable September day. She didn't look like a colonel—perhaps because she wasn't in military garb as by then she'd retired from active service. However, she still worked in the Pentagon for Jim Haynes as a civilian lawyer. Perhaps it was the generous overcoat that seemed large enough to hide her altogether; perhaps it was the lack of confidence, a vulnerability. "She was never a happy person," a former JAG told me, "there was always a cloud over her."

The third time we met she had stopped working for Haynes and had a new job, as the main lawyer for the American Forces Information Service, which produces news, feature articles and TV reports on all aspects of military life. On this occasion she was jollier and far more relaxed; and she was happier to talk. She described in detail her year at Guantánamo, from the summer of 2002, the key period. She then returned to the Pentagon, where her jobs were administrative. Legal advice on the war on terror occupied her for several years.

She'd always wanted to join the U.S. Army. The Women's Army Corps was created during the Second World War to allow women to enlist, but was disbanded in 1978, when women were first allowed to join the Reserve Officers' Training Corps. The ROTC provided scholarships to pay students to attend college, after which they would complete a period of service in the Army. Beaver was among the first group of women to be granted an ROTC scholarship. She was animated in her description of the male world of which she became a part. She studied in Bloomington, Indiana, and, after graduating in 1979, started work as a military police officer. She spent three years in Germany, based in Nuremberg, and visited the courtroom in which the Altstötter trial had taken place.

On her return to the United States she was posted to Fort Riley, in northeast Kansas. For many years this was the home of the 1st Mechanized Infantry Division, known as "the Big Red One"—it symbolized machismo. "The 1980s was a difficult time for women in the Army," she explained. "All of a sudden a large number of males were confronted with women who were doing a better job than them." Sexism was rampant. It was assumed that the women were easy and looking for one thing only. Beaver was a good runner, but stopped running with one of her male colleagues because of all the gossip.

Then she reached the glass ceiling. As a woman she wasn't going to be promoted to company commander, but didn't want to be a prison officer for the rest of her life, so she decided to get out. She went to the law school at Washington University in St Louis, Missouri, paying the tuition fees herself: she enjoyed constitutional law, but never studied international law. "Law school taught me to think more critically," she reflected, "It provided me with new skill sets." However, she hadn't given up on her military aspirations and joined the Army reserves, the 10th Psychological Operations Battalion. After law school she had interviews with various law firms, but decided that wasn't the life for her. She then served as a law clerk to Andrew Jackson Higgins, who became Chief Justice of the Missouri Supreme Court.

That year gave her time to think about her career. The Army was changing, and becoming more open to women. It would have been difficult to get onto active duty, so in 1987 she took the bar exams and applied to join the Judge Advocate General Corps, known as the JAG. The JAG makes sure that military law—set out in the Uniform Code of Military Justice—is complied with. Her JAG training began in October 1988, at Fort Lee in Charlottesville, Virginia, after which she was assigned to Fort Bragg in North Carolina, with the 4th Psychological Operations Battalion. Fort Bragg happened to be the home of SERE training, so she knew all about that but wasn't involved. She obtained jump wings, and later assignments included the invasion of Panama in December 1989. The following year she was deployed to Saudi Arabia in the run up to the Gulf War, serving in Special Operations Command. This gave her some initial contact with counter-intelligence operations and the work of the CIA, and since she had had no training in intelligence law she often called friends at Fort Bragg to prepare for her assignments. This gave her a better understanding of what was to come at Guantánamo.

In the 1990s she was promoted to major and awarded a Bronze Star. She moved to the Office of the Judge Advocate General in the Pentagon, and then on to Fort Riley, Kansas, where she served as a Deputy Staff Judge Advocate. She was disappointed to be passed over for promotion to colonel and took it as a sign that her time in the military was coming to an end. To prepare for a return to civilian life she took up a legal position as chief of the Eastern torts branch. She was working as a claims lawyer at the Pentagon when the planes hit the World Trade Center and the Pentagon. Although she could have retired from the military at the end of 2002, she wanted to contribute to the war on terror, especially with her background in special operations in the first Gulf War. She was told about a new Joint Task Force that was being established in Miami and knew General Tom Romig, the highly regarded Judge Advocate General for the Army, who helped recruit her onto the Joint Task Force assignment dealing with detainees. They would need lawyers, and so finally she made it as a Staff Judge Advocate, a role she had always wanted. "I think it's going to be six months in Miami," Romig told her: Cuba wasn't mentioned.

Her mother lived close by in Fort Myers and so she packed up, took her cat, and headed to Miami. "Oh boy," she exclaimed as she got to this moment of the story, "little did I know what was in store for me." A rare smile passed her lips. Miami meant SOUTHCOM, which had responsibility for Guantánamo Bay, but no one told them what was going on. Days and weeks passed and then they were told they were heading off to Cuba, and that they would be there for a year. By January 2002 she and the rest of the world knew from the media that detainees were arriving at Guantánamo Bay from Afghanistan. Preparations were limited, almost nonexistent. Her last day at SOUTHCOM in Miami was a Wednesday, in early June. At 5 P. M. she and the other lawyers were called to a meeting by Manny Supervielle, SOUTHCOM's Staff Judge Advocate. One of the lawyers got out a butcher-block size pad of paper and said "This is your guidance." On it he wrote a few words, and some bullet points.[1] A few stuck in her mind: "ICRC access"; "Repatriation?/prosecution?/Relationship with CITF and Military Commissions Interrogation Mission"; "Training"; 160/170. "That was it, a few words on a large sheet of paper, those were our instructions." She puffed out her cheeks and blew the air out. "That was our SOP," she exclaimed, "our Standard Operating Procedures." The paper came with no briefing or explanation or anything useful. "Because it was so ridiculous I took it with me and kept it as a reminder of the outstanding support I received from the SJA, SOUTHCOM." Later she sent me a photograph of the paper.

Beaver struck me as a careful and methodical person, used to well-organized processes, proper procedures. This was different. "I've been a leader," she declared, "I've never failed to accomplish my mission." She wanted to get it right. She arrived in Guantánamo in June 2002 and was assigned to JTF–170, with Mike Dunlavey as her boss. She raised her eyes on my first mention of his name. She confirmed the real tension that existed with JTF–160, whose lawyer was a reservist trained in the usual Geneva rules on POWs. One of her problems was that these rules didn't apply to her interrogations. The President had decided that none of the detainees would be able to claim any rights under the Geneva Conventions. Doug Feith's handiwork gave Beaver a real headache: no alternatives were offered to the Geneva rules.

General Hill hadn't yet taken command of SOUTHCOM (he only arrived in August 2002). Beaver knew little about Baccus or Dunlavey, or what they had been instructed to achieve, and their personalities made things harder. She thought that Baccus wasn't up to the job, and Dunlavey's management skills were pretty limited to say the least. There were also other problems, like too many reservists at Guantánamo. Reservists had limited training and experience and so their presence made things more difficult. On the intelligence side the staff were generally good at what they did, but there was insufficient experience. The people from the Defense Intelligence Agency were the only ones who'd done interrogations for real, she said. Dunlavey also referred to the key role played by the DHS, the Defense Humint Service, which was part of the DIA. "We had folks with skills, but then throw into it the President's memo on Geneva and we were in a new area."

Compliance with the interrogation rules was one of her main responsibilities as Staff Judge Advocate for JTF–170. When she arrived at Guantánamo there were no special rules in place. The military were following *FM 34–52*, which was what she was brought up on. The FBI was concerned with prosecutions, however, and the need to ensure that evidence from interrogations would be admissible in criminal proceedings. By the time she arrived there was already pressure to go further in the interrogations, and her arrival also coincided with the discovery of al-Qahtani, who had "gone up to the brig" (i.e., he'd been placed in isolation). They weren't getting anything out of him so the military intelligence people, the DIA, started looking at other options. "Could we go further?" she was constantly asked. "I never got help from anyone in dealing with that legal question," she told me. She knew she was being put in an impossible situation.

In many respects, Beaver's account of what happened in the late summer of 2002 confirmed what Dunlavey had told me. More aggressive interrogation techniques were wanted, going beyond those identified in *FM 34–52*. The *Field Manual* hadn't been updated since 1992 and it dealt with different circumstances. She didn't know if the initiative to go beyond the *Field Manual* came from outside Guantánamo. She thought that techniques were not imposed as such directly from Washington, but it was clear that Washington was closely involved. She thought it possible that Washington's views were being fed into the process by people on the ground at Guantánamo, like the DHS representative, but she had no direct evidence of that. Her sense of the pressure coming from Washington was confirmed by other documents I came across later. The Interrogation Control Element (ICE) was the body that oversaw all the military interrogations at Guantánamo, under the DIA. The ICE chief, Dave Becker, told an Army investigation that many of the aggressive interrogation techniques requested in October 2002 were "a direct result of the pressure we felt from Washington to obtain intelligence and the lack of policy guidance being issued by Washington."[2]

In September 2002 there were a series of brainstorming meetings, some of which were led by Diane Beaver. This coincided with the first anniversary of September 11, which was marked at Guantánamo with a special ceremony run by Dave Becker, the ICE chief. The aim of these sessions was to gather possible new interrogation techniques. "I kept minutes, I got everyone together, I invited, I facilitated," she told me. The CIA were down there recruiting, and they came in on the sessions, as did the DIA. Where were the ideas coming from? All over the place, she said. Discussion was wide-ranging. Some ideas came from people's own training experiences: several people had been on SERE courses, but no one in the group was a SERE expert. Some colleagues, then went off to Fort Bragg, SERE's home, including a Gitmo psychologist and psychiatrist. Others had experience in the Joint Personnel Recovery Agency, which was charged with recovery of detained U.S. personnel and oversaw SERE training for the services. This was confirmation for me that SERE had indeed played a significant role despite the Administration denying that this was the case.

Ideas also came from other sources and Beaver mentioned one that surprised me. I noted the words "24—Jack Bauer," but didn't immediately follow this up with her. It was only when I got home that I realized she was referring to the main character in Fox Channel's popular series *24*, which everyone watched. Jack Bauer is a fictitious member of the counter-terrorism unit in L.A. who helped to prevent many terror attacks on the

United States; for him torture and even killing are justifiable means to achieve the desired result. "Rules don't apply to Jack Bauer," another character says in one episode, "he does what he wants, when he wants, and he doesn't care whose life it affects." Bauer had many friends at Guantánamo Bay, Beaver said, "he gave people lots of ideas." Later on I watched the second seson of 24, that started broadcasting in October 2002, with my son. The first episode opened with a scene of a man being tortured, apparently with chemicals. The information he divulged—that a nuclear device was to be exploded in Los Angeles within the next twenty-four hours—was the basis for the series. The message was clear: torture works. I raised this with Beaver when I next saw her. "We saw it on cable," Beaver explained, "people had already seen the first series, it was hugely popular." She believes the scene contributed to an environment in which those at Guantánamo were encouraged to see themselves as being on the frontline—and to go further than they otherwise might. Nowadays she can't watch 24 any more.

The information on the sources of the new techniques was unconventional, to say the least. In the absence of formal guidance from the Pentagon the group at Guantánamo turned to SERE and were inspired by a television program. The CIA's involvement in the brainstorming sessions to identify techniques was consistent with news reports that suggested high-level coordination between the CIA and the Pentagon in developing aggressive new interrogation techniques. Later allegations also suggested a role for three CIA-employed psychologists—James Mitchell, Bruce Jessen and R. Scott Shumate—in the development of these new techniques.[3] Not everyone was enthusiastic, however. Beaver mentioned that the FBI and the Criminal Investigation Task Force declined to get involved. And one of the Criminal Innvestigation Task Force (CITF) psychologists, Mike Gelles, raised concerns based on second- and third-hand information, Beaver believed. When she asked him for facts he couldn't provide any.

Under Beaver's guidance a list of ideas slowly emerged. The Chief of the Interrogation Control Element recalled a meeting with Beaver on the maximum length of an interrogation session, no more than twenty hours in a twenty-four-hour period. "We came to that number after reading about the United States Army Ranger Course," he explained, in which "our soldiers are subjected to twenty-hour days and are apparently only required to have four hours of sleep."[4] If that was OK, he explained, "then in our minds it was OK to subject the terrorist to twenty-hour interrogations," although keeping a detainee awake for five days straight "would be sleep deprivation," which was prohibited.[5] But they set no limit on the number of twenty-hour days; two or three was one thing, but twenty or thirty or fifty was quite another.

They saw less difficulty with other potential techniques, for instance taking the detainees out of their usual environment, so that they didn't know where they were or where they were going; the use of hoods and goggles; the use of sexual tension, which was "culturally taboo, disrespectful, humiliating and potentially unexpected"[6]; creating psychological drama. Beaver recalled that smothering was thought to be particularly effective, and that Dunlavey, who'd been in Vietnam, was in favor because he knew it worked. I recalled a photograph that had been published on the front page of the *Washington Post* in January 1968, and showed the use of a waterboarding technique on an "uncooperative enemy suspect." She thought it came from the Navy SERE training program, where waterboarding was part of the curriculum (water is passed over a detainee's face to create "a flooding sense of suffocation and drowning, meant to make him talk"[7]; it has been used around the world, and was graphically depicted in the 1966 film *The Battle for Algiers*). Supporters of techniques like this were macho and tough, Dunlavey among them: "he's a tough guy," she said cynically. And a lawyer, I thought.

These brainstorming meetings at Guantánamo produced animated discussion. "Who has the glassy eyes?" Beaver asked herself as she surveyed the men around the room, thirty or more of them. She was invariably the only woman in the room, keeping control of the boys. The younger men would get particularly agitated, excited even: "You could almost see their dicks getting hard as they got new ideas." A wan smile crossed Beaver's face. "And I said to myself, you know what, I don't have a dick to get hard, I can stay detached."

As the new techniques emerged, it was Jerry Phifer's job to compile them into a list. According to Beaver, Dunlavey was willing to make a decision then and there at Guantánamo: "He didn't really sit down and think about things." He was frequently in conflict with Baccus, and wanted to show that he was in charge. She was sure, though, that he didn't mean to harm anyone. None of them did. Eventually she and Phifer convinced Dunlavey that the list of techniques had to go up to Washington for approval.

By then it was September and there was no question in Beaver's mind that Washington was closely involved. She confirmed what Dunlavey had told me, that toward the end of the month a delegation of senior lawyers came down to Guantánamo, well before the list of techniques was sent up to Washington. Among the lawyers was David Addington, Vice President Cheney's lawyer. He talked a great deal and it was obvious to Beaver that he was a "very powerful man," "definitely the guy in charge" with his booming voice and confident style. Addington was accompanied by Alberto Gonzales, President Bush's lawyer, who was quiet and said almost nothing. Jim Haynes was there too, and seemed especially interested in the military commissions that were being contemplated to prosecute some of the detainees. Haynes came down at least twice. John Rizzo, a CIA counter-terrorism lawyer, and now CIA Acting General Counsel, was also with them.

I asked how she felt when she first met Haynes. She replied without a moment's hesitation: "Scared," although he seemed a "very nice man," and very bright, and she was keen to make a good impression. Later, in June 2004, Haynes hired her as an Associate Deputy General Counsel in his office and she worked closely with him on revisions to FM 34–52.

The senior Administration lawyers were down there for an orientation visit, to get a better feel for Guantánamo. They talked to the intelligence people, they even watched some interrogations. They were interested in the proposed military commissions, but they also talked to Beaver about the new interrogation techniques. Talking about this visit made Beaver anxious; like Dunlavey she didn't want to give details. But, she said, the lawyers were given an intelligence briefing, and they knew all about al-Qahtani. They also probably believed that FM 34–52 was not "sufficient," but, according to Beaver, "we weren't at a point where we could discuss anything with that group of lawyers." One thing she did recall: the message they got from the visitors was that they should do "whatever needed to be done," meaning a green light from the very top—from the lawyers for Bush, Cheney, Rumsfeld and the CIA.

By the first week of October, the list of eighteen techniques was more or less completed and it fell to Beaver to provide the legal sign-off. She told me that Dunlavey thought verbal approval would be fine, contradicting his account to me. She said that he was worried that if the request went to General Hill he might say no. "I was asked to approve the new techniques orally, but I wasn't comfortable with that." (Later I went back to Dunlavey and he denied vigorously that he had at first asked Beaver for a verbal legal sign-off.) It wasn't so much that she had doubts about what she was being asked to approve, but she thought so important a decision needed to be properly written up: there needed to be a paper trail, and ultimately there needed to be authorization from the top. She was conscious of her relatively lowly position, "the dirt on the ground," as she put it too self-deprecatingly, but also acutely aware of the time constraints, the pressures, her responsibilities. And she knew her own limitations.

The beginning of October was a time of terrible strain for Diane Beaver. Relations with Dunlavey were now very tense and she thought he might be "losing it." "I never prayed so hard in my life as in October 2002," she whispered, and relieved her stress by diving in the waters off Guantánamo. It was rumored that Dunlavey was leaving, that he'd become paranoid, lost the plot. At the same time, as a lawyer with relatively limited experience of intelligence law and no background in international law, Beaver was being asked to sign off a whole new line of interrogation techniques. "I just wasn't comfortable giving oral advice. I wanted to get something in writing. That was my game plan. I had four days. Dunlavey gave me just four days. But I was in Guantánamo, there wasn't access to much material, books and things."

She tried getting help from more senior lawyers, starting with Manny Supervielle at SOUTHCOM, but got nowhere. "I heard nothing from Manny," she said, "so I called some of the lawyers in Washington, but no one got back to me." At the time, Jane Dalton was the main lawyer for the Joint Chiefs of Staff, General Myers's lawyer, and next in the chain of command, but Beaver sensed that Dalton wanted nothing to do with this. "She wasn't going to play," Beaver said, "she didn't want to tread on the toes of the 4-star generals, she said you should talk to Manny Supervielle, not me, talk to SOUTHCOM." Beaver called the DIA in Washington; they said "we do de-briefing, it's all based on *FM 34–52*." She didn't know who to call at the CIA so she called the JAG school, but again without success. "I would have appreciated some strategic level guidance from senior people." So she ploughed on alone, working for four days preparing her own advice, doing the best she could with the most limited resources and no assistance. "I wanted to get something in writing, out to SOUTHCOM in Florida." She also believed that more senior lawyers in Washington would review her advice—and override it, if necessary. It never occurred to her that on so important an issue she would be the one writing the decisive legal advice. As far as she was concerned, her victory "was getting it up the command," in the face of Dunlavey's opposition.

The legal advice was completed just before the Columbus Day weekend. She signed off on Friday, October 11. Dunlavey had reviewed earlier versions, but had not imposed any significant changes. The final version was addressed to Dunlavey, as Commander of JTF–170, and came with a four-line covering note, entitled "Legal Review of Aggressive Interrogation Techniques." I wondered who had chosen the word "aggressive." The note was crisp, in length and in tone. Beaver reviewed Phifer's list of interrogation techniques and agreed that "the proposed strategies do not violate applicable federal law." The word "agree" stood out, suggesting confirmation of a policy decision already taken. Beaver had been put in a situation in which Dunlavey—who would have reminded her not only that he was a lawyer but also a judge—had already concluded that the new techniques were fine and he just wanted her sign off. Here was a loyal soldier, in uncharted waters on these new and complex legal issues, confronted by a powerful, macho personality who was on a mission to save America from the next attack.

The legal brief was attached to the covering note. Like any advice, hers began with the issue she was asked to address: "To ensure the security of the United States and its allies, more aggressive interrogation techniques . . . may be required in order to obtain information from detainees that are resisting interrogation efforts and are suspected of having significant information essential to national security." As stated, the issue was not balanced and skewed the advice toward a desired result.

Beaver began her memo with 'the facts': none of the detainees were protected by Geneva; the detainees had developed resistance strategies because they could communicate among themselves; there was no established, clear policy for interrogation limits, but interrogators felt they shouldn't do anything "controversial." By the time she set out her views on the law the list of techniques was in final draft. Some of these facts came to her directly: she had observed many interrogations, seen the resistance strategies. A key fact was the President's decision of February 7, 2002, which set aside Geneva. Beaver proceeded as though this automatically set aside all the rules of international law. "I opened the book, went to the section on 'unlawful combatants,' found that the pages were blank," she told me. Marooned on Guantánamo, without access to a proper library or other military lawyers, Beaver was told to draft the rules hereby.

She was stuck with the President's decision on Geneva, which required her to proceed on the basis that Geneva provided no rights for the detainees. "It was not my job to second-guess the President." I put it to her—unfairly perhaps—that in such circumstances her responsibility was to give independent legal advice, and if necessary to second-guess the leader. It was her job to make sure that the interrogators and her soldiers didn't end up in the dock. She disagreed. That was a job for more senior lawyers; acutely aware of her rank and status, she proceeded on the basis that "no international body of law directly applies." The President had set aside Geneva; moreover, she concluded that the Torture Convention and various human rights treaties didn't apply, either, because the United States had entered reservations that gave primacy to U.S. federal law, or because the treaty was not "self-executing" (meaning that although it might bind the United States under international law it didn't create rights that the individual detainees could enforce before U.S. courts). Beaver ignored customary law altogether. All that was left was U.S. law, which is what she turned to.

Given the circumstances in which she found herself, the advice had a certain desperate, heroic quality. At first sight Beaver seems to give *carte blanche* approval to all the new interrogation techniques. But a more careful reading shows nuanced advice, with numerous caveats and conditions. Beaver proceeded methodically through the eighteen techniques. Each was tested against the standards set by U.S. law, namely the Eighth Amendment of the Constitution (which prohibits "cruel and unusual punishments"), the federal Torture Statute, and the military law of the Uniform Code of Military Justice. A common theme ran throughout: the techniques were fine "so long as the force used could plausibly have been thought necessary in a particular situation to achieve a legitimate government objective, and it was not applied maliciously or sadistically for the very purpose of causing harm." The legitimate government objective was, of course, national security and the imminent threat of further attacks. Beaver's standard was elastic—it could accommodate just about anything. It was difficult to imagine much that would be prohibited, short of an intentional desire to cause maximum pain without any plausible benefit. The federal Torture Statute, Beaver wrote, would not be violated so long as none of the proposed techniques were "specifically intended to cause severe physical pain or suffering or prolonged mental harm." Legality was thus boiled down to intent. That was not what the Torture Convention said, of course, but since it didn't apply that didn't matter.

Each of the three categories listed in Lieutenant Colonel Phifer's memo was tested. The two Category I techniques were straightforward. An interrogator could yell at the detainee so long as he did so without any *intent* to cause severe physical damage or prolonged mental harm. Deceiving the detainee was fine because the law imposed no obligation "to be truthful while conducting an interrogation."

The twelve Category II techniques required a little more work. Everything was fine so long as no "severe physical pain" was inflicted or prolonged mental harm intended. Physical pain that was not "severe" was permissible. Mental harm that was not "prolonged" was fine. The reader would look in vain for guidance as to the meaning of the words "severe" and "prolonged" as Beaver did not define them. In the time available, it wasn't possible to draw precise lines, to help an interrogator distinguish between pain that was "severe" and pain that was not. The assumption was that none of the techniques crossed that line. I pointed out to Beaver that under international law the pain threshold was set far lower. "I know," she countered, "but the President decided those rules didn't apply."

Yet even here the advice was defensive. The techniques were justified because there was "a legitimate governmental objective in obtaining the information for the protection of the national security of the United States, its citizens, and allies." The ends always justified the means, and it wasn't difficult to see where this path would lead, or why Beaver felt a pressure to give the advice she did. Rumsfeld had described the detainees as "the worst of the worst"; Dunlavey thought that some of them wanted "the destruction of our culture as we know it, our way of life." And Beaver herself had unambiguous views about some of them: "Psychopaths," she told me, "skinny, runty, dangerous lying psychopaths." For those people the Category II techniques seemed almost too decent. Beaver had no problem making a detainee stand for four hours, or isolating him for up to thirty days, or interrogating him in different environments. Taken on its own, each technique was legally permissible so long as it was not used for the malicious and sadistic purpose of causing harm. She had no evidence that prolonged mental harm would result from their use. For the same reasons the deprivation of light and auditory stimuli and hooding during transportation and questioning were permissible.

Beaver expressed no need to set limits on these techniques. She did not address the possibility that the techniques could be used cumulatively, or over extended periods of time. The use of twenty-hour interrogations was fine. There was no legal requirement to give detainees four hours of sleep a night, but as a cautionary measure they should receive "some amount of sleep" to avoid severe physical or mental harm. There was no need to provide religious or other comfort items (although the situation was different if the detainees were U.S. citizens with rights under the First

Amendment). Shaving of facial hair and other "forced grooming" was permissible so long as it wasn't intended to punish or cause harm. Clothing could be removed, along with hot meals. The detainee's phobias could be used. The reasoning was thin, almost to the point of non-existence.

The four Category III techniques provoked a little more restraint on her part. Threats of imminent death or severe pain were permissible, so long as there was a "compelling government interest." Nevertheless, this technique required some caution: the U.S. Torture Statute specifically mentioned making death threats as an example of inflicting mental pain and suffering. How Beaver distinguished between "death threats" which would be prohibited, and the construction of a scenario in which death was imminent, which would not, was unclear and she was unable to explain the difference to me. It was for the interrogator to work it out.

Likewise, "exposure to cold weather or water" was permissible with appropriate medical monitoring. It was not clear what was meant by "exposure to water"—and Beaver provided no detail. No limits were identified in Phifer's list, and Beaver suggested none. The words seemed innocuous: who could object to a few splashes of water? On the other hand they might mean waterboarding, creating the perception of drowning. Nor did Beaver have a problem with the use of a wet towel "to induce the misperception of suffocation." Again, there had to be no specific intent to cause prolonged mental harm and no medical evidence that it would. However, this technique prompted an unusually strong cautionary note in Beaver's advice. Foreign courts had "already advised about the potential mental harm that this method may cause": she'd dug up some case law from the European Court of Human Rights, the body that Dunlavey had told me would have given him pause for thought. Beaver must have known that the European Court had ruled that these kinds of techniques were abusive or worse. She must have known that they were prohibited. She alerted Dunlavey but still failed to advise categorically against the use of such water-related techniques that could bring the United States into disrepute. Dunlavey, meanwhile, turned a blind eye, assuming he read the advice.

That left one final technique in Category III: mild non-injurious physical contact, otherwise referred to as pushing and poking. Beaver advised this would "technically constitute an assault" under the Uniform Code of Military Justice, but she did not draw that observation to its logical conclusion. She did not advise that the technique be actually outlawed, prohibited. On my reading, she was saying that assault was apparently permissible if it was "technical."

Beaver therefore recommended that all eighteen techniques be approved. Her most striking omission was the failure to consider what the use of two or more of the techniques together or cumulatively might mean. She did, however, enter some caveats. The interrogators had to be properly trained. Since the law required examination of all facts under a "totality of circumstances" test, all proposed interrogations involving Categories II and III methods had to undergo a "legal, medical, behavioral science, and intelligence review prior to their commencement." This suggested concerns about these new techniques, including whether they would be effective. Dunlavey passed on her advice in full, but this final, important recommendation wasn't included in Haynes's recommendation to Rumsfeld a month later. Why not, I asked? She didn't feel able to answer the question and suggested I put it to Haynes directly.

⊷⊷⊶

Time and distance did not improve the quality of the advice. I thought it was horribly wrong when I first read it, and horribly wrong when I re-read it. Nevertheless, the circumstances surrounding Diane Beaver's advice were now much clearer. She should never have been put in that position: a more confident individual would have refused. Beaver struck me as honest, loyal and decent. She did what she did in difficult circumstances, under pressures from her commanding officer at Guantánamo and against the background of even greater pressure from Washington. She stood by her advice, at least in the circumstances in which she had found herself in October 2002. Did it occur to her that her advice could expose her to legal proceedings? "No. We never thought about it like that. It was October 2002, the anniversary of 9/11. There were real pressures. We had these people. We believed they had more information. We were just doing our jobs." Yet there was no help for her, at least from Washington. She stood by her advice. She did not oppose more aggressive techniques of interrogation. But as we parted there was a palpable sense of grievance about the way her advice had been handled. "I thought that Manny Supervielle would give an opinion. But he didn't write one. I thought that Jane Dalton would give an opinion, but there was none from her either."

Beaver was put on a faraway island and told to get on with it. She explained what she had tried to do, and her sense of shock about the way in which her advice was made public. "They gave me an hour's notice, no warning, no preparation." They left her name on the advice when they released it: Haynes could have blacked it out but didn't. She took the flak and the lawsuits personally. I had a distinct memory of her sense of grievance during our first conversation. She was let down, by weaker men, and she, the author of the legal review that Gonzales and Haynes would rely on, knew it.

There was one other matter. When he released Diane Beaver's legal advice Alberto Gonzales also made available two other legal advices that had been written for the Administration in August 2002 by John Yoo and Jay Bybee, the Justice Department lawyers. Was she aware of those documents when she prepared her opinion? No, she only became aware of them when they were put in the public domain by Gonzales in June 2004. She did remember, however, that the "CIA said we had an opinion, it took DOJ some time to do." This was perplexing: why was she not told that more senior lawyers in Washington had put their minds to the very same legal issues she was being asked to address?

As I gave my thanks and said goodbye to her, I noticed a framed certificate on the wall of her office. It was the Defense Medal for Exceptional Civilian Service, given to her by Donald Rumsfeld and signed by Jim Haynes. The citation identified her as a "noted expert on matters related to the detention of enemy combatants in the Global war on terror" and commended her for her "unique combination of legal skills, experience and enthusiasm."

INTERROGATION LOG OF DETAINEE 063
Day 22, December 14 2002

0001: Detainee's hands were cuffed at his sides to prevent him from conducting his prayer ritual. . . .

0025: Lead taped picture of 3 year old victim over detainee's heart . . . Control drips a few drops of water on detainee's head to keep him awake. Detainee struggles when the water is dropped on his head. . . .

0120: Interrogators take a break and detainee listens to white noise. Detainee goes to bathroom and is exercised while hooded. . . .

1630: Corpsman checks vitals—gives three bags of IV . . . Detainee broke down crying. . . .

9

In August 2002, as Mike Dunlavey and Diane Beaver grappled with the new interrogation techniques, they were in the dark about what was going on elsewhere. Despite Beaver's efforts to procure the advice of more senior and experienced lawyers, no one told her that lawyers at the Justice Department were on the case. With his decision of February 7, the President removed Geneva and its Common Article 3 from the American book of rules for Guantánamo. However, there were other international rules that also constrained interrogations at Guantánamo.

In 1948, shortly before Geneva was adopted, Eleanor Roosevelt led the U.S. delegation in the negotiation of the Universal Declaration of Human Rights. Article 5 proclaimed a new international commitment: "No one shall be subjected to torture or to cruel, inhuman or degrading treatment or punishment." Two decades later that principle was enshrined in a binding legal text, Article 7 of the International Covenant on Civil and Political Rights. By the 1980s it was broadly accepted that the prohibition reflected customary international law, with no exceptions or limitations. All that remained was the need to flesh out the details and provide enforcement mechanisms.

In 1984 the United States and other governments adopted the Convention against Torture and Other Cruel, Inhuman or Degrading Treatment. Article 1 defined torture broadly, as "any act by which severe pain or suffering, whether physical or mental, is intentionally inflicted on a person," carried out by a public official to obtain information or a confession. The Convention was also categorical that there were no circumstances—even a war against terrorism—in which torture could be justified, a principle ignored by Professor Dershowitz and the makers of 24. All acts of torture are treated as criminal offenses. According to Article 4, "any act by any person which constitutes complicity or participation in torture" is also to be treated as a criminal offense.

(left) Jay Bybee, Assistant Attorney General, Office of Legal Counsel, U.S. Department of Justice

(above) John Yoo, Deputy Assistant Attorney General, Office of Legal Counsel, U.S. Department of Justice

The United States joined the Convention in 1994. Eight years later, its provisions concentrated minds in Washington. Detainees in the 'war on terror' caused the White House and Alberto Gonzales to request the lawyers at the Office of the Legal Counsel (OLC) at the Justice Department to advise on the Torture Convention. A legal opinion from the OLC is decisive and final: it trumps all other legal advice. Traditionally, OLC advice is prepared with input from other governmental departments which may have specific expertise. In this case, the State Department lawyers that particular knowledge of the treaties in question, yet they were not invited to contribute and were cut out of the process, under the direction of the White House. This can only have been because it was known that they would have objected strenuously.[1]

In August 2002, Gonzales received legal opinions from Jay Bybee, who headed the OLC at that time, and John Yoo, one of Bybee's deputies. When Alberto Gonzales released the Haynes memo and its related documents in June 2004, in the heat of the Abu Ghraib scandal, two of the opinions were made public. A third was not. None of the opinions was prepared with the benefit of any input from the State Department or other lawyers, bypassing the particular expertise that would usually have flowed from the inter-agency process.

The first legal memo on the definition of torture was signed by Bybee, the Assistant Attorney General.[2] A deeply religious man, Bybee studied law at Brigham Young University, the Mormon university in Utah.

Before moving to the OLC he spent time in private practice and taught constitutional law in Louisiana and Nevada. From 1989 to 1991 he was Associate Counsel at the White House to the first President Bush. With no background in international law or issues of war or interrogation, and excluded from the "War Council," he turned to John Yoo for assistance in drafting what has come to be called the Bybee/Yoo memo. According to Jack Goldsmith, who served as Haynes's Special Counsel from September 2002 and knew Yoo well, Bybee "tended to approve Yoo's draft opinions with minimal critical input."[3] Yoo had joined the Justice Department from Berkeley Law School in California, where he taught international law. Widely regarded as a skeptic on international law, a prerequisite for membership of the "War Council," Yoo was concerned about constraints on American power and sovereignty. After the Geneva decision, his views on the treatment of the Guantánamo detainees were reported in the press. "What the Administration is trying to do is create a new legal regime," he said.[4] Other colleagues also contributed to the drafting of the memo, including David Addington, Alberto Gonzales and Tim Flanigan, Gonzales's deputy.[5]

Michael Chertoff, at the Justice Department and now Secretary of Homeland Security, also seems to have been involved. He advised the CIA on the legality of coercive interrogation techniques based on the Bybee/Yoo memo.[6] Chertoff liked a tough approach and was a fan of Jack Bauer, the lead in 24, and his fictitious counter-terrorism unit colleagues, praising them for showing the kind of character and tenacity that would help America defeat terrorism.[7] For Chertoff, it seemed, there was no line dividing fiction from reality. "That is what we do every day," he said of 24, "that is what we do in the government, that's what we do in private life when we evaluate risks."[8]

The purpose of the Bybee/Yoo memo was left ambiguous. "As we understand it," it read, "this question has arisen in the context of the conduct of interrogations outside of the United States." This apparently referred to DoD interrogations at Guantánamo, as well as interrogations by the CIA in faraway places that would come to be associated with extraordinary rendition. However, the compass of the memo was not limited to CIA interrogations, although Yoo apparently believed it should have been. "I always thought that only the CIA should do this, but people at the White House and at DoD [an apparent reference to David Addington, Alberto Gonzales and Jim Haynes] felt differently."[9]

The fifty-page memo was dense—but length is no substitute for analysis or substance. Bybee and Yoo concluded that U.S. law prohibits only "extreme acts." Similarly, the Torture Convention prohibited only the most extreme acts by reserving criminal penalties solely for torture, not for acts of "cruel, inhuman or degrading treatment or punishment" that caused less suffering. They considered the case law of various courts, including the decisions of the European Court of Human Rights that Diane Beaver had considered. But they chose selectively. From these "international decisions' on sensory deprivation techniques," they concluded that there was a "wide range" of such techniques that didn't reach to the level of torture. They also considered the possibility of prosecutions under U.S. law. The U.S. Congress could not interfere with the President's conduct of the interrogation of enemy combatants; laws that prevented the President from gaining intelligence necessary to prevent attacks upon the United States would be unconstitutional. Moreover, criminal law defenses of necessity and self-defense were available to prevent a direct and imminent threat to the United States and its citizens. This overrode the Torture Convention's absolute prohibition on torture: the U.S. Congress must have intended to permit the "necessity or wartime defense" for torture. Whatever the merits of those arguments—it is hard to discern them—Bybee and Yoo failed to address the possibility of criminal proceedings outside the United States. Nor did they consider their own potential complicity in advising on the legality of techniques prohibited by international law.

The heart of the Bybee/Yoo analysis was that the current definition of torture set an absurdly high threshold of suffering. So they ignored the definitions applied by the U.S. military in *FM 34–52* and in international law. Torture covered only the most extreme acts, limited to severe pain that is difficult to endure. "Where the pain is physical," they wrote, "it must be of an intensity akin to that which accompanies serious physical injury such as death or organ failure." Anything less would be permissible. Where the pain was mental, then it required suffering "not just at the moment of infliction but it also requires lasting psychological harm, such as seen in mental disorders like posttraumatic stress disorder." These were surprising conclusions, given the language of the Torture Convention. Nevertheless, the most senior lawyers in the Administration concurred. Acting CIA General Counsel John Rizzo, who joined Addington, Gonzales and Haynes on the trip to Guantánamo, thought the memo was "persuasive." "My reaction was that it was an aggressive, expansive reading," he explained, "but I can't say that I had any specific objections to any specific parts of it."[10]

A second legal opinion was signed by John Yoo,[11] dealing with the question: would interrogation methods used on captured al-Qaeda detainees which were lawful under a U.S. statute none the less violate the 1984 Torture Convention? They would not, he concluded, because of an "understanding" that the United States had added to the 1984 Convention, giving form and content to the Convention's amorphous concept of mental pain and suffering. This "understanding" ensured that the bar on mental torture would rise to a severity comparable to that required for physical torture, and create a valid and effective reservation to the Torture Convention's broad definition. On Yoo's analysis, each party could substitute its own definitions for those of the Convention by setting out its "understanding" of what the Convention required. But Yoo misunderstood what the United States did when it ratified the Convention. It did not enter a 'reservation' redefining torture and setting the bar at a higher level: it could not change the international legal obligation. Without the benefit of any input from the State Department, Yoo confused a "reservation" and an "understanding," noting that Germany had commented on the U.S. "reservation" but 'did not oppose any U.S. reservation outright'.[12] In fact that was not what Germany did. Germany stated that the United States's understandings "do not touch upon the obligations of the United States of America as State Party to the Convention," making it clear that the United States could not impose its own definition of torture. The definition in the Convention—the international definition—is the only one that matters internationally.

A third opinion was also sent to Gonzales at this time. To this day its precise contents remain secret. Written by Bybee and Yoo at the request of John Rizzo, and sometimes referred to as Bybee II, the eighteen-page memorandum, dated August 1, 2002, drew on the Bybee/Yoo memo to advise the CIA on specific interrogation methods it could use against al-Qaeda members.[13] Asked about the relationship between the Bybee/Yoo memo and this more specific document, CIA acting General Counsel John Rizzo confirmed that they "play off each other."[14] One former Pentagon official who was aware of its contents told me that it set out a list of interrogation techniques that were largely similar to those set out in the Haynes memo. Bybee II concluded that techniques akin to the eighteen—including waterboarding—did not constitute torture, although threatening to bury a prisoner alive would.[15] The interrogation techniques assessed by the Justice Department were provided by John Rizzo's office.[16] Rizzo believed all of the techniques were "humane,"[17] a view he took with him to Guantánamo. The evidence of this opinion was highly significant because it confirmed the OLC's sign-off on the techniques. Its existence provided a safety net for Haynes, who would know he didn't have to go beyond Beaver's advice.

These opinions sent an unequivocal message to Alberto Gonzales and the White House, that there was much that could be done by way of interrogation that wasn't constrained by international obligations. The fact that the opinions came from the OLC, that they were binding and dispositive, provided even greater reassurance to those who knew the contents. The OLC opinions were sent to Gonzales, and kept within a tight group. When the group of senior Washington lawyers, led by David Addington, visited Guantánamo in September no mention was made of the OLC opinions to Beaver and Dunlavey.[18]

When Diane Beaver told me she didn't see those memos I believed her. She thought the similarities came from "people's common experience of interrogation techniques, a group of folks that had the same experience and training." And of course there was the possibility that the techniques that the OLC signed off on in Bybee II influenced the eighteen techniques in indirect ways, communicated through the CIA and DIA personnel down at Guantánamo. In any event, Addington, Haynes, Gonzales and Rizzo were well aware of the contents of all three OLC opinions and as they discussed interrogation techniques with Dunlavey they would have known that they already had approval by the OLC. So it didn't really matter what Beaver wrote, although her legal opinion would provide useful cover later.

Four years on, Beaver saw Addington at the Pentagon. He recognized her immediately, even though they hadn't seen each other since Guantánamo. "Great minds think alike," he said with a smile.

INTERROGATION LOG OF DETAINEE 063
Day 24, December 16 2002

Day 24

0220: Detainee began to fall asleep and water was used to assist him in maintaining his attention with interrogator. . . .

0530: Detainee required to sit and watch as interrogator and linguist played checkers. Laughed and mocked detainee throughout game. . . .

0630: Detainee was instructed to clean the room. Interrogator told detainee that he will not be allowed to leave trash all around and live like the pig that he is. He picked up all the trash from the floor while his hands were still cuffed in front of him and the interrogator swept the trash towards him.

0650: Corpsman drew detainee's blood. . . .

10

Shortly after Addington, Gonzales and Haynes visited Guantánamo, General James T. Hill received Dunlavey's memo. It was Friday October 11. Hill didn't know that the D.C. lawyers had visited Guantánamo, or that Bybee and Yoo had given their own advice and had signed off on interrogation techniques equivalent to the eighteen. Hill had only taken up the post of Commander of U.S. SOUTHCOM in Miami a couple of months earlier and was not yet fully up to speed on the machinations at Guantánamo.

Dunlavey's memo had set alarms ringing for Hill. The request for approval of the eighteen new techniques received his immediate attention. Hill had his own intelligence officers and staff lawyer (Manny Supervielle, who briefed Beaver as she had left Miami for Guantánamo) and he wanted to be sure that his people reviewed the materials. Straightaway he recognized the significance of what was being asked. He knew too that SOUTHCOM's reputation was on the line, along with the entire U.S. military establishment. So it was no surprise that Dunlavey's memo spent a few days in Miami and was not immediately forwarded on to Washington. Despite the apparent urgency, it remained in Miami for two weeks as Hill pondered.

General Hill was known to his friends as Tom. He was smart and he was careful. As a commanding officer he was acutely aware of the different roles he played, as a "soldier-diplomat," and he knew that perceptions were often as important as facts. He'd devoted his life to the U.S. military and wasn't about to degrade its reputation or expose his own men and women to the risk of abuse. In the 1970s he had served in Vietnam, so was well aware of the dangers of captivity. His later career had taken him to many of

General James T. Hill, Commander, U.S. Southern Command

the world's most serious trouble spots. In the first Gulf War he commanded the "Always First" 101st Airborne Division during Desert Shield and Desert Storm, then served as deputy Commanding General of U.S. forces in the UN Mission in Haiti. Command of the U.S. Southern Command was his final posting before retirement. It brought huge responsibilities, including overseeing military operations in more than thirty countries of Central and South America, from Mexico in the north, through the Caribbean, down to Argentina in the south. An accident of geography—and decisions taken in Washington in the days after September 11—caused Guantánamo to fall into his lap.

In November 2004 Hill retired from Guantánamo, the U.S. Southern Command and the U.S. military and moved to Coral Gables, Florida, a few miles from SOUTHCOM headquarters. His home is close to the Biltmore Hotel, a monumental 1920s pile that reflects Miami's glory days, boasting the largest resort swimming pool in the United States. The first time I called his home, I left a message, not too hopeful about a response. I tried again a few days later and spoke to Mrs. Hill. She was friendly and not in the least fazed by my call. Her husband was away, she said; he'd call back.

A few days later he did. My nine-year-old daughter ran to the kitchen. "Dad, there's a man on the phone who says he is a general." Hill agreed to meet me. I booked a flight to Florida and the evening before the trip he emailed to say that we could spend an afternoon talking, and go into the evening if necessary. But before we could meet an unexpected "intervening event" occurred. Tom Hill had a Mike Dunlavey moment. In the cab between the Miami airport and the Biltmore hotel I called to arrange where to meet, as we'd agreed. His wife was surprised. Had I not received the phone messages before my flight? Hill had been called away on unexpected business. He had left a message on my American cell phone, but that phone didn't work in London. I only received the message after speaking with

Mrs. Hill. Could she try to track him down? I had not hidden my over-whelming sense of mortification at being ditched after so long a journey. A few minutes later she called back: Hill would meet me at the Biltmore at 5 P. M. "I don't think he'll have very long," she added.

Hill arrived at five o'clock on the dot. He was impeccable: tanned, wearing glasses, an open-necked, blue shirt and polished shoes. It was pretty clear, though, that he would rather have been anywhere but in the lobby of the Biltmore with me. I wasn't quite sure why. His response to Dunlavey's request—in a memo to General Myers, the Chairman of the Joint Chiefs of Staff—had been equivocal and suggested to me he had nothing much to hide. Perhaps a headline in that morning's *Miami Herald* had caused discomfort. "Germany to Consider Probe of Rumsfeld,"[1] for abuse at Guantánamo, amongst other places. I invited him to my room and we sat under a reproduction nineteenth-century map of Central and South America that showed SOUTHCOM's jurisdiction. It gave us something to talk about, to break the ice, to build rapport. He had been to most of the countries on the map. We talked about Tegucigalpa airport in Honduras, probably the most frightening airport in the world, arrived at by descend-ing in ever-diminishing circles into the mouth of a volcanic crater, an expe-rience we both remembered well. His recollection wasn't always so clear on Guantánamo issues and occasionally he asked me to stop taking notes. Three times he took a note of something I had said, after mention was made of someone I'd spoken with.

Hill took over command of SOUTHCOM in August 2002. He vis-ited Guantánamo a week before he took up his command, but had not fol-lowing closely all the comings and goings as the issue of new interrogation techniques rose up the agenda. From the outset he was aware of major ten-sions—between JTF–160 and JTF–170; between Baccus and Dunlavey; between the military and the FBI and the CITF. There was "a lot of fric-tion," mostly relating to the soldiers' living conditions, and also to the treatment of the detainees. Hill discussed the problems with General Myers and agreed a solution was needed. Around that time others had also seen problems. Myers instructed Brigadier General John Custer, the Deputy Commanding General of the Army's Military Intelligence training school at Fort Huachuca, Arizona, to go down to Guantánamo and take a look at what was going on. Custer's report made numerous recommenda-tions on better training for interrogators. Others who expressed concerns included a Republican Congressman, David Hobson, and the Pentagon's Director of Administration and Management, Ray Dubois. They returned with "some pretty unfavorable remarks about Guantánamo." As these reports reached him, Hill became increasingly concerned about a "dysfunctional" command leadership. He worried that the full intelligence value of the detainees might not be fully exploited. He was also concerned that the interrogators hadn't been properly trained. "They were just kind of swimming by themselves," he said.

Hill wanted to remove Baccus immediately. Instead he decided to combine JTF–160 and 170 into a single unit, JTF-GTMO. He concluded that neither Baccus nor Dunlavey was suitable to command the new integrated unit, a view that was shared at the Pentagon, and so he was open to a new appointment. Eventually the decision was to go for Major General Geoffrey Miller, although he had not been on an original list of possible replacements provided by General Shinseki, the Army's Chief of Staff. Later Shinseki called him and asked if Miller would be acceptable. Hill did not hesitate. "He was my guy. I knew him personally. I trusted him explicitly and I knew he'd do a great job." Yet he was surprised that Miller took the job, thinking that his wife Pam would say no. By the time Miller arrived in November 2002 Guantánamo was not in good shape. "They didn't have the right housing. They didn't have the right standards. It was a mess. In all candor, it was a mess." But they were about to get new interrogation techniques.

Dunlavey's request arrived on Hill's desk on October 11, together with Beaver's legal advice and the list of eighteen techniques. Hill didn't know much about Dunlavey other than that he was an intelligence officer, and had been selected and assigned by Rumsfeld. The request from Dunlavey for new techniques was their first formal contact regarding interrogations. Hill had visited Guantánamo and knew about al-Qahtani. So he was aware of the pressure to take the interrogations beyond the limited, non-coercive techniques that *FM 34–52* allowed. Dunlavey's request did not come out of the blue. But none of this made him more comfortable.

As far as Hill knew, Dunlavey had made the initial request for the development of the new techniques. He was frustrated with the lawyers, and the limits they imposed on the conduct of interrogations. "I've got one lawyer that tells me I can't even offer this guy a hamburger to get him to talk to me," Dunlavey told him, "so how do I build rapport?" Other lawyers could tolerate different standards and Dunlavey managed to find some who were more supportive of his need for flexibility: "I'm going to go out on my own, my guys are buying fish burgers from McDonalds and bringing them in because we finally got a lawyer that said that was OK." Hill knew

Dunlavey wanted to go further and that he was under considerable pressure from Washington—meaning Rumsfeld—to deliver results.

The timing of Dunlavey's request was significant. The anniversary of September 11 had come and gone and there was a widespread fear of more attacks. A "general mood" of anxiety pervaded the country. "We just didn't know what we didn't know," Hill recalled, and as a result, he didn't feel under any particular pressure to decide things a certain way. He had been told that some of the detainees had information, and he had no reason to doubt that. "We really believed—and I still believe—that there are people that have lots of information that is still relevant information that we haven't gotten." He was also acutely aware of the requirements of FM 34–52. These were exceptional times, however, that justified different actions. "We were in uncharted waters. We'd never done this. The Army had never done strategic interrogations like that. We knew we had our manuals, but the guys there had their manuals too, because we had in fact the al-Qaeda training book [the Manchester Manual], for how to evade interrogations."

Hill wasn't directly involved in the elaboration of the proposed techniques. As far as he knew, the ideas had been gathered at Guantánamo, under the direction of Dunlavey. He was aware, however, that there would have been input from different sources. "My recollection," he said, "is that it was developed at GTMO. Vetted with my lawyers and my J2." Efforts had also been made to improve the techniques on the basis of Brigadier General Custer's report, which was finalized at the end of September. That provided more ideas for the list that eventually emerged. Beyond that he had no detailed knowledge of where the techniques came from, "no idea who conjured them up." Hill was clear that the Department of Defense would have vetted the eighteen techniques *before* they were finalized at the end of October. "The JTF guys and my lawyers and the J2 would have taken it up there and let the staff see it . . . at the Pentagon." This was important. It confirmed that Dunlavey didn't send his request into a void. By the time the eighteen techniques arrived in D.C. the Secretary of Defense already knew what was on the list—and knowledge implied approval. This was also clear from the letter Hill sent to Myers on 25 October. "Our respective staffs, the Office of the Secretary of Defense, and Joint Task Force 170, have been trying to identify counter-resistant techniques that we can lawfully employ." I'd missed this point of detail and it was Hill who reminded me of the exact words. This was written, contemporaneous evidence confirming that Rumsfeld's office, including the lawyers, were *already* involved by that date. This meant that documents Gonzales made public contradicted his own narrative in June 2004.

Hill also knew that there was a connection with the SERE program that trained American soldiers to resist interrogation. A group from Guantánamo had visited Fort Bragg, South Carolina, in mid-September, although Hill had only learned about the visit after it had taken place. Fort Bragg was home to Army's John F. Kennedy Special Warfare Center and School, and it ran a number of SERE courses. Broaching this subject was delicate, since SERE training was never intended to teach soldiers how to interrogate individuals. When pushed, however, General Hill said that he saw no difficulty in drawing upon SERE training, it was an appropriate thing to look at. "In the process of determining the techniques, that would be a sensible thing to have done." That did not mean, however, that SERE techniques should be dispositive. What was not sensible, however, was the suggestion that the Pentagon made to Hill that he should be the one to approve of the new techniques. This was yet another nugget of evidence that Rumsfeld and Haynes knew about the new techniques before Dunlavey's request reached the Pentagon. He refused. "I said no, no, no. This is way too important to leave at our level." He pushed the decision back to Washington.

He had discussions with General Myers, to "keep him abreast," but on this particular issue he had no discussion with Paul Wolfowitz, who was Rumsfeld's Deputy, or with Doug Feith, who was responsible for policy at the Pentagon. Having decided to punt it up to Washington, it wasn't going to go to just anybody. "I had my staff draft a letter personally from me to the Secretary. And the reason I did that was to put it in the hands of the Secretary right off the bat. Not a staff guy." His letter to Rumsfeld stressed the importance of the work that needed to go on at Guantánamo. "The staff thinks that there's a list of interrogation techniques that they think are legal." Hill had reservations. "I said, I personally don't think all of them are [legal], nor even if they are that they should be used." These changes had such significance in his eyes that he wanted a decision from Rumsfeld personally. "There ought to be a major policy discussion on this and everybody ought to be involved. And he was the only one that could do that."

The issue was so important that he also wanted top-level legal support. "I wanted this material out. I wanted transparency." He knew there were bound to be serious legal questions and he was not comfortable relying on Beaver's advice alone. She was far too junior. His own lawyer, Manny Supervielle, had looked at the documents and insisted on a more senior review. Although Addington, Gonzales, Haynes and other senior Washington lawyers had visited Guantánamo in late September, Hill wasn't present so didn't know what their views were, or what advice they had given or received. Only later did he learn of their visit. Hill was also thinking about the reaction of other, friendly states to the new techniques. He wanted to do the right thing, the legal thing. He wanted his soldiers "to be able to look themselves in the mirror and know that they had done the correct and legal thing." Supervielle reviewed the documents and they both agreed that they needed more legal advice.

On Friday October 25 Hill wrote to General Myers, the Chairman of the Joint Chiefs of Staff. He forwarded the list of eighteen techniques, the Beaver advice and the Dunlavey request. His covering note was carefully crafted. It had an anxious air and voiced serious concerns, and I noticed that General Hill didn't actually request anything himself, beyond a further review by more senior lawyers. I pointed that out to him. He looked at me. "You obviously read things carefully." The memo consisted of four crisp paragraphs. JTF–170's activities had provided "critical intelligence support," but some detainees had tenaciously resisted current interrogation methods. This was a reference to al-Qahtani and another detainee whose identity was—and remains—classified and secret. "Our respective staffs, the Office of the Secretary of Defense, and Joint Task Force 170 have been trying to identify counter-resistant techniques that we can lawfully employ," he wrote. The line confirmed Rumsfeld's prior involvement and signaled concerns about legality. It undermined the Administration's claim that the techniques had emerged at Guantánamo alone, that they were merely the product of the creative thinking of an aggressive major-general. In their rush to get the materials out, Gonzales and Haynes hadn't thought through all the consequences or been sufficiently attentive to the words used by careful men like Hill.

Hill thought that the first two categories of techniques were legal and humane, but he was uncertain whether all the techniques in the third category were legal under U.S. law. He was concerned about the absence of judicial interpretation of the U.S. Torture Statute, and was particularly troubled by the use of implied or expressed threats of death of the detainee or his family. He wanted to have as many options as possible at his disposal, so he requested that "Department of Defense and Justice Department lawyers review the third category of techniques." The reference to the Justice Department was highly significant, since normally it would be left to the Defense Department lawyers—meaning Jim Haynes—to sign off. It was consistent with what he had told me about his ignorance of the fact that the OLC had already given opinions. His words should have set alarm bells ringing: some of the techniques looked like torture. He told General Myers that Diane Beaver's legal review was not a sufficient basis for proceeding, that he wanted these issues to be looked at very carefully, that it should go beyond Jim Haynes, and that the Justice Department had to be involved. Hill wanted a thorough review of JTF–170's proposed strategy. He was open to other suggested interrogation methods, and wanted to provide the interrogators with "as many legally permissible tools as possible." His concluding sentence was prophetic: "I am cognizant of the important policy ramifications of some of these proposed techniques."

At the Biltmore Hotel we went over the techniques, the documents spread before us. He had been concerned about some of them; the Category III techniques certainly, but also some of the Category II techniques. That was why he asked for more legal advice. "I wanted to be totally covered." But Hill never heard anything more about the legal advice he requested; he didn't see any legal advice from the Justice Department or the OLC or from Haynes. He assumed that the lawyers at the Justice Department and the Defense Department had got on with it but he never saw the legal advices from Bybee and Yoo. "The first I knew of Yoo's advice was when it was in the press."

Geoffrey Miller took over command on November 8 and Dunlavey left Guantánamo on November 14. JTF-GTMO was established. These were positive developments, Hill thought, they needed unity of command. He didn't want to denigrate Dunlavey, who had done a decent job—he had pinned a medal on him when he left Guantánamo—but his praise was less than lukewarm.

On December 2, five weeks after he sent his note to Myers, Hill received a copy of Haynes's recommendation, duly signed by Donald Rumsfeld. The approval came from the top as he had wanted. The techniques that had really bothered him weren't given blanket approval, although they weren't rejected, either. He saw Rumsfeld's handwritten question ("I stand for 8–10 hours a day. Why is standing limited to 4 hours?"), and assumed that it was being "a bit jokey" and didn't mean anything much. "I didn't interpret it in any way."

Did they cross a line? My question troubled him as it was one he had frequently asked himself. The President had decided that none of the detainees had protection under the Geneva Conventions. They just had to be treated humanely, but the President provided no guidance on what that meant. So the interrogators were just "swimming by themselves," Hill said. More detailed guidance was a good thing, but of course there were "lots of different views" on what humane treatment was. What was the standard? "Beatings, physical beatings with a stick, that's not right. That's torture. Throwing a chair against a wall, not aimed at the detainee. Is that torture?" So how would Hill define "humane treatment"? In another interview he answered: "We should as a nation and as a military treat everybody with a degree of respect irrespective of who they are. And you can't physically hurt somebody, even minor. . . . that's the standard by which we all grew up in the military. That's my recollection of how I grew up. And as a citizen."[2]

The new techniques were not considered by that standard. I asked Hill if he would be comfortable with any of these techniques being used on American detainees or POWs. He didn't want to answer that question. I reminded him of the test that the authors of FM 34–52 provided to help an interrogator distinguish between lawful and unlawful interrogation: would a reasonable person in the place of the person being interrogated consider that his rights were being violated? Would they be violated if the same actions were used on an American detainee? Hill was silent. All he said was: "They behead us."

I persevered and asked if he was comfortable with the new techniques that Rumsfeld had approved. Another, longer pause this time. "There were many techniques in there that I would not have used under any circumstances." And then, as we parted, he opened up a little. "You know," he ventured, "some of the techniques on that list I would never authorize, under any circumstances." We looked at each other and there was a moment of understanding. "I shouldn't have said that to you, but many of the techniques I would not authorize. Never."

INTERROGATION LOG OF DETAINEE 063
Day 25, December 17 2002

0120: Control shows detainee photos from a fitness magazine of scantily clad women. . . .

1400: Detainee was shown numerous 9–11 tribute videos. . . .

2100: Detainee appeared to have been disturbed by the word homosexual. He did not appear to appreciate being called a homosexual. He denies being a homosexual. He also appeared to be very annoyed by the issue of his mother and sister as examples of prostitutes and whores. . . .

2200: He appeared disgusted by the photos of [Osama Bin Laden] and a variety of sexy females. . . .

11

General Hill's memo reached General Dick Myers, Chairman of the Joint Chiefs of Staff, on October 25, 2002. Myers knew this was serious. Hill was top-notch, a "very impressive" Combatant Commander, and he had intelligence that could save American lives. Myers told Jane Dalton, his main legal adviser, that the request was "radioactive." "We've got to get an answer back to him that is the right answer."

Myers had served as Chairman from October 2001 and was the most senior person in the U.S. armed forces. He rose through the ranks, joining the Air Force in 1965, seeing duty in Vietnam, flying more than 600 combat hours in an F–4 fighter plane, and eventually becoming Vice Chairman and then Chairman of the Joint Chiefs of Staff. In that role he knew that the decisions on Geneva and detainee interrogations were among the most important and difficult issues that he would have to deal with in his four years as Chairman. As principal military adviser to the President he was not in the chain of command. For Guantánamo the chain ran from the President, to the Secretary of Defense, to General Hill as Commander of SOUTHCOM, and then straight down to Dunlavey. Myers's role on detainee interrogations at Guantánamo was therefore advisory. In carrying out this role he was keenly aware that whatever was decided would have serious implications for U.S. military personnel.

I located General Myers by an indirect route. A letter to a home address in Virginia came back marked "addressee unknown." Eventually I found an email address for his wife, Mary Jo. A few weeks later I met General Myers in Washington. We agreed on an academic venue, the University of Georgetown Law School. Myers was a tall man, well over six feet,

General Richard Myers, Chairman, Joint Chiefs of Staff

with an easy, friendly, open face. His manner was unassuming, a generous and open spirit, happy to listen, not pushing any agenda. Rather different from Doug Feith, I thought, as he talked freely and candidly on any topic I cared to put on the table. No subject was off-limits. He frequently suggested it would be helpful to speak with Jane Dalton early in our conversation and said: "It would be good if Jim Haynes would at least talk to you." I understood the suggestion to be an indication of the key role that Haynes played. I had written to Haynes but his office turned down my request. "Unfortunately, because of his extremely busy schedule," wrote Colonel Kelly Wheaton, his Senior Military Assistant, "he regrets that he will not be able to meet with you."

My conversation with Myers ranged far and wide, but we focused on two key issues: the decision on Geneva, and the new interrogation techniques. He was keen to remind me of the context: the unprecedented ruthlessness of al-Qaeda's attacks and their impact on the psychological make-up of the decision-makers, which should not be underestimated, plus the desire of those in charge to make sure it never happened again. As Chairman he felt a great responsibility to protect the population. "There was a sense of urgency that in my forty years of military experience hadn't existed in other contingencies," he explained. There was also the real fear that one of the detainees might know when the next attack would happen, and that they would miss vital information. These were legitimate concerns, and it was abundantly clear that Myers spoke in good faith.

The first big decision was Geneva. Myers confirmed Feith's role, although he didn't exactly suggest they became bosom buddies. Myers too was involved, although by the time the issue reached him the Administration was "either close to a decision or had made a decision." He didn't think it was just a legal issue, it was more a question of principle on which he had clear views. "When I found out that there was a decision pending that the Geneva Conventions would not apply, I thought that was contrary to everything we've ever been taught." He was referring to Rumsfeld's decision of January 19, supported by Haynes and Gonzales. It would put the U.S. military in a bad position if they were picked up on the battlefield. For historic, cultural and training reasons he had insisted that Geneva should apply, even to a rogue, lawless actor like al-Qaeda. It was about values and reciprocity. "More robust debate would have been helpful," he said, but his position was clear. He remembered a key meeting with Powell and Rumsfeld and their lawyers, Will Taft and Jim Haynes. He didn't take Jane Dalton, because it was an issue of principle on points he could argue. "So I had nobody." There was no doubt in my mind about his attachment to the idea of Geneva, even if his knowledge of the subject was fuzzy.

Then our conversation took an unexpected turn, as it became clear that General Myers was a little confused about the decision taken. He claimed to be satisfied with the President's decision of February 7, 2002. "After all the arguments were done, the decision was, we don't think it applies in a technical sense, but we're going to behave as if it does." This surprised me. That wasn't what the President decided. The actual decision distinguished between the Taliban—to whom Geneva applied, although detainees could not invoke rights under it—and al-Qaeda, to whom it didn't apply at all. This was Feith's confusing formulation. The effect was that no Guantánamo detainee could rely on Geneva, even its Common Article 3. I explained this to Myers. "I have to think about that for a minute because this is a heck of a time, we were certainly discussing both the Taliban and al-Qaeda in those days and, I thought we'd said, I'm fairly certain, we said that Taliban was different from al-Qaeda but in the end, for both groups, we would treat them as if it did apply, to include . . ." "As if it *didn't* apply?" I interrupted, emphasizing the word "didn't" and correcting what I thought he said. "No, as it *would* apply," he responded, "as it *did* apply." I was surprised by his error. He went on: "I thought the compromise was that the Taliban was a little bit more of an organized military force, so they were entitled, al-Qaeda was not entitled but we treat them as if they were."

Feith's formulation had confused me, so it was no surprise that it should have confused others, including the Chairman of the Joint Chiefs of Staff, the most senior military officer of the most powerful country in the world. Nevertheless I was taken aback. Had Myers understood what had been decided? Did he appreciate the consequences for interrogation techniques? If the Chairman of the Joint Chiefs of Staff was confused about what had been decided on Geneva, then inevitably soldiers in the field would also be confused. With confusion comes uncertainty, and with uncertainty a greater likelihood of abuse. And, of course, Feith's formulation may have been *intended* to confuse, leaving the decision-makers, or some of them, thinking they'd decided one thing when in fact they'd decided another. If that was the intention, it worked magically. As one seasoned observer of military affairs put it to me, Myers was "well and truly hoodwinked"—perhaps because he was an Air Force guy and had no direct experience of ground wars and Geneva.

Myers went on. "I don't know what part they dissented on, but once the decision's made, the decision's made—you've made your best case and the Justice Department sits there, the Attorney General sits there, White House Counsel sits there, they've worked it through in their minds, and the President has to make a tough call." The President's tough call did away with Common Article 3, its legal restrictions on cruel treatment and torture, on "outrages upon personal dignity," and on humiliating and degrading treatment. New interrogation techniques were the logical and inevitable next step. With General Hill's memo they landed on Myers's desk. "I guess we knew it was coming up, because I probably talked to General Hill," he told me. But still he was surprised when it came. "I really hadn't expected it, I suppose."

Faced with the abandonment of FM 34–52 and established techniques of interrogation, and Hill's request for more legal advice, Myers turned first to Jane Dalton. On all these difficult issues he and Jane were "pretty much joined at the hip." He had the highest praise for "this diminutive lady," having long understood that a military commander needed proper legal advice. "Are we inside the railroad tracks?" was a question he often asked Jane and he would usually get a pretty straight answer. On this issue, however, it seems she missed a trick or the process was short-circuited.

⊷

By the time I met Myers I'd begun to understand the complexities surrounding the giving of legal advice in the Pentagon. The last word in legality rested with the General Counsel to the Secretary of Defense, Jim Haynes. He could receive input from the General Counsels to each of the services (Army, Navy, Air Force) and the Marine Corps, who were directly below him. He could also receive sideways legal input from the military lawyers, the Judge Advocate Generals, as well as from the lawyer to the Chairman of the Joint Chiefs of Staff—in the form of advice. On the question of interrogation techniques these lawyers would have had different views, and it was already clear that there would be a split between the military lawyers and the civilian legal advisers. The bottom line was that within the Department of Defense Haynes was the decision-maker.

Hill's memo coincided with another issue that caused huge tension at the Pentagon between the civilian and military side. Rumsfeld, Wolfowitz, and Haynes wanted to streamline legal advice, so that one General Counsel would speak for the whole department. They wanted the legal office of the Joint Chiefs of Staffs, and the other military JAGs, to be placed under (rather than alongside) the office of the Secretary of Defense's legal counsel. Such a change would have transformed decades of practice and would have dispensed with the tradition and safeguards of independent legal advice for the Joint Chiefs and the military. Differences of view would not be tolerated. The effect would be to make Rumsfeld's General Counsel even more powerful, centralizing all decision-making in a hierarchical structure that would stifle dissent. A political appointee would provide legal advice to the Chairman. In the 1990s, when he was General Counsel to the Army, Jim Haynes had once before "tried to subordinate the Army TJAG to his office," a former TJAG told me, but that effort had failed.

These proposed changes were vigorously opposed by Myers and most of the military lawyers. Myers stood firm in wanting his own legal advice; he valued Dalton's independence. "I think the services felt they didn't have a big enough voice," said Myers, "and they had trouble getting access." On this key issue Myers prevailed, but it left lingering distrust between the two distinct groups of lawyers.

Another legal source at the Pentagon told me that Jane Dalton was not entirely comfortable with Haynes's approach to the interrogation techniques. I also learned that she was less than fully comfortable with Diane Beaver's opinion, which did not surprise me. Yet Beaver told me that when she sought assistance from Dalton in early October it was not forthcoming. "She said you should talk to Manny Supervielle, not to me, talk to SOUTHCOM," said Beaver. "She wasn't going to play." At this later stage Dalton did get involved. "My main interaction on all this," Myers said, "was with Jane, General Hill to some degree, and then meetings with the Secretary and Jim Haynes as we were trying to struggle with what's the right thing to do." Rumsfeld wanted to work through the issue. "He would not have conviction right away," Myers explained, "He would say, OK, let's discuss it." Haynes, according to Myers, was also "always counseling caution, as a conservative approach, as was I."

I reminded Myers of the wording of the Haynes memo, to jog his memory and reconstruct what happened before Haynes had finished it on November 27. "This memo is interesting," Myers said, "I remember, I had a comment on this memo, but I can't remember what it is." He paused, took the sheet of paper and carefully read through the one-page memo. After reading "I have discussed this with the Deputy [Paul Wolfowitz], Doug Feith and General Myers," Myers eventually said sharply: "You don't see my initials on this." Normally, he explained, he would have initialed a memo to indicate approval. This memo was signed by Haynes and Rumsfeld and copied to Myers. But there was no confirmation Myers saw the memo or approved it before it went to Rumsfeld. "You just see I've discussed it," he said quietly. He paused and reflected, thinking back to that frenetic period four years earlier. "That's why I have a problem with thinking that this is how it all worked out, because I've discussed it. This was not the way this should have come about." Haynes didn't follow the usual path: normal procedures were circumvented.

Myers was clearly troubled by this unorthodox document. He leaned forward. "I'm thinking, why did I never approve that point? Where did that October thing come from? This is where the approval came from, but it was not . . ." I interrupted. Did he ever talk about these issues with Wolfowitz and Feith? Was there a meeting of all the key players, together in one room, as had happened with the Geneva decision? "No," said Myers, "that's the problem."

Myers was candid. His honest face reflected real concern, almost as though the penny was dropping for the first time. It was as though he had been cut out of the process. "I thought this was very strange when I looked at it. There's something in my stomach that is turned over saying, it wasn't a well staffed . . ." His sentence tailed off. The TJAGs complained they were never consulted on the issue. There was never a meeting in "the tank," the room where the Joint Staff meets. Crucially, the General Counsel of the Navy at that time, Alberto Mora, later shared with me that Jane Dalton told him afterward that "Jim pulled this away; we never had a chance to complete the assessment." In other words, Haynes short-circuited the usual process.

Later I got further confirmation that the Haynes memo was not a normal action memo. A former Pentagon official told me that General Bantz

Craddock, who was Rumsfeld's Senior Military Assistant at the time, noticed that it was missing a buckslip. This is the essential routing slip that would show the document's circulation, on which everyone usually signed off. The Haynes memo had no accompanying "legal chop" (signature) from the General Counsel's office. So it went back to Haynes, who later returned it with a note that said "good to go." Myers never did get a chance to sign off on it.

I took General Myers back to Hill's memo and the request from Dunlavey for aggressive interrogation techniques. Myers knew Dunlavey; he had been involved in his selection. "I know him well; he looked like the perfect candidate, pretty darned good given . . . his background." But things didn't work out. There were management problems, leadership issues that were alluded to but unspoken. As Myers was deciding what to do with Hill's request, Dunlavey was replaced. On November 8 General Miller took over command at Guantánamo. Myers was involved in that decision too and welcomed Miller, even if he had no background in human intelligence sources. "This is not his expertise, this is not what he does for a living," Myers explained, "but we put him in there because he's a good leader."

Miller was not involved in overseeing the choice of new techniques that appeared on the list: that was Dunlavey's job. Miller would just apply them. Myers wasn't involved in the choice of techniques, and knew little about the process that led to it. "I was not aware of those debates with Dunlavey and his legal counsel," he said, although Jane Dalton "might have been." He didn't know if Dalton was in direct contact with General Hill or with Haynes, at an earlier stage, but suspected that Haynes would have been in contact with Dunlavey and Manny Supervielle, Hill's lawyer.

So what did Myers think about the new techniques? We had the list on the table before us. "We thought, OK, all the techniques came out of the book, there weren't any techniques invented." I stopped him. "Out of which book?" I asked. "Out of 34–52," Myers replied, "I think all of these are in the Manual." They were not—not one of them. "They aren't?" he asked, surprised. Not only that but most of them violated Geneva's Common Article 3. Again, such an answer from the Chairman of the Joint Chiefs surprised me. He really had taken his eye off the ball. Haynes and Rumsfeld had been able to run rings around him.

We went down the list of eighteen techniques. He said many were familiar to him, from his own training. "They're going to yell at you, they're going to deceive you, you're going to have different techniques, they're

going to give you false stuff, in our training we'd go through stress positions." He picked out MREs (meals, ready-to-eat). Colin Powell's lawyer
at the State Department, Will Taft, had told him that forcing detainees to
eat MREs was tantamount to torture. Myers didn't agree. Maybe Taft was
being ironic, I suggested. Later on Taft told me he remembered the conversation and confirmed that he was not being serious.

As we walked through the list of techniques Myers became increasingly hesitant and troubled. At forced grooming and dogs he became defensive. "Dogs were only to be present, never to be . . ." his words tailed
off. "Exploit phobias, claustrophobia, in my training that's what we'd do,
see if you're claustrophobic, removal of all comfort items, what our folks
went through in Vietnam, from hot rations to MREs, removal of clothing
would be less fun, but forced grooming . . ." The words tailed off, again. It
was obvious to me he was appalled. How did this get past, he seemed to be
asking himself?

In fact, he suggested, nothing really happened after the eighteen techniques were approved. Another pause. Except "maybe in one case." Did he
have al-Qahtani in mind? "Maybe in two cases," he said. "There was lots of
detainee abuse." Then he thought again. "Not lots, but there are cases of
detainee abuse." And maybe even a case or two of torture, I inquired.
"Who was that?" Myers asked. "al-Qahtani?" I replied, "depending on how
you read the interrogation log." "Before or after guidance?" Myers asked.
"Between November 23, 2002 and January 15, 2003," I replied. I got the
impression he hadn't seen the interrogation log.

There was another way of looking at this. I remembered FM 34–52.
Was Myers comfortable with the thought that these techniques might be
used on American personnel? Without hesitation, his clear, one-word
response was: "Inappropriate." The Chairman of the Joint Chiefs did
not want these techniques used on Americans. Nor did General Hill, I
said, so the sixty-four million dollar question was . . . This time Myers
interrupted me. "Why would you authorize it? I'd have to look at these
one by one again." And in combination, I added. Hill had also wanted
more legal approval, and Myers obviously shared his concerns. "When
you see this, you say, holy mackerel," he exclaimed. The United States
didn't do torture. "We never authorized torture, we just didn't, not what
we would do." The Field Manual allowed some flexibility, it had nuances. If
these techniques were approved then the interrogations were OK. But
what about combinations of the techniques used together, I asked. He
had discussed this fully with Rumsfeld, he replied, which was surprising,

since the memo as approved was completely silent on the use of multiple techniques.

I told him that it struck me as curious—astonishing even—that so important a decision would be taken on the basis of legal advice from a relatively inexperienced Staff Judge Advocate—Diane Beaver—down at Guantánamo. "That's not what happened," Myers replied. "[Jim Haynes] had advice from DOJ, he had advice from the military service JAGs, advice from the chairman's advisor, so he had lots of advice." Up to a point Myers was correct, but there was nothing to suggest that the military service JAGs were involved at that time. They had been cut out. The crucial point, however, was Myers's belief that Haynes had approval from the Justice Department. Had he known that their lawyers were working on definitions of torture and cruel treatment? "Yes, I knew that," he said, although he did not know much. Did he meet Jay Bybee or John Yoo? "Not unless it was in the National Security Council meeting, which might have been the case, but not in working at the staff positions." "I've recommended Jim talk to you," he offered for the third or fourth time during our meeting. "He would be the one who would have known about the Justice effort." Did he know how close Haynes was to Cheney's lawyer, David Addington, that Addington had been best man at Haynes's wedding? "I knew they were close." Did he know that Haynes and Addington traveled together to Guantánamo shortly before Dunlavey had sent his memo? Apparently not.

Myers had views on the opinions from the Justice Department. "I do know that that was guarded," he said of the opinions, "for whatever reason." The Bybee/Yoo memo—the organ failure advice—was in the public domain after June 2004 but Bybee II, signing off on specific techniques, was not. "I would have to agree, that was not a happy piece," Myers suggested. According to that opinion, and the standard it set out, the decision on the eighteen techniques were fine. "But it wasn't fine," said Myers. Bybee II looked at individual techniques, but Myers was not sure he had seen that later memo. He thought the Secretary of Defense would adopt more of a common-sense approach to the definition of torture, rather than a technical or legalistic view. "There may be a point there where [Haynes] changes his line, but his advice to the Secretary was always, whatever we do today, this is not about yesterday, this is about long term, we've got to think about that."

Nevertheless he was aware of discussion behind closed doors. "I'll call it 'intrigue' that was going on," he said, "that I wasn't aware of, and Jane wasn't aware of, that was probably occurring between Jim Haynes, White

House General Counsel and Justice." He stopped himself from going further. "We didn't see the organ failure thing." Yet as the senior military man he took comfort from the fact that the Department of Justice, the Attorney General and others were working on these issues. He assumed there was a serious effort on their part to ensure compliance with the Torture Conventions and other international laws. "What gave me some comfort in all of this was the fact that Justice was looking at these things. That's another party."

In the end no other written legal advices directly relating to Rumsfeld's decision emerged, beyond Beaver's and those written at the OLC. Jane Dalton didn't give written legal advice on the issue, nor did the TJAGs, who were not asked for their input. Jim Haynes wrote the Haynes memo, which made it look as though Diane Beaver's legal advice constituted the final word was dispositive. Later on that caused her considerable grief, because the public presentation made it look as though her legal advice was the basis for Haynes's recommendation and Rumsfeld's decision. She was given no notice when the documents were put in the public domain, in June 2004, nor was Mike Dunlavey. This was the first time Myers had heard this and he looked unhappy. "That's too bad."

Little by little, my understanding of Myers's role was becoming more focused. He hadn't pushed for these new techniques, but he didn't resist them, either. The deliberative process was informal; he didn't ask too many questions, or inquire too deeply, and kept his distance from the decision-making process. Myers had recognized that things had gone wrong in the process of deciding on the new techniques, although not as badly as some were saying. His demeanor and his words made that clear. The military had behaved reasonably; restraint was an important value. I put it to him that problems in the decision-making process may have been on the political side, at the point at which the proposals had initially emerged and that it was here that the decision-making may have been dysfunctional. "Early on," he suggested, "I would say it was true."

The issue of protecting America was always on people's minds. Myers frequently gave public presentations and his audiences expressed their concern. "They say, why don't we just go do this, serious middle of the road Americans say, well, we've just had enough, have we ever considered nuclear weapons? I say, you can consider them but, they're killing innocent men, women and children and that's one of our issues here, are we going to be just like them?" He paused. "By the way," he offered spontaneously on the subject of interrogation techniques, "I don't think pulling the tongue out [was on the list], I'm not sure that's going to be effective."

General Myers struck me as a decent person, but he appeared out of his depth with these sharp political appointees. He seemed bothered by the fact that Dunlavey and Beaver had not been warned about the release of the documents in June 2004.

"Are you saying," he asked, "that by releasing his documents they are kind of pointing to, well look, it's these folks at Guantánamo?" Dick Myers was the most powerful military man in the world. I wondered how the system had allowed Doug Feith to have hoodwinked him.

INTERROGATION LOG OF DETAINEE 063
Day 27, December 19 2002

0300: Interrogators had detainee look at picture of women in bikinis and identify if the women were the same or different. Detainee refused to look at girls and began struggling. A few drops of water were sprinkled on his head to gain compliance. . . .

1100: Happy Mohammed mask was placed on detainee and he was yelled at when he tried to speak. . . .

1940: SGT M had shown the detainee a picture of Mecca, there were thousands of Muslims congregated in this photo. The detainee broke down and cried at the sight of this picture. . . .

2320: He attempts to resist female contact. He would attempt to pray as she spoke into his ear about his continuous lies. . . .

12

While Myers was reflecting on General Hill's memo, it circulated for comment to the Director of the Joint Chiefs of Staff for Strategic Plans and Policy (J5). On October 30 it was passed for comment to a select group within the Joint Staff, including the Office of Legal Counsel and those responsible for intelligence and operations. It did not go to the TJAGs for the three services and the Marine Corps. It did go to Jim Haynes, who was expecting it.

Haynes reported to Rumsfeld that he had also discussed the request from Guantánamo with Paul Wolfowitz and Doug Feith. He already had Beaver's advice and did not, apparently, feel any need to seek further written legal advice, whether from Jane Dalton or the General Counsels of the Navy, Air Force or Army. Doug Feith was Undersecretary of Defense for Policy and Haynes knew him well. They had agreed on the approach to Geneva—that it shouldn't be available to any Guantánamo detainees—now they could focus on interrogation techniques. Policy decisions on detainee interrogations should have been at the top of Feith's list of priorities. He didn't need to bother with any other rules of international law, such as the convention prohibiting torture and abuse: the Justice Department lawyers at OLC had given him a free rein. "The President said humane treatment," Feith told me, "and I thought that was OK, perfectly fine phrase, that needs to be fleshed out, but it's a fine phrase—humane treatment."

Feith could not claim a lack of familiarity with the legal process. He had studied at Harvard as an undergraduate and obtained a law degree from Georgetown University in Washington. He then worked as a lawyer and became the managing attorney of his own law firm, Feith and Zell. Yet it seems he never really wanted to flesh out the meaning of the words "humane treatment," though he was prepared to put time into the issue of circumventing the Geneva Conventions. By his own account, he felt no burning desire to immerse himself in the details of the eighteen techniques, as became clear during our conversation in his office at Georgetown. He was happy to talk at length about the February moment and his triumph in ensuring that none of the detainees could rely on Geneva. During our conversation he was less comfortable discussing the interrogations and his role in November 2002—on the preparation of the new techniques, on their humanity, on their legality, he was positively bashful and timorous.

When I mentioned the name of Mohammed al-Qahtani, Feith blanched. "I'm not even sure I knew that he existed," was the initial and over-quick reaction, before, he added: "I had nothing to do with that." So he knew who al-Qahtani was and, presumably, what was done to him. He knew enough to want to distance himself. To me his line was that he wasn't sure if he knew anything about the coercive interrogation of al-Qahtani until late on; he wasn't sure that he ever even got briefed on any of this. Some of the people in his organization at the Department of Defense may have been doing something on these issues: he wanted me to know that he was responsible for more than 1,500 people at the Pentagon. He didn't have time to check the details of what everyone was doing.

He claimed to have had no involvement in interrogation issues until later in the autumn of 2002, after October. Dunlavey's request was passed on by General Hill and then to General Myers and finally to Haynes. Only when Haynes finally wrote to Rumsfeld on November 27, Feith told me, did he first get involved in discussing interrogation. Until then, this was an issue mainly for Haynes and Stephen Cambone, who worked for Rumsfeld as Director of Program Analysis and Evaluation. Cambone's name came up in other conversations, and he was closely involved, even if not mentioned by name in the paper trail. His name invariably provoked a strong adverse reaction when I mentioned it to anyone in the military. Feith's mention of his name seemed to be a way of passing the buck. He told me he didn't know the names of the people at Guantánamo; he didn't see their interrogation reports; he wasn't asked about their interrogation techniques.

This sounded improbable and didn't square with what others had told me. Dunlavey, for example, had said that he first met with Feith in February 2002 in Washington, and they'd been in regular contact. Dunlavey had told Feith that half the people at Guantánamo posed no threat, were unconnected with terror, and should be sent home. According to Feith, he had seen Dunlavey "when he came through Washington," and perhaps met him "once or twice." I asked him if he met Dunlavey, whose job was interrogation at Guantánamo from February to October 2002. Feith didn't respond. We had reached a turning point in our conversation, the first of several. I later asked my assistant Jenny, who transcribed the audio recording of this conversation, what she thought of this moment. "Squirming," she said, "the squirming."

I also knew that Feith had visited Guantánamo. "Much later," was all he would admit to. I reminded him about the Haynes memo and handed him a copy. I might as well have slapped him or poured a bottle of cold water over his head. "My recollection is that I became aware of the interrogation issues for the first time when this memo came to the Secretary. And, I remember there was a round table, you see this is me"—he pointed at the bottom left-hand corner, marked "cc: USD (P)"—"and I think that's when I first learned of this issue." But that couldn't be right. Haynes's memo stated explicitly that he'd *already* consulted Feith. I read out Haynes's words: "I have discussed this with the Deputy, Doug Feith and General Myers. I believe that all join in my recommendation that, as a matter of policy, you authorize the Commander of SOUTHCOM to employ, in his discretion, only categories I and II and the fourth technique listed in Category III ('Use of mild, non-injurious physical contact such as grabbing, poking in the chest with the finger, and light pushing')." Feith looked at me, as I waited for a response. Silence. Then he told me I'd mispronounced his name. "Pronounced 'Fife,' by the way," he said.

Doug Feith, head of policy at the Pentagon, apparently didn't feel the need to ask too many questions about the policy implications of abandoning *FM 34–52* and embracing aggressive interrogation techniques. He displayed none of the anxieties or concerns that had troubled General Myers when we spoke. The implications for American soldiers were not at the forefront of his mind. Moreover humanity or inhumanity of the eighteen techniques didn't seem to trouble him.

What was his reaction when he first saw the list of new techniques? "I don't think there was a list of techniques at this point," he said. That was plain wrong and he must have known it: there was a list at that time, the document said so. Dunlavey's memo came with the list of eighteen techniques attached and it was attached to Haynes's draft. "At this point," Feith asked, "or was it later?"

Feith was digging himself into a hole. Now he provided me with an explanation that was preposterous. Nobody ever actually explained precisely what each of these techniques was. That was curious, I said, since none of the techniques could be said to be really ambiguous: stress positions, thirty-day isolation, light deprivation, forced grooming, exposure to water, use of a wet towel. Faced with the hopelessness of his own argument he shifted tack again. "I didn't get involved in military operations. I didn't get involved in intelligence operations. I didn't tell military people how to point their guns, or how to do things. I'm not going to tell interrogators how to do things. That's an operational thing. Policy people don't tell operational people what to do. We don't have the skills to do that." I suppressed a laugh.

Did the list of eighteen techniques not set alarm bells ringing when he first saw them? I reminded him that General Hill's note forwarding Dunlavey's request expressed serious concerns and asked for further legal review. "To tell you the truth," he responded, "I'm not sure I remember seeing this before I got into the Secretary's office—this was not something that I remember staffing personally." Haynes had discussed the new interrogation techniques with Feith, but Feith now had only a limited recollection of this. So what exactly was discussed with Haynes? Feith saw his role as discharging his responsibilities and not doing other people's work. Haynes was the lawyer and as such responsible for the legal issues. Feith's job was to sort out the "policy equities," of which there were two. One was a policy interest in effective interrogation, the other was a policy interest in obeying the law. Feith saw his task as ensuring that they were not disrespectful of the law "in a way that a policy person would say." He never seemed to ask himself what the implications of this new policy would be for America's international standing, what the incidental consequences might be. Surprisingly, he didn't mention other major policy interests, like coalition-building and protecting U.S. troops from reciprocal treatment. These were huge policy questions, not legal issues.

Feith presented me with a couple of questions while we were discussing the interrogation techniques: "I would like to know, does anybody think that these proposals are not serving our intelligence interests—question 1? And, secondly, are the people who are responsible for legal judgments, satisfied that what we are doing is lawful?" The context was significant, he reminded me. There were extremely important intelligence interests in adopting the new techniques. "Here we are," he reminded me, "we've been attacked, we're concerned about the next attack." The only way to fight this war was to get the intelligence about what the enemy was doing. During the Cold War intelligence could be obtained from satellites looking at military formations. "In this war the intelligence is all in people's heads. So interrogation is as important as our eyes in the skies during the Cold War." The difference between satellite imagery, which showed real-time information, and the knowledge of detainees who had been off the battlefield for a year ought to have been striking to the head of policy, but no, the intelligence that was needed to fight the War on Terror, to defend the country, to protect millions of people from attacks by smallpox or anthrax, that intelligence was in the heads of the people detained at Guantánamo. "We need to extract it."

I pondered Feith's words and thought back to what Cheney had said five days after the attacks, about working through the "dark side." "It's going to be vital for us to use any means at our disposal, basically, to achieve our objective,"[1] Cheney had said. I also remembered what Rumsfeld told Dunlavey. "Maximize the intelligence production." Extracting information was the primary policy objective. That being agreed, Feith's role was limited. "So my job as the policy advisor would be to say, Mr. Secretary, you cannot make this decision without talking to the lawyers." But, he added, "I didn't have to say this, because he knows that."

On this premise the role of the No. 3 man in the Pentagon consisted of no more than getting the right people to the table. "Once I decided that the intel people were essentially at the table, and the lawyers were at the table, at that point I was not going to second-guess the intel people on their judgments or the lawyers on their judgments, so that's why I had a very minor role in this."

Thus head of policy at the Pentagon was a glorified facilitator. Feith's words spoke for themselves. Being a stickler for legality, he threw himself enthusiastically into investigating the legal issues surrounding the detainees' rights under the Geneva Conventions—to make sure they had none. He then went to war against the contrary legal arguments put by Will Taft, Colin Powell's lawyer at the State Department. Feith was not a man who shied away from expressing his views forcefully. "I will tell you when you are right and when I think you are wrong," he said to me apropos his general philosophy. But when it came to the design of specific interrogation techniques, he was immovable: that was not a matter for him to be involved in; that was for the lawyers, for Haynes. He dealt with Haynes a lot, but didn't know him that well. He tried not to rate Haynes as a lawyer because he was there to address issues of policy. "He had his business, I had mine."

"There was not a team of lawyers in the room," Feith continued, "so he's [Haynes is] the General Counsel, and what I wanted to know, is, have the lawyers looked at this?" "Yes" was the response he received and it was not his job to find out which lawyers had worked on it; it was not his job to second-guess Haynes. Yet on the materials before him, the only written legal advice that had been obtained had come from the relatively lowly Diane Beaver, and her advice was somewhat equivocal. General Hill saw Beaver's advice and thought it insufficient and wanted more from DoD and DoJ lawyers. Didn't that trouble Feith? Did it not give him pause for thought?

By now Feith was becoming testy with me. "Look—the thing is, you don't understand, I'm not gonna sit there and—if the General Counsel says, this has gotten proper legal review—do you know how many decisions we work on in a given day?—if somebody says this has gotten proper review, you don't say to them, stop. I want to know what you consider to be proper legal review and I want to know who worked on it—you don't do that." But then he went further, and confirmed that Haynes had received more legal advice. "It was clear, this was not a matter that was being done by DOD lawyers without interagency work," he explained, "this was a thoroughly interagency piece of work for the lawyers, as far as I understood, from day one." Feith made it crystal clear that Justice Department lawyers were involved in *these* issues. The connection came through Haynes, who told Secretary Rumsfeld that "the lawyers who need to review this have reviewed this." General Hill had asked for Justice Department approval; it wasn't for Feith to call on Haynes to explain himself to provide those further legal analyses. He didn't work for Haynes, he worked for the Secretary, Donald Rumsfeld. This was a crucial moment in our conversation. Like Myers, Feith had confirmed that Haynes had had access to advice from the Justice Department lawyers who supported him: he didn't *have* to rely on Beaver's advice.

Feith painted a picture of the people who sat around the table, involved in "good faith discussions about really difficult issues." They were good Americans, interested in human rights and individual rights and constitutional principles and everything else that mattered. "Nobody around the table was a totalitarian, nobody around the table is a Jihadist, nobody around the table is a murderer and a racial superior. . . ." Yet I detected no qualms about any of the techniques, no regret for Haynes's recommendation, no hesitation about Rumsfeld's approval. Feith didn't object to the use of any of the eighteen techniques on U.S. detainees who didn't meet the standards required for POW status. People out of uniform weren't entitled to the same protections that people in uniform received. The United States was fighting enemies who wouldn't provide

Geneva-style protections anyway, so there was no point in worrying about reciprocity from al-Qaeda.

Could the techniques be used on an American who failed to meet the conditions of Geneva, I asked. "Sure, that's the whole point. It's absolutely understood that they are not entitled to POW treatment if they get caught." No exceptions? "As a matter of law, that's the risk they take, they can be shot. We know that." The best that could be said about these comments by Feith was the absence of any double standard. This would help to cement America's moral authority, and Feith believed that moral authority mattered. Faced with a difficult problem, the decision to approve the techniques was taken in good faith. The United States had been attacked and was now trying to head off the next attack; they were grappling with hard issues and "gigantic, large, constitutional issues that were a brooding omnipresence over the whole subject."

Feith seemed to be dissembling. Under pressure and on the defensive, he reminded me of Paul Wolfowitz when he appeared before the U.S. Senate Armed Services Committee in the summer of 2004, shortly after the Abu Ghraib photographs emerged. Senator Jack Reed of Rhode Island put a series of questions to Wolfowitz on the meaning of humane treatment:

> *Senator Reed:* Mr. Secretary, do you think crouching naked for 45 minutes is humane?
> *Mr. Wolfowitz:* Not naked, absolutely not.
> *Senator Reed:* So if he is dressed up that is fine? . . . Sensory deprivation, which would be a bag over your head for 72 hours. Do you think that is humane?
> *Mr. Wolfowitz:* Let me come back to what you said, the work of this government . . .
> *Senator Reed:* No, no. Answer the question, Mr. Secretary. Is that humane?
> *Mr. Wolfowitz:* I don't know whether it means a bag over your head for 72 hours, Senator. I don't know.
> *Senator Reed:* Mr. Secretary, you're dissembling, non-responsive. Anybody would say putting a bag over someone's head for 72 hours, which is . . .
> *Mr. Wolfowitz:* It strikes me as not humane, Senator.
> *Senator Reed:* Thank you very much Mr. Secretary.[2]

Away from public scrutiny, two years earlier in November 2002, Wolfowitz had lent his support to techniques that might be even more abusive. Haynes had consulted him. "I have discussed this with the Deputy," he

Paul Wolfowitz, Deputy Secretary of Defense

wrote in the Haynes memo. Wolfowitz had signaled his approval of hood-ing, sleep deprivation, humiliation. The new techniques recommended by Haynes were no more humane than those that troubled Senator Reed, yet Wolfowitz didn't push for more legal advice, or more humanity.

This seems to be his modus operandi. A few years later the World Bank's executive directors investigated how Wolfowitz, as President of the bank, had dealt with a possible conflict of interest issue arising from his re-lationship with his girlfriend, Shaha Riza. The bank's directors set up an ad hoc group to examine the facts: they found that Wolfowitz had subverted the established governance structure of the bank by avoiding legal advice that would be unhelpful. He did this in a four-step process. First, he deter-mined that "no rules applied to the situation, and therefore no rules could have been broken in resolving the matter as he did." Then he decided "not to consult the World Bank General Counsel, or any other staff of the World Bank Legal Vice Presidency." Next, he directed others dealing with the issue not to consult the General Counsel or any other members of the World Bank legal office. Finally, he referred the matter to outside lawyers whom he had chosen himself.[3]

An identical approach had been applied to the eighteen techniques, as I was discovering as I gradually peeled away at the layers. First it was decided that the Geneva Conventions did not apply, so there were no rules. Then the military lawyers were cut out and the decision was put in the hands of Jim Haynes, with support from other political appointees at the Justice Department. Were the normal processes of governance subverted? Were decisions taken that led to a loss of moral authority? Doug Feith didn't like such questions. "The problem with moral authority," he said, was "people who should know better, like yourself, siding with the assholes, to put it crudely."

INTERROGATION LOG OF DETAINEE 063
Day 28, December 20 2002

1115: Told detainee that a dog is held in higher esteem because dogs know right from wrong and know to protect innocent people from bad people. Began teaching the detainee lessons such as stay, come, and bark to elevate his social status up to that of a dog. Detainee became very agitated. . . .

1300: Dog tricks continued and detainee stated he should be treated like a man. Detainee was told he would have to learn who to defend and who to attack. Interrogator showed photos of 9–11 victims and told detainee he should bark happy for these people. Interrogator also showed photos of al-Qaeda terrorist and told detainee he should growl at these people. A towel was placed on the detainee's head like a burka, with his face exposed, and the interrogator proceeded to give the detainee dance lessons. . . .

2200: The detainee was strip-searched. Initially he was attempting to resist the guards. After approximately five minutes of nudity the detainee ceased to resist. . . . He stated that he did not like the females viewing his naked body while being searched and if felt that he could have done something about it then he would have. . . .

13

Siding with the assholes would have meant awaiting a formal written decision to be taken on General Hill's request. That didn't happen. On November 8, 2002 Dunlavey was replaced by General Miller, with four days for a handover. Around the same time Jerry Phifer, the J2 intelligence officer who had prepared the list of new techniques, was replaced by a full-time civilian from the Defense Intelligence Agency.

A detailed plan for the interrogation of al-Qahtani was finalized by the Defense Intelligence Agency's Defense Human Intelligence Service, based on the eighteen techniques. Al-Qahtani was separated from the general detainee population on August 8 and placed in an "isolation facility."[1] Apart from occasional interrogations he was "totally isolated" in a cell that was always flooded with light.[2] Diane Beaver told me that his interrogation plan was rewritten at least ten times, while they waited for Pentagon authorization. General Hill told me that the interrogation plan was sent up to Rumsfeld personally, for his approval. The fact that the Secretary of Defense was "personally involved" in the interrogation of this one person, with the support of his "General Counsel system," was later confirmed by army investigator Lieutenant General Randall Schmidt.[3] The unsigned but approved interrogation plan was completed by November 12, well before Haynes sent his memo to Rumsfeld.[4] Now it was just a question of getting approval for the new techniques.

By the time the request made its way up to Haynes and Rumsfeld, and their written authorization had been given—on December 2—Mike Dunlavey was out of the picture. He left Guantánamo on Thursday, November 14. Baccus was removed a month earlier, two days before Dunlavey sent off his memo to General Hill. When I asked Dunlavey whether this was coincidental he looked at me and said nothing. As for the circumstances of his own removal, four years later that was still a painful subject.

Major General Geoffrey D. Miller, Commander, JTF-GITMO (from November 2002)

He had wanted to command the Guantánamo Task Force that combined JTF–160 and JTF–170, but Rumsfeld took the decision to bring in Major General Geoffrey Miller, after consulting General Hill. Dunlavey found it galling that Miller, an artillery man with no background in intelligence or interrogation, could be brought in over his head. "When I showed up at GTMO," said Miller, "I had never before" witnessed an interrogation.[5]

Why was Dunlavey removed? "What I was told was that the reason I did not take command was because I fought with everybody. I fought with Baccus. . . . I don't think that I was being looked upon as the good soldier by those above me. I was obstructive. I am who I am. I am a lawyer. I am a soldier. I believe I did the right thing." He believed that he had had the respect of Rumsfeld, up to a certain point, but then lost it. He'd seen through the changes that were needed, including the new techniques of interrogation, and he was proud of that. But others were glad to see the back of him: Diane Beaver had described Dunlavey as paranoid, to the point that he believed that the foreign workers brought in from Jamaica and elsewhere were out to kill him.

Miller arrived to contend with a command climate that he described as "the most dysfunctional" he'd ever seen and he set about sorting out that problem. He supported the new techniques of interrogation: the detainees were "ruthless, murderous people."[6] but he was "uncomfortable" with the Category III techniques, which would "not help develop intelligence rapidly and effectively from detainees." However, they'd already been approved from the top. "They were approved but not directed," he explained to a senior military official, and "I had latitude to use them. It was an order that came down through SECDEF."[7] He didn't question Rumsfeld's office about the use of the new techniques of interrogation, despite speaking to the Office of the Secretary of Defense "almost every day," including "informal conversations."[8] It was clear from Miller too where the pressure was coming from.

Against that pressure, the FBI and the Criminal Investigation Task Force prepared an alternative interrogation plan, one that made no use of aggressive techniques. They shared their information with the DIA and Miller, although Miller later denied seeing or receiving a memo from the FBI that commented on any Special Interrogation Plan. Miller came down in favor of aggressive interrogation. He recognized the "significant friction" between the FBI and CITF and the Joint Task Force on "how the interrogations were done."[9] The FBI thought that Miller was "biased in favor of DHS's interrogation methods."[10] On Saturday November 23 Miller received a "VOCO," authorizing him to start with the aggressive interrogation of al-Qahtani. This was four days before the Haynes memo was finalized, five days before Thanksgiving, and nine days before Rumsfeld signed the Haynes memo.

What's a VOCO, I asked Diane Beaver. "A vocal command to allow the interrogation to begin," she explained. Why was it given? "Urgency." But she didn't know who issued that command: she thought maybe it had gone to General Miller from General Hill, but must originally have come from Washington since the Pentagon was so closely involved. I asked General Hill about the VOCO. He had racked his brain on this one, fruitlessly. "None of us can recall who gave that," he said, "it's a gap." He thought he might have discussed it with Myers. "I know that people asked the Chairman about it. There are some notes. Some cryptic notes the Chairman wrote during a combatant commander's conference. So maybe the Chairman and I discussed this issue. But I don't know."[11] Finally, I asked General Myers about the VOCO. "It rings a bell," he said, "I'm trying to think, I just can't tell you."

Later on Rumsfeld was questioned by an army investigator. "Did I approve that before I actually signed it?" he asked quizzically. He couldn't remember. They went around the table to all the people that were in the room for that period. No one could remember. It was safer to assume that Rumsfeld had approved it. The army investigator, Lieutenant General Randall Schmidt, concurred with that conclusion. "Rather than call an entire line of people liars, we said that probably happened. You just can't prove it. So it's unknowable."[12]

So with Rumsfeld's oral approval and Haynes's support, the interrogation of Mohammed al-Qahtani began, even before there had been formal written approval, even before the usual processes of deliberation had been completed. The interrogation log for November 23 recorded the first moment. "The detainee arrives at the interrogation booth at Camp X-Ray.

His hood is removed and he is bolted to the floor. SGT A and SGT R are the interrogators. A DoD linguist and MAJ L (BSCT) are present."

INTERROGATION LOG OF DETAINEE 063
Day 29, December 21 2002

2103: As we discussed taking the wrong path the discussion lead into the consequences for taking the wrong path, lead to discussion of torture, beating and killing according to the Manchester document. At this point of the discussion I was forehead to forehead with the detainee and he stated that he would rather be beaten with electrical wire than to have me constantly in his personal space. . . .

2223: I began to engage closeness with the detainee. This really evoked strong emotions within the detainee. He attempted to move away from me by all means. He was laid out on the floor so I straddled him without putting my weight on him. . . . The detainee began to pray loudly but this did not stop me from finishing informing the detainee about the al-Qaeda member, Qaed Salim Sinan al Harethi aka Abu Ali, that was killed by the CIA. When the linguist mentioned this killing she informed me that the detainee told her to get out of his face. She did not move she continued to interpret as usual. . . .

COMEBACK

14

The first interrogators of al-Qahtani were from the military and the Defense Intelligence Agency. In the background was an Exploitation Team charged with assessing the information that emerged. The team was set up by the Defense Intelligence Agency's Joint Intelligence Task Force for Combating Terrorism (JITF-CT), overseen by Cal Temple in Washington. Interrogators from other services present at Guantánamo didn't get involved in this phase of the interrogation: the FBI was there from the outset, for example, with behavioral psychologists and interrogators, but didn't participate; nor did the Naval Criminal Investigation Service. As Thanksgiving approached, and al-Qahtani's special interrogation plan was prepared, alarm bells were ringing with the FBI and the NCIS, even before the VOCO arrived. One of the FBI's behavioral psychologists called headquarters in Washington. Eventually the call reached Spike Bowman.

Spike Bowman's real name is Marion. "I've never forgiven my mother for that," he said with a grin that may or may not have been genuine. I reminded him that James Bond once impersonated a Scotsman called Hilary, and that he might have fewer problems in Britain. He grinned again. "Everybody calls me Spike," he said, "you do the same." We were in London, where he was attending a law enforcement conference. A tall, solid man in his late fifties, when I told Linda, our perceptive receptionist, that he was with the FBI, she replied "Yup, looks like it."

Quiet-spoken and deliberative, Bowman joined the U.S. Navy in 1969, and worked in intelligence for several years before going to law school in Idaho. In 1979 he became the first ever Judge Advocate at the National Security Agency. He prosecuted espionage cases, taught international law at the U.S. Naval War College, worked at the U.S. embassy in Rome, and litigated cases for the Navy. In 1995 he went over to the FBI.

On September 11 he was in his office at the FBI headquarters in northwest Washington, D.C. The attacks surprised him, but he hadn't expected the rule-book to be torn up. For the FBI, terrorism was both an intelligence matter and a criminal matter. FBI investigations were carried out within the law, so that intelligence could be used as evidence in criminal proceedings. But that wasn't the only reason the FBI objected to aggressive interrogations. "You need to maintain the quality control of that information," Bowman explained, "so that you can put it together with other information that may be found in subsequent years." Working within the law preserved the integrity of the information and its usefulness. The FBI had long believed that the only way to interrogate was by building rapport. Behavioral scientists figured out a plan for each detainee, focused on the individual, his background, his family, which provided specific issues to aim at.

In late October, or perhaps early November 2002, Bowman first became aware of serious concerns at Guantánamo among FBI staff. This was after the memos from Dunlavey and Beaver went to General Hill, although Bowman was unaware of them. He also knew nothing about the Bybee and Yoo memos. If they had reached the FBI they would have come to him, since they raised issues of international law. "As far as I know," he said, "the FBI was cut out of that process, completely." By November the FBI had an entourage of about twenty staff at Guantánamo, not counting the behavioral scientists. The FBI supervisor and interviewers were on relatively short tours of duty, between thirty and forty-five days, as compared with the DoD's military interrogators, who were there for six months, which meant that the FBI team had less continuity and influence. There would have been one person who was relatively more senior than the others, an assistant special agent in charge from some field office, but the others were street agents. Nevertheless everybody with the FBI at Guantánamo was experienced in interrogation.

In October concerns were raised by an FBI Special Agent who'd been at Guantánamo since mid-September. When the agent arrived al-Qahtani was already "incarcerated in a darkened cell in the naval Brig."[1] He was interrogated by the FBI, and the plan was for military personnel to interrogate him for twenty-four hours straight. The FBI agent objected but was told that this technique was approved by "the Secretary," meaning Donald Rumsfeld. This confirmed Rumsfeld's involvement even before the VOCO. al-Qahtani was moved to a plywood interrogation hut in Camp X-Ray, where he was "aggressively interrogated by military reservists," according to the FBI Special Agent, under the direction of a civilian who was with the military and who wanted to do things that were "off the charts." The FBI Agent described how "the reservists yelled and screamed" at al-Qahtani, and "a German shepherd was positioned at the door of the interrogation hut and made to growl and bark at the detainee." At one point a copy of the Koran was placed in front of al-Qahtani while he was handcuffed to a chair, and an interrogator "straddled the Koran." The detainee became very angry, but still refused to provide any information. The agent later told investigators that al-Qahtani exhibited "bizarre behavior," observing remote objects and displaying extreme ranges of emotion. On November 22, the day before VOCO, he put this in writing in an electronic communication that was sent to the FBI's Counterterrorism Division.[2]

Around this time, Bowman was contacted. "I got a call from our behavioral scientists telling me that they thought that the military was going down the wrong path," he told me, "that they were going to have dysfunctional interrogation techniques." The FBI's behavioral scientists—psychologists—believed that Bowman had a direct line to the Pentagon, something few people in the FBI had. Bowman called the DoD's Acting Deputy General Counsel for Intelligence, Bob Dietz, an old friend, who had come over from his permanent position at the National Security Agency. This was the 10th or 12th of November, and it was the first of three calls he made. Dietz told Bowman that he wasn't working the issues, but that Haynes's deputy, Dan Dell'Orto, was. "In that conversation Bob said he already knew there were concerns," said Bowman, "by then they had heard complaints through military channels."

A few days later, around November 19, well before the VOCO and Thanksgiving, Bowman made his second call, to Dell'Orto. "I told him about it, and he said that he was aware of information, that he was still looking into it, which seemed fine to me." Dell'Orto told him he would get back to him. Was it possible that these concerns hadn't yet reached Haynes, I asked. Haynes told a Senate Committee he didn't recall "specific FBI complaints at the time of the November 27, 2002, memorandum" although he knew there were concerns about the appropriate means of questioning the detainees at Guantánamo "at that time."[3] "Impossible," said Bowman. He leaned across the table and pulled over a paper napkin. He drew two parallel lines, to show a corridor, then he drew a little square to show Dietz's office, and on the other side of the corridor, just across from the first square, he marked out a second square to show Haynes's office. So there were just a few feet between the two offices? "Correct," he replied, "It was impossible for Haynes not to have known."

A couple of weeks later Bowman got another call from the FBI psychologists. "I was being told that they had gone down and offered to help them construct an interrogation routine, and that they had been rejected, saying that they didn't have time to do rapport building—they needed to get information from these people immediately." By now Bowman was aware that new interrogation plans were well advanced for two detainees, including Detainee 63, whose name he didn't know. "They were certainly the ones that they concentrated on, but I don't think the techniques adopted were limited to them. 063 was one that clearly they were focused on." Bowman didn't know the identity of the second detainee, who turned out to be Mohammedou Ould Slahi, a Mauretanian who was subject to a special interrogation plan in the spring of 2003.[4]

Dell'Orto didn't get back to Bowman. "I hadn't expected him to really," he said, "I thought he'd just take care of it." But later he received a second call from the psychologists, saying the situation was getting worse. Their concerns were now that the interrogations were dysfunctional and there was mistreatment. "They didn't say it was bad mistreatment, they didn't say whether he was being hurt, but you have to understand that the FBI has a very, very strict way of interrogating, so anything that falls outside it is going to raise significant issues within the FBI."

Bowman's chronology of events was confirmed by a document I saw after our first meeting: an email from the Behavioral Analysis Unit at the FBI's Critical Incident Response Group (CIRG) that was copied to Bowman. Written in May 2003, it described events at Guantánamo a few months earlier, in November and December 2002, as observed by an FBI Special Agent. It referred to serious tensions between the FBI and the Defense Intelligence Agency's Defense Humint Services (DHS), who "were being encouraged to use aggressive interrogation tactics" that were of questionable effectiveness and at odds with legally permissible interviewing techniques. The email claimed that military interrogators had "little, if any, experience eliciting information for judicial purposes."[5]

The FBI personnel clearly objected to these new techniques, but their arguments were met with skepticism and resistance by senior DHS officials at GTMO. Things came to a head on November 21. The DIA's interrogation plan for Detainee 063 was complete and was based on the eighteen techniques outlined in the memo sitting on Jim Haynes's desk. The FBI and the Criminal Investigation Task Force now prepared a separate interrogation plan and in draft form shared it with the DIA (it was finalized the following day). Their plan did not use aggressive techniques. There was an animated discussion between the FBI and the DIA about the differences between the two plans, addressing, among other things, "legal problems" that could arise. According to the FBI group, the DIA team was "adamant" that its more aggressive plan was preferable, despite the absence of evidence that such techniques worked.

Later that day—November 21—the email described "an awkward teleconference between GTMO and Pentagon officials." According to the FBI Special Agent, the Army Colonel who oversaw military interrogations "blatantly misled the Pentagon into believing that the [FBI's Behavioral Analysis Unit] endorsed DHS's aggressive and controversial Interrogation Plan" for Detainee 063. This caused the FBI supervisor to write a letter to Major General Miller, Dunlavey's replacement, correcting the misstatement during the teleconference and requesting an urgent meeting. At this meeting, Miller acknowledged the positive aspects of the FBI plan, but "it was apparent that he favored DHS's interrogation methods," despite FBI assertions that such methods could easily result in unreliable and legally inadmissible information. The FBI concluded that Miller was "biased in favor of DHS's interrogation methods."

At that time Bowman was unaware of Dunlavey's memo and the list of eighteen techniques. "However, I think it is possible that the behavioral scientists were aware of this," he said. He explained: "The reason why that's relevant is that when I had the second phone call from them I told them that I'll make a call to the Pentagon, but in the meantime can you give me something in writing—lay out your views on this, because I wanted to be able to very concretely explain to people in the Pentagon, the General Counsel's Office, why they thought the interrogation techniques would be faulty." Bowman told me that he didn't get that written document until much later, in March or April 2003. Why did it come so late? "Probably in their mind it wasn't the most important thing," he countered, "I think they felt like me, that we should be able to straighten this out." But they didn't straighten it out. "I think if I had known that I wasn't going to have any effect with the phone calls, then I think I would have had to take the issues at least to Director Mueller of the FBI." John Ashcroft was Attorney General then, he added, so that might not have worked. Apparently the documents were sent to the FBI office at Quantico and not forwarded to Bowman until much later.

Bowman told me that the second phone call from the psychologists at Guantánamo probably came to him because he was thought to have influence at the Pentagon. This prompted him to call Dan Dell'Orto again—by now it was early December. Dell'Orto wasn't available, so he asked for, and got, Jim Haynes. "Jim basically blew me off. He said, 'Dan's handling that. I don't know what's going on with that—you'll have to talk with him.'" A short conversation? "A very short conversation, he did not want to talk about it at all, he just stiff-armed me." I was curious that he had direct access to Haynes. "Haynes didn't want to talk to me about what the FBI was saying." The significance of the encounter was that Haynes knew early on there were concerns. He couldn't claim ignorance.

Bowman's account was consistent with what General Myers had told me. I had asked Myers whether he was aware of the concerns expressed by the FBI at that time, even if he hadn't dealt directly with Bowman. "Yes, I did hear some issues," Myers said. Had that given him pause for thought? "Yes, absolutely, we wrestled with that, tried to reconcile all that."

So Bowman had come across Haynes before. "He didn't want to engage himself in anything that was controversial. It was very clear that he was trying to keep his name below the radar screen." Bowman knew Haynes's style. He had been involved in the investigation of Larry Franklin, a Pentagon civilian later charged and convicted of communicating classified U.S. national defense information to the American Israel Public Affairs Committee, a lobbying group.[6] Franklin had worked for the Office of Special Plans, which was (coincidentally) led by Doug Feith. "I came to the opinion that he was not the person we needed in the Pentagon," was Bowman's attitude to Feith.

At an early stage of the Franklin investigation, Bowman went to see Haynes to brief him. "We took a report with us on what they'd found. I gave the report to Jim. He declined to look at it, saying that he couldn't unread anything once he'd read it, so he didn't want to read anything." Did he turn a blind eye? "He couldn't turn a blind eye to it because we had given him a report, an oral report on what was going on, he just didn't want to get too deeply involved in it." Bowman could see why Haynes had met Rumsfeld's selection criteria. "He would not have appointed anybody who he did not think was going to do what Rumsfeld wanted him to do. He would not appoint anybody to anything who wouldn't toe the line." That also applied to Dunlavey.

—◆—

The conversation in early December 2002 was the last that Haynes and Bowman had until the spring of 2003, when Bowman received a bundle of

documents from the FBI's behavioral analysis unit. He went to see Haynes. "I
told him what I had, I said there are some papers here that you really ought to
look at." Haynes responded that he'd seen those papers, about abuse at Guantánamo, including the documents concerning al-Qahtani's treatment in the
days before November 23. "I never heard from him again." By now, however,
Bowman had formed a clear view of Haynes, who was insisting that every
lawyer in the Department of Defense, uniformed or otherwise, work directly
for him. Haynes didn't want to leave any room for independent thinking, and
liked to leave no tracks. Bowman did not know whether anybody had come to
Haynes about the issue of interrogation early on or not (he was unaware that
Haynes had visited Guantánamo in September). "But," he added, "I would
think that the way he was trying to run things this would not have come as a
surprise, because he tried to control what everybody was doing there. I don't
know whether he listened to anybody else on any of this or not." He paused.
"But I don't think he was of a mind to say 'no' about anything."

Bowman objected to aggressive interrogation techniques. In his mind
the function of interrogation was to obtain information that was reliable,
that could be used. For him, developing rapport with the detainee was the
only thing that worked: that was the criteria against which the eighteen
techniques should have been tested. Bowman did not see the list until later
in 2003; he had no idea where the techniques came from. Some were recognizable, similar to ones used on him in SERE training (he went through
Navy SERE training during Vietnam; "not fun" was all he would say about
that experience). "I did not see any rational process—or any thought
process—that went into the idea of how you were going to get information
out of a person." Drawing up a list of authorized techniques without having something in mind for particular individuals was irrational. "You have
to ask the question, what's it going to give me? If you can't answer that
question, then the technique isn't harmless, it's dysfunctional."

Some techniques raised serious concerns for Bowman, namely stress
positions. "If you are going to cause people physical discomfort, they're
going to get pissed off, they aren't going to talk to you as readily." The same
went for sleep deprivation. It didn't produce results: "I don't have much
difficulty with a 20-hour interrogation, but if you do it for four or five days
in a row, the person who is not getting enough sleep isn't going to have co-
herent thoughts in a very short period of time." I asked about fifty-four
days on the trot. Bowman raised his eyebrows. "If you do it for a week,
you're going to come out with a guy on the other end who doesn't know
what he's talking about."

We moved on through the list. Forced grooming? Objectionable because it was culturally significant. Phobias and dogs? "Absolutely unacceptable." Mild non-injurious physical contact, like grabbing and poking? "It looks intuitively non-problematic," he said, "unless the person doing the pushing is a female." When I first saw the list that had not occurred to me. And, he added, a lot of the females that were down at Guantánamo were there for precisely that purpose. Al-Qahtani's interrogation log was filled with references to female interrogators and the use of girly magazines.

Bowman objected because these techniques would not produce meaningful information. "If it were me being harassed with some of these techniques, I might be tempted to give them any kind of spurious information to get them to stop." Even worse than the absence of limits, he said, was the fact that the techniques weren't geared to elicit a specific response. "What you are doing is giving these techniques to a bunch of young soldiers who don't have a clue about interrogation, who are told this is OK, but not told why it's OK, or what they are going to get from it." This was in contrast to the FBI interrogators, who knew how to interrogate and knew what al-Qaeda was all about. The FBI were able to tell the Commanding General what to look for, who were the key figures, their training, what they'd been doing, who to go after.

A particular interrogation technique was used because you expected to elicit a response that was directly connected to your objective: that was the aim of behavioral analysis. Some of these techniques might work on the battlefield—where you had somebody who was probably grateful to be alive and not sure they were going to remain that way—and might have immediate tactically significant information that could be scared out of them. "But if you put somebody behind bars," Bowman suggested, "and they know that they're not going to be killed . . . then this stuff becomes more harassing than it is productive."

Bowman thought two things had gone wrong at Guantánamo. The first was that after September 11 there was "a very high degree of urgency to try and get information to head off something else." That feeling of urgency had to be taken into account, but it was allowed to dominate. The second factor was a lowering of standards of training for the treatment of prisoners in times of conflict. Bowman was exasperated by this. "I find it almost mind boggling that it could have eroded as fast as it has, considering how much effort went into that for such a long period of time."

There were plenty of experts on military law around, but they weren't used or even consulted—anywhere. The military lawyers were cut out by the civilians, by Haynes and the like, who bore particular responsibility for what followed. "The General Counsel has a responsibility to make sure that he is completely steeped in all the issues," said Bowman. "The fact that the first Bybee memo came out as it did gives you an indication that there was a lack of understanding." For Bowman the buck stopped with Haynes. "If he perceives that there is an illegality going on and he can't stop it, then his responsibility is to resign."

And the signs of illegality were there, even as the Haynes memo was being written. I showed Bowman a document entitled "Legal Analysis of Interrogation Techniques." It was a photocopy of an undated and unsigned three-page document that was sent by fax on November 27, 2002. At the top of the first page, almost illegible, it said: "Drafted by SSA ███████ FBI (BAU) at Guantánamo Bay and forwarded to Marion Bowman, Legal Counsel, FBIHQ, on 11/27/2002."[7] This was one of the documents that Bowman said only reached him much later. It concluded that ten of the eighteen techniques were examples of coercive interrogation that were unlawful under the U.S. Constitution. These techniques included hooding, twenty-hour interrogations, the removal of clothing, stress positions and dogs. The analysis went further: these interrogation techniques could violate the U.S. Torture Statute. "It is possible," wrote the unnamed author, "that those who employ these techniques may be indicted, prosecuted, and possibly convicted if the trier of fact determines that the user had the requisite intent. Under these circumstances it is recognized that these techniques not be utilized." All these techniques were used on al-Qahtani.

Bowman looked at the document. He recognized it; there was no doubt about its authenticity. "It was drafted by someone at Guantánamo, yes." It was part of a three-quarter-inch package of documents sent him by a Special Agent to take to the Pentagon, and also included an opinion by some Judge Advocates, deploring the treatment of detainees. However he didn't receive it until the spring of 2003, probably because it was sent to the FBI's Behavioral Analysis Unit at Quantico to be forwarded on to him. Bowman thought the legal analysis wasn't drafted by the Special Agent, but by someone else at Guantánamo, almost certainly a lawyer. "I know the procedures for the FBI, no supervisory special agent would have drafted this on his own. He would have asked one of the attorneys to look at what's going on and to draft something." The legal analysis made it quite clear that some lawyers at Guantánamo were concerned enough about the new techniques to express their opposition in writing.

Bowman knew there was a problem—and he reacted—but in the end he didn't do enough. This thoughtful and phlegmatic man finally concluded:

"The lawyers are the gatekeepers. The question is, whether you've got the right lawyers."

INTERROGATION LOG OF DETAINEE 063
Day 30, December 22 2002

0030: Lead (the leading interrogator) began the "attention to detail" theme with the fitness model photos. Detainees refused to look at photos claiming it was against his religion. Lead poured a 24 oz bottle of water over detainee's head. . . .

Day 31, 23 December 2002

0001: Upon entering booth, lead changed white noise music and hung pictures of swimsuit models around his neck. Detainee was left in booth listening to white music.

0030: Lead pulled pictures of swimsuit models off detainee and told him the test of his ability to answer questions would begin. Detainee refused to answer, and finally stated that he would after lead poured water over detainees head and was told he would be subjected to this treatment day after day. . . .

0230: Detainee requested that lead add wearing the towel over his head to list of detainee problems. Detainee related that he already knows where he is, so why does he continue to wear a towel over his head. . . .

1115: Detainee was offered water and refused, so the interrogator poured some of the bottle over the detainee's head. . . .

15

Getting the right lawyers was also on Mike Gelles's mind. Gelles was from the Bronx, in New York. He became a clinical forensic psychologist, and since 1990 had worked for the Naval Criminal Investigation Service (NCIS), the primary law enforcement and intelligence arm of the U.S. Navy. He first visited Guantánamo in February 2002, where he worked closely with the military, the FBI and the CITF; there he saw firsthand what was taking place.

Gelles was a man with abundant energy and clear views. Tall, balding, and genial, his specialization was operational psychology—understanding what motivates or causes human behavior—and his work had a strong forensic component in the sphere of counter-terrorism and espionage. He had plenty of experience by the time he got to Guantánamo: he'd been involved in the aftermath of the 1993 bombing of the World Trade Center and a few years later in the bombings of the U.S. embassies in Nairobi and Dar es Salaam. This experience influenced his approach. "I really learned that it was necessary to think differently about how we talked to terrorists," he told me when we met at the Tabard Inn in Washington, "and how we conducted interviews and interrogations." For Gelles, the personal, critical moment came with the bombing of the USS *Cole* in the Yemeni port of Aden in October 2000 in which seventeen sailors were killed. "2000 was more significant for the Navy than 9/11," he explained, because it caused the NCIS to rethink law enforcement techniques. In particular, they needed to look again at the most useful way to interrogate terrorists. Existing approaches were too limited. "I'll give you a little bit of credit," he said sheepishly, "you guys in London have sort of struggled with much more of a diverse ethnicity in that regard than we have here, while we have been a lot more focused on violent crime, which leads to different ways of thinking about people and how you approach them."

At the NCIS, Gelles worked closely with Mark Fallon, a case officer. Their approach to interrogation was not based on the *U.S. Army Field Manual*. "FM 34–52 never came into our life, never," he said, "that was designed for combatants." For Gelles and the NCIS—as for Bowman at the FBI— the focus was on interrogation models that provided information and evidence to be used in U.S. courts. "I'm a forensic psychologist, everything should be acceptable, reliable, valid in a court of law." He paused and took a breath. "Here lies the big problem we're coming to."

Gelles was at Guantánamo from the outset, even before Mike Dunlavey arrived, and he knew that large numbers of suspects were being detained in Afghanistan and many were on their way to Guantánamo. They needed to decide what to do with these people. "So they stood up the Criminal Investigation Task Force, the CITF," Gelles explained, describing the establishment of the Force under the auspices of the Secretary of the Army's delegated leader Major General Don Ryder, a military lawyer and the most senior officer in the Army's Criminal Investigation Division. The CITF included investigators from the Army, Air Force and the Navy's Criminal Investigation Service (NCIS) of which Gelles was part. The head of the NCIS was Dave Brant, for whom Gelles's affection was clear. Brant brought Mark Fallon on board: Fallon was the main case agent on the investigation of the bombing of the *Cole*. They had two primary responsibilities: to develop new interrogation models and to train interrogators.

Gelles was based in Washington, where he established a team from various agencies and developed a training model. His team included ten psychologists and a couple of psychiatrists. They called their group the "behavioral consultation team," the BSCT, known as "biscuits." His "biscuits" went down to Guantánamo and trained alongside the military. "We'd do a couple of days with them, get them up to speed, here are the tactics, here are the steps, things you have to think about, here's how you remain disciplined." Gelles's team wrote papers, prepared PowerPoint slides, assessed what had and had not worked. They modified the training on the basis of what worked—it was a constantly evolving process. Gelles identified three phases: a first phase up to June 2002, during which initial interrogations were conducted; a second phase to November 2002, as new interrogation techniques were being thought through; and a third phase after November 23, when the new techniques were applied.

But Gelles had concerns from the outset. He was immediately unimpressed by Mike Dunlavey, the Army Major General handpicked by Rumsfeld, and his opinion didn't improve over time. The deep antipathy was mutual. "He was just way over the top, just totally out there," Gelles said. Dunlavey was no more complimentary: "He may have been a psychologist, but he had no knowledge of those people." Gelles had expected a different approach from a lawyer. Dunlavey looked to him like a "judge coming out of locker one," a man so "consumed by himself and his own ego" that he saw himself as the General Patton of Guantánamo. He didn't want to doubt Dunlavey's intentions. "Come on!" he exclaimed, "I'm not saying it wasn't to protect America, but let's put it in perspective; as professionals, we are required to be disciplined in the way we think." That was a major part of the problem, the lack of professionalism, of critical thinking, of a disciplined approach. The difficulties were compounded by the pressure from the Pentagon to get results. The military were under instructions to obtain information—that was clear to Gelles—and it created an intense sense of self-belief about what they were doing. The military interrogators identified themselves as "the tip of the spear in the struggle against an existential threat to the United States." Dunlavey was the point at the very tip of the spear, making it clear who was running the show. "I'm the General here, I'll ask for things and it'll happen, and I will define what's happening." Gelles was unsure about Dunlavey's relationship with Rumsfeld, although Dunlavey was constantly reminding him of his high-level contacts and Gelles knew there were trips up to see Rumsfeld and others in D.C.

Gelles's account was broadly consistent with what others told me. The people at Guantánamo were under intense pressure from Washington to get results and they were following orders rather than generating their own. Things got out of control. "Diane Beaver was following orders," Gelles said. "She was doing what she was told and then she dug in." Gelles was more impressed by her than by Dunlavey, but still he had questions. "I don't really dislike her, she seems like a nice professional, just kind of curious as to where she was coming up with these legal arguments because I had other lawyers on the CITF side saying 'this is ridiculous.'"

By June the numbers at Guantánamo had grown to more than 500 detainees and interrogations were underway. Were they getting any useful information? The expression on Gelles's face suggested not. Even assuming they had the right people, nobody discovered what they knew. "I remember being down in Camp X-Ray and wandering around," Gelles recalled, "and seeing a couple of very psychotic folks and thinking 'What's going on here?' Why would you fly a guy who's flagrantly psychotic from Afghanistan to Guantánamo Bay? It didn't make any sense." The best that could be said was that the interrogations produced incomplete information. The interrogators listened to the stories: some were probably true, others obviously not. "The bad guys were using natural stories for why they were there," Gelles explained, "so it was difficult to differentiate—are you telling the truth or not?" Gelles was acutely aware of the dangers of coercion and false confessions. He wanted to protect the integrity of the information.

Despite the absence of detail about many of the detainees' backgrounds—a crucial component of an effective interrogation, and something that Dunlavey had also complained about—by June they had enough information to designate a small number as "high level" cases. Gelles would talk to the interrogators and look at specific cases, the "high value targets," as they came to be known, including Detainee 063, but he didn't conduct the interrogation. He looked at the file, met the interrogators, observed behavior, watched interrogations on video; then he would suggest ways to proceed. But he never went into the room. "Psychologists don't go in," he said, "I looked through a door or usually would sit in a corner, but there was no reason for psychologists to be in the room, no sense." This struck me as strange, since al-Qahtani's interrogation log had identified the presence of a behavioral psychologist from the very start. Major L (BSCT) was Major John Leso, a psychologist who was not part of Gelles's team and who Gelles thought was "basically a good guy" who was in over his head because he had "no real background in interrogation." The presence of BSCTs is referred to frequently in the log.[1]

Gelles learned that there was "a parallel process" underway. Alongside his team's interrogations and efforts to gather information, he became aware of other efforts at "intel-collection": interrogations of the same detainees were being carried out by the military interrogators, using the *FM 34-52* techniques. Gelles began to pick up information about a divergence of opinion, on the approach to some "high value detainees." There was a growing gap between the work of the military interrogators extracting intelligence and the work of the FBI criminal investigators—the cops—gathering evidence. For the most part the military interrogators seemed to be eighteen- and nineteen-year-old kids passing through on short rotations. They'd gone through a six-week training program and were mechanically following the techniques allowed by the Army manual. Gelles believed this would not produce results. Interview interrogation required particular assessment skills; the interrogator constantly had to assess emerging information and then make decisions as to the right approach, based on the detainee's answers and behavior, and the stances he took. That wasn't happening, largely because the interrogators lacked experience and insight. But that wasn't the only difficulty. "As you move forward, based on the information," he explained, "it's a constant feedback loop. These kids were pulling techniques off a list, so they were interviewing and interrogating by technique. Here lies the problem."

Gelles thought the military interrogators had limited real-life experience. In June he had met with Dunlavey, who wasn't receptive to Gelles's ideas. "It didn't obviously have much of an impact because there were a lot of naysayers," Gelles recounted. He faced strong objections to his softly, softly approach, as well as his focus on the need to obtain sound evidence. "If you ever talk to Diane Beaver," he whispered, "you're not going to get a lot of kind words about me. She feels I was totally obstructionistic to the process." That was indeed her view. Nevertheless, Gelles thought Beaver had tried to rein in some of the greater excesses. "She tried to cool it, but basically she was so immersed and so lost . . ." Gelles's words trailed off. "She drank the Kool-Aid."

The existence of two parallel approaches—"intel" versus the cops—had immediate consequences. Dunlavey wanted Gelles's team more deeply involved, but under his command. "He said, 'Love what you're doing, I want you here, I need you here fulltime.' I looked at him and I go: 'Not gonna happen.' 'What do you mean it's not gonna happen?' I say, 'It's not gonna happen.'" Gelles had told Dunlavey that his team was small and they could not devote themselves exclusively to Guantánamo, which was not the be all and end all of American efforts to combat terrorism. Dunlavey didn't like that. "So what does he do? He says, alright, I want my own biscuit [BSCT]. And what he does is he then proceeds to pull in medical folks from the army hospitals on orders to come and be his biscuit. Here lies a grave error."

So, according to Gelles, Dunlavey created his own team—although this is a claim that Dunlavey disputed. Gelles told me that most of Dunlavey's team had no background in interrogations of this kind: they may have been great people, great doctors, great clinicians, but they had no training in interrogation. They would come in and support the interrogators. There were then two sets of BSCTs: the trained and experienced group, Gelles's group, and the untrained and inexperienced group gathered by Dunlavey. And later on in the press it would be Dunlavey's group that garnered the attention. "That was the other biscuit. That's the biscuit (BSCT) that they talk about in the news all the time, which you can imagine, sets this little Bronx kid up and on fire. That's what happened." According to Gelles, Dunlavey was not a big fan of his after June.

June 2002 was the turning point. The military interrogators decided they were going to step up the pressure. Detainee 063, al-Qahtani, was of high value. By now he was under FBI interrogation, even if not everyone knew his identity. The interrogation was moving slowly, but it was moving. "They all move slowly," Gelles explained. "They are not like interviewing westerners, talk to Scotland Yard, they'll tell you. They move slowly, it's a different process." The apparent lack of progress increased the tension. "Everybody was looking to destroy this enemy that attacked American soil," said Gelles. Meanwhile Dunlavey's narcissistic tendencies became more exaggerated, and the contribution from outside Guantánamo, from Washington and beyond, didn't help the forces of restraint and reason. Gelles singled out the background noise made by people like Harvard Law School Professor Alan Dershowitz, who didn't help with his ticking time bomb theories all over the media. "I remember having a discussion with him once in the men's room at Harvard about that," Gelles recalled, his words laced with scorn.

And it was only much later that Gelles would understand Washington's real role, when he went to see Jim Haynes in D.C. "I met with him, I met with Billingslea," he told me. Marshal Billingslea was Rumsfeld's main civilian adviser on counter-terrorism efforts against al-Qaeda and other terrorist groups. Gelles was circumspect about Haynes. He didn't have anything negative to say about him as he had had insufficient exposure to form a clear view. "I thought that he was very respectful, polite, corporate, listened." He also remembered his interaction with Billingslea, which came much later, who was curious about Gelles's alternative approach. In the end, Gelles told me, Marshal Billingslea was "like the rest of them—political appointees who were following leadership's perspective—this was driven by Rumsfeld."

As summer proceeded, Gelles and his team started hearing more and more about the need for new interrogation techniques. Some of it was "ridiculous stuff," he said. "Eventually, we learn that they're coming out with these increased, enhanced, tactics." The cops had not prevailed. General Hill did not take up his post until late August, by which time the push to introduce the new interrogation techniques had begun. "There was a suspension of critical thinking," which even a "good guy" like Hill could not halt. In September 2002 there were brainstorming sessions on the new techniques, involving Defense Intelligence Agency people from Defense Humint Services (DHS), as well as others on the base, including the CIA. Gelles stayed out of those. He knew about a visit to Fort Bragg, to learn more about SERE training, about which he was scathing. "They saw SERE as a potential option because SERE is search evasion resistance training and basically, if you can teach people how to tough it out, maybe you can use those techniques to get people to talk. Although on the surface that makes sense, it's totally illogical. SERE is built for evasion, not for elicitation." Later, Gelles would tell the psychologists and psychiatrists (whose identity he kept to himself) who were present during the interrogation of Detainee 063 to be careful, very careful about what they were doing. And he doubted the value of the effort. "The half life for some of this stuff is six months to a year, then it's gone."

Was Gelles aware in September that the military were looking at new techniques for Detainee 063? He tensed up and gave an unusually curt response. "Yes." Was he aware that Dunlavey's team was in liaison with Washington and with Rumsfeld's office about the new techniques? "Probably." Did he have trouble recalling? "It's better for me not to recall because I know a side of this that I can't talk about."

In October 2002 he became aware of the list of eighteen techniques. There was a fourth category—rendition to another country—but that fell by the wayside. "Maybe somebody thought it was kind of stupid to put it in writing." "Category II and III were pretty stupid to put in writing too," he quickly added. What problems did Gelles have with the new techniques? Basically he had the same concerns as Spike Bowman: the new techniques would produce "unreliable information," they were immoral and they'd "set a pattern that was clearly going to impact our folks overseas, too, when they were captured."

As for as al-Qahtani was concerned, this meant he couldn't be tried and none of the information he produced could be used in courts. Beyond that, the total absence of limits on the use of techniques troubled Gelles greatly. "How do you build thresholds into a slap?" he asked, "How do you build thresholds into standing?" He recalled Rumsfeld's handwritten note on the Haynes memo. He hadn't paid much attention to it: it was ridiculous, arrogant, sarcastic. It probably didn't mean much. "It gave some insight into the fact that there obviously wasn't a whole lot of real thoughtful thinking going on about this," he added. It was a knee-jerk type of reaction. "As a psychologist, how could I say these techniques weren't going to traumatize somebody?" To introduce coercive techniques would undoubtedly have an impact on mental stability. Was al-Qahtani traumatized by the new techniques? How could you say that he wouldn't be? Was it torture? Gelles wasn't going to start defining what torture was or what torture wasn't—that was more of a legal thing. For Gelles the concern was simple: "Why are you going to do this? Are you going to get some information from him? We didn't believe it would be reliable."

I told Gelles that I'd spoken to Feith, Dunlavey, Beaver, Hill, Myers and others. The Administration's narrative—that the new techniques had come from a bottom-up process that started at Guantánamo—struck me as implausible. Gelles livened up. "That's not accurate." So, I asked, were there people right up at the highest levels in Washington who were basically saying, get the new techniques, here are some ideas? "Correct." Here were two competing stories: one described the emergence of techniques from the DHS and the Secretary of Defence's office; the other ascribed a more passive role to Rumsfeld and those around him, as they reacted to new techniques emerging from Guantánamo. Gelles had clear views, and they related to signals he'd picked up from Beaver and Dunlavey. "I don't believe it was Gitmo that sorted it out. That's my impression. I think it's the first one. That they had already developed them." He was silent for a time, then added: "This was not done by a bunch of people down in Gitmo, no way."

By November the new techniques were on Haynes's desk in D.C. As Washington deliberated, in the period before Thanksgiving, a detailed interrogation plan was coming together for al-Qahtani. It was at the tail end of Dunlavey's period in charge of making Guantánamo a front line in America's war on terror. Dunlavey left in early November 2002, though by then there weren't too many questions to be asked. "People recognized he was over the top, I'm just going to leave it at that." Dunlavey's replacement was Geoffrey Miller. Gelles met him several times and didn't feel he was much of an improvement. "I remember sitting at the table," Gelles recalled, "and Miller said to me 'If you want to be on the team you've got to wear the right jersey.'"

"It was before Thanksgiving that things were really starting to take off." Five days before Thanksgiving, I reminded him, on November 23. He paused. "We couldn't stop them." FBI emails corroborated his account. Gelles went to Mark Fallon and together they approached Dave Brant, the head of NCIS. Brant was robust and didn't hesitate: it was time to do something. "I don't want my agents in on this type of crap," he told Gelles, "if they are going to start doing this we're not going to be in the same room as them." Brant called Don Ryder. "I'm hearing some not good things, the bottom line is I'll pull my people out if they don't meet our interrogation guidelines," he told him. As a result Gelles and Fallon separated their agents from Dunlavey's team.

They knew what was coming. Gelles's needle went to danger when he saw al-Qahtani's interrogation plan, based on the eighteen techniques. "No way, no way," was how Brant reacted. He maintained this went beyond even his level of seniority and they needed to go higher. He could pull his agents out, but he didn't want to make a big deal down in Guantánamo. "This is Rumsfeld," he told Gelles. Already worried that the techniques could be used more widely, they looked for someone they could go to. Later they identified Alberto Mora, the General Counsel to the Navy.

Gelles's team had written a counter-plan, before November 23; by the time they had completed it, the aggressive interrogation of al-Qahtani was underway. "At the same time we were simultaneously fighting this, we're writing, meeting, talking." They wrote "a nice plan, simple," a sixty-page document, setting out a different approach, an alternative to coercion. But by then it was too late. The saving grace for Gelles and Brant was that they knew they weren't alone. "There were a lot of other people down there that were thinking 'Oh my God, what's going to happen here.'" And there were people in Washington, people like Alberto Mora. "Thankfully there was Alberto," said Mike Gelles.

INTERROGATION LOG OF DETAINEE 063
Day 32, December 24 2002

0001: Control entered booth, changed music playing, and hung binder of fitness models around detainee's neck. . . .

1145: Detainee initially refused water so control poured a little on detainee's head. . . .

2100: The detainee is thinking a lot more on the themes when presented to him, seems to be on the verge of breaking. . . .

Day 33, December 25 2002

0230: Interrogator poured one half bottle of water over detainee's head and yelled that the detainee was not in control in the booth, that the interrogator decided everything that happened to him, but the detainee could take that power away by simply telling the truth. Detainee yelled back that the interrogator did this to him and the rest of the bottle was poured over the detainee's head to illustrate the point that the interrogator was in control. . . .

0300: Detainee offered water and refused. Interrogator poured some water on detainee's head. . . . Detainee started falling asleep so interrogator had detainee stand up for 30 minutes. . . .

Detainee was subjected to white noise (music) waiting for his IVs to be completed. . . .

16

I first met Alberto Mora unexpectedly in November 2005. I was passing through Washington on a lecture tour and an acquaintance in the U.S. Department of Defense suggested that I might want to meet the General Counsel of the Navy. This would mean a trip to the Pentagon, which I'd never visited, so I jumped at the opportunity.

So great is the inner extent of the Pentagon that my escorted journey from the visitor's entrance to Mora's office took nearly fifteen minutes. We walked past shops and supermarkets, navigated endless corridors, past a wall lined with portraits of all the Secretaries of Defense—two of Rumsfeld—and past Rumsfeld's office. Mora was delightful: a sharp and witty man with a terrific sense of humor. There was warmth in his eyes, and a twinkle suggesting a propensity to do mischief. I later learned that his family heritage was a mix of Cuban and Hungarian, two countries that have produced some of my favorite and most entertaining friends. Mora was comfortable with the message of *Lawless World,* my previous book, even if there was much he disagreed with. He supported the Iraq War, for example. At our first meeting he said nothing at all about any role he had played in the short life of the Haynes memo. After I left his office I was escorted back to the visitor's entrance. As we approached, the officer who had accompanied me asked if he might share a private word. "Excuse me for saying this, sir," he said gently, "but I wanted to let you know that many of us in the services are grateful for your efforts."

By the time Mora and I saw each other next, he'd stepped down as Navy General Counsel and was now General Counsel for the international operations of Wal-Mart, living in Bentonville, Arkansas. I flew to Fayetteville. "They say this is going to be like L.A. in ten years," said my cab driver, but that wasn't immediately obvious. We drove past flatlands, Charolais beef battles, many articulated Wal-Mart trucks, and topsoil for

*Alberto Mora, General Counsel to the U.S. Navy
(Photograph courtesy Tom Fitzsimmons/JFK Library
Foundation)*

sale in quantities that would have covered the whole of the British Isles. With a few hours to kill before my meeting with Mora, I looked around in the central square of Bentonville. It was a perfect square, in every sense. I went back the next day with Mora's wife, Susan Talalay, who entertained me with comparisons of life in Washington and Bentonville, and provided her own perspective of events back in 2002.

I visited the Wal-Mart Visitors Center, surely one of the great small museums of the world, right up with the Musée du Pruneau in Agen and the British Lawnmower Museum in Southport. The Wal-Mart center is a monument to the foresight of the small investors who turned a few dollars into millions in the space of a generation or two. The highlight was the re-creation of Sam Walton's office, with his blue cap still perched on the simple wooden desk. Walton founded Wal-Mart in 1962, and it is now the second largest corporation in the world. Mora's office was about one-tenth the size of his office at the Pentagon, but he had no regrets leaving.

Bentonville seemed a world away from the threats of international terrorism, and the events that caused Dave Brant to walk into Alberto Mora's office on the afternoon of Tuesday December 17. Mora talked freely about that visit, which came without warning. He'd worked with Brant, trusted him, and knew nothing at that time about any Haynes memo or other changes to military interrogation practices. Brant told him about the abuse, but didn't mention al-Qahtani or any other individual detainees. They would not have known that by then al-Qahtani was into the fourth week of his new interrogation regime, which included a day of dehydration and hospitalization, 9/11 tribute videos, and taunts about his homosexuality. Brant said the NCIS agents were getting information that the abusive actions had been authorized at "high level" in Washington and he wanted Mora to check out what was happening. Brant's group refused to be involved in abusive, unlawful interrogations; if they continued, the NCIS would have to consider whether to remain at Guantánamo at all.

This was the first that Mora had heard about the abuse. He'd been down to Guantánamo a couple of times, first in January and then later in the year, when he saw Baccus and Dunlavey. Neither had overly impressed him. "He visited me down here," Mike Dunlavey confirmed. When Brant came to talk to him, Mora was unaware of any authorizations, from the Pentagon or elsewhere in Washington, and had no inkling of any decision to go beyond the military's traditional approaches to interrogation. The following day, December 18, Mora met Brant again and Mike Gelles joined them. Gelles told him that the interrogators were under pressure to achieve results. Guards and interrogators were using physical contact, stress positions and coercive psychological procedures; one detainee had been dressed in female underwear. Gelles told Mora about the interrogation logs he'd seen, and they showed him some fragments. Gelles was concerned that the techniques being used by young and inexperienced military interrogators violated the law, and that there was a real danger that the abuse would escalate and spread. He described the phenomenon of "force drift," where interrogators using force come to believe that if some force is good then more is even better. Gelles and Brant also said that their concerns were shared by others at Guantánamo, including the FBI and some military personnel.

Mora was dismayed. The interrogation techniques described to him violated U.S. law and international law. At the very least they were inconsistent with Common Article 3. Knowing that the army had responsibility for Guantánamo, he called Steve Morello, the Army's General Counsel. Morello said he had information—"I know a lot about this"—and invited him over to discuss the issues. They met later that same day, December 19. "There was a worried air about him, showing me the papers he gave the impression that he was doing something he shouldn't have done, but it was weighing on his conscience," said Mora. He went into his room, Morello shut the door, and they sat at his circular table. Morello pushed the papers across to Mora. "Look at this," he said, "don't tell anyone where you got it." Morello showed him a copy of the Haynes memo, signed by Donald Rumsfeld. Morello seemed to know about the evolution of the documents and told Mora they'd tried to stop it. "We were told to go away," Morello told Mora. Mora also saw Dunlavey's originating request, Diane Beaver's opinion, and General Hill's memo. Mora didn't question Morello in detail on what he knew and when. Probably Morello had found out because the

Army was the executive agency running Guantánamo, so the material would have come to him through Tom White, the Secretary of the Army. Mora took copies of the documents.

Returning to his office, he spread the documents on his large desk. He was horrified by what he read—by the list of techniques, by the absence of limits, by Beaver's advice. "I was astounded that the Secretary of Defense could get within 100 miles of this issue," he told me. Only later did he come to appreciate that the Haynes memo contained several clues. The reference to the discussions with Wolfowitz, Feith and Myers was notable, confirming what Myers had said. "The Joint Staff never got a chance to formally approve this," was how Mora later understood the process. Certainly the services' General Counsels and the senior JAG lawyers were by-passed, and never had an opportunity to express their views. Mora learned that the Joint Staff circulated General Hill's memo and the attachments to the Staff of the Chief of Naval Operations (OPNAV), where it was reviewed by a navy captain on November 2. The captain was not a lawyer and cannot have understood the full import of what was being proposed. Nevertheless, he concurred with the proposal, but he too recommended the need for a more detailed inter-agency legal review. That never took place. The documents never reached Mora or any other senior military lawyers in the Navy. "My guess," said Mora, "is that they understood what should have happened didn't happen."

Mora confirmed the sequence of events I was now becoming familiar with. The documents would have been passed to SOUTHCOM's JAG lawyer, Manny Supervielle, but what was highly surprising to Mora was that the only legal opinion was from Diane Beaver. Mora knew Supervielle as an acquaintance; they were both from the Cuban-American community. He called him before the suspension of the interrogation techniques but Supervielle never returned the call. Mora was surprised, "You know, a Colonel never failed to return a call to a service General Counsel like me." "My assumption is that there is no other legal opinion from service lawyers, it is likely that none exists." This was very unusual: there should have been written legal advice from Supervielle or from Jane Dalton. "I have the highest regard for Jane," Mora told me, "but I wondered whether she'd focused fully on all the issues." Mora came to learn that it was Jim Haynes who short-circuited the normal approval process. "I heard that from Jane Dalton," he said. "She said to me 'Jim pulled this away, we never had a chance to complete the assessment.'" A senior military lawyer closely involved in the process confirmed to me that that was precisely what had happened.

Mora thought Beaver's legal advice was shocking. "I was looking for the language of limitations," he told me, "and it just wasn't there." The advice was a "wholly inadequate" analysis of the law and a "poor treatment of this difficult and highly sensitive issue." The Haynes memo that Rumsfeld had signed was "fatally grounded" on Beaver's "serious failures of legal analysis." At the time Mora did not know about the Justice Department's Bybee/Yoo memos: he only learned of those when they were made public, two years later. Contrary to the Administration's line, by his reading the Bybee/Yoo memo *did* apply to Guantánamo. There was nothing to suggest that it was intended for—or limited to—use by the CIA outside the United States. He also believed that David Addington, Vice President Cheney's lawyer, was involved, even if he was not tainted by the paper trail. Did Mora think that Haynes would have known about the Justice Department opinions? "I think Jim was in the loop," he told me, "because he knew of detainees in DoD custody."

He was equally appalled by the new interrogation techniques and believed they should never have been approved. Some of them could produce "effects reaching the level of torture," whether applied singly or in combination. And even if they didn't cross the line of torture, they "almost certainly would constitute 'cruel, inhuman or degrading treatment.'" By either standard they were illegal; they did not meet the standard of humane treatment that Mora thought the President had committed himself to on February 7, 2002 in his Geneva decision.

At the same time Mora understood the dilemma the military lawyers faced with the Geneva decision. "They thought this was an abomination," he said, "but it's a very, very serious matter to disobey an order." If a military officer questions orders this is insubordination—you just don't do it. But Mora wasn't in uniform. "I can't say that I wouldn't have executed Rumsfeld's order," Mora said, "but my utility to the service JAGs was that I wasn't in uniform so I wasn't under those constraints." Diane Beaver had spoken powerfully about the authority of a decision that had been taken personally by the President or the Secretary of Defense, and her view was echoed by Lowell Jacoby, the DIA Director whose people were on the ground at Guantánamo. He told me that the decision on the new interrogation techniques was "a painful experience" for him because it adopted a path that was "counter-cultural." A senior Congresswoman once asked him why he hadn't resigned. "I said 'Madam, I received a lawful order, it came down from the National Security Council, it was an order relayed to me by the Deputy Secretary of Defense, my job was to execute lawful orders, I couldn't resign because things were tough or political.'" Like Diane Beaver, Jacoby believed that "where policies came down from the Secretary of Defense my role was to make sure that the execution was in accordance with the policy." No more, no less.

Mora adopted another route, however, because he believed implementing the techniques would have severe ramifications. They would harm U.S. foreign policy and its military and legal practices. They would make it more difficult to prosecute a global response to terrorism. He decided to act, by briefing the Secretary of the Navy, Gordon England. He would also take his objections directly to Jim Haynes. The next morning he met briefly with England, who was not aware of Rumsfeld's decision. England told him he could raise his concerns with Haynes. "Use your judgment," he said. Mora met Haynes that afternoon and told him he was surprised that Rumsfeld had signed the Haynes memo, since the new techniques were tantamount to being considered torture. Haynes disagreed. Mora told him to think about the techniques more closely. Could a detainee be held in a coffin? Could phobias be applied until madness set in? He went through the list while Haynes listened. He told Haynes that individual techniques could be torture, so could their use in combination. The fundamental problem with your memo, he told Haynes, "was that it was completely unbounded—it failed to establish a clear boundary for prohibited treatment." That boundary was crossed the moment cruel or unusual treatment began. Beaver's legal advice was inadequate and should not have been relied on.

Mora also told Haynes that Rumsfeld's handwritten comment about standing for hours would cause problems. Even if it was intended to be jocular—and Mora knew Rumsfeld's style—lawyers would interpret it otherwise. The fact that Rumsfeld had signed it meant he would be summoned as a witness in any proceedings brought by the detainees, and he would be asked whether the words were a coded a message, "a written nod-and-a-wink to interrogators . . . that they should not feel bound by the limits set in the memo, but consider themselves authorized to do what was necessary to obtain the necessary information."[1] That chimed with what Dunlavey had told me about his meeting with Rumsfeld in February 2002, nine months before he signed the memo. "He wanted me to 'maximize the intelligence production,'" Dunlavey had said. He wasn't told that the gloves were off, but he understood that the Geneva Conventions didn't apply and the usual constraints on interrogation were removed. Mora's fears coincided with Dunlavey's instructions.

Haynes listened attentively to Mora and said he would consider Mora's concerns. "You could never know what Haynes was really thinking," Mora told me. What Mora didn't know was that Haynes strongly supported the decision to get rid of Geneva, that he had knowledge of opinions from the Justice Department confirming that the new techniques were lawful, and that he supported the use of the new techniques. "I had entered the meeting believing that the December 2 memo was almost certainly not reflective of conscious policy but the product of oversight," said Mora, "a combination of too much work and too little time for careful legal analysis or measured consideration." He did not realize at the time how far off the mark that was: he did not know that the Joint Chiefs of Staff had provided no written legal advice, or that Haynes was aware of the decision-making relating to Guantánamo interrogations well before the request was first sent on October 11. He did not know that Addington and Haynes had visited Guantánamo together. Knowing none of this, he left the meeting with Haynes confident that authorization of the eighteen techniques would be quickly suspended. They were not.

Mora went on holiday to Miami with his family. Halfway through his holiday Brant called to tell him the abuse hadn't stopped. They agreed to deal with it as soon he was back from vacation. Mora was back in his office on Monday (January 6). Brant told him that the detainee mistreatment was continuing and authorization had not been suspended or revoked. Mora was shocked. He had assumed Haynes would act immediately. For the first time it dawned on Mora that the new techniques were the product of a conscious policy decision that had been taken at the highest levels. There were people around Rumsfeld who supported aggressive interrogation, people like Stephen Cambone, a Program Director in Rumsfeld's office who was appointed Undersecretary of Defense for Intelligence in March 2003, and who was not popular with the military. "If we were being overrun by the enemy and I had one round left," one general reportedly said, "I'd save it for Stephen Cambone." Marshal Billingslea, Rumsfeld's Principal Deputy Assistant Secretary, was also said to be unapologetic and vehement about the need to interrogate Guantánamo detainees without restraint. A former Pentagon official who was close to all these events described Billingslea to me as "the worst creature in the Department of Defense." "Guys, wake up, smell the coffee, take your gloves off," Billingslea said of the new interrogation rules at one meeting of JAGs. After Billingslea left the Pentagon, his next job was as an Assistant Secretary General at NATO, in Brussels.

In the face of such opposition from the political appointees on the civilian side, Mora knew he had to build a constituency of opposition. Gordon England was leaving to become Deputy Secretary at the Department of Homeland Security, so Mora had a meeting with the Deputy Secretary of the Navy, Susan Livingstone—and was impressed. "If Gordon and Susan had said 'Don't get involved,'" he explained, "it would have been difficult, but they didn't, in their view it was a matter for the lawyers and it needed to be done right." He recommended an NCIS briefing and Livingstone agreed. Later that day Brant and some colleagues gave the briefing and Livingstone was in full agreement with Mora's approach. Navy JAG lawyers produced an initial legal memo, concluding that the techniques were unlawful, should not be used, and could expose perpetrators to criminal proceedings. As Mora explained, the content of this legal memo was severely constrained by the President's decision on Geneva. "The President's sneering contempt for Common Article 3 was striking and significant," Mora said of the President's reaction to later court decisions, adding that "to address that provision as binding law was to repudiate the President directly." This was the same problem that Beaver had faced. "With Geneva out of the picture," Mora said, "it was surprisingly difficult to cobble together an argument, particularly since any appeal to customary law would have been seen as weak with these people." Questioning the President, the Commander-in-Chief, was tantamount to insubordination.

A couple of days later Mora went to see Jaymie Durnan, a Special Assistant to Rumsfeld, and Wolfowitz. Durnan expressed "serious concern" and asked for copies of the memos, about which he seemed to be unfamiliar, and said he would look into what was happening.

On January 9, 2003 Mora had a second meeting with Haynes and told him he was surprised that the techniques hadn't been stopped. He gave Haynes a draft copy of the Navy JAG lawyers' memo to Mora. Haynes was intransigent. He provided no explanation as to what had happened in the three weeks since they had last met and merely said that some U.S. officials believed the techniques were necessary to obtain information from key Guantánamo detainees who, it was thought, had been involved in the 9/11 attacks and had knowledge of other planned al-Qaeda operations. Mora now recognized that "some U.S. officials" included the person with whom he was speaking, Jim Haynes, so he shifted tack. He recognized ethical concerns. "I was not sure," he said, "what my position would be in the classical 'ticking-bomb' scenario." If he was in the position of interrogator, he might well resort to torture, but he would do so with the full knowledge of potentially serious personal consequences, including criminal charges. Even then it would not be right to change the laws to make torture lawful. But this was not the situation they faced in January 2003 at Guantánamo. The issue should have been decided at a higher level: it was not for the Pentagon to make unilateral decisions on such crucial questions.

Again Haynes said little in response. On all points he remained impassive: the possibility of leaks to the media about abuse, the dangers of altering the U.S. military's core values and character, the risk of federal courts exercising jurisdiction, even the British experience in applying "virtually the same techniques" against the IRA, which the European Commission on Human Rights had ruled to be torture and the European Court of Human Rights had characterized as "cruel, inhuman and degrading treatment." The British would think twice about cooperating on aspects of the war on terror if they were to be seen as abetting illegal activity, said Mora, and there was risk of the United States being seen to have jettisoned its commitment to human rights, a core element of its foreign policy since the Second World War.

Haynes's total lack of reaction left Mora deeply frustrated. He told Haynes that the interrogation policies threatened Rumsfeld and could damage the President. "Protect your client," Mora told Haynes. Again he had no inkling what impact, if any, he had made. "He promised to get back to me," Mora wrote to Jaymie Durnan, "but didn't say when." But Mora must have had some impact because the following day, Friday January 10, Haynes arranged various meetings. Mora met first with Jane Dalton, to break the ice on this issue. She had called the meeting at Haynes's request. That, thought Mora, was positive. At that time, he didn't really know what role Dalton had played, and that Haynes had short-circuited her involvement and didn't question her on the history of the decision, or her involvement in the process. Mora made his points. "My sense," he told me, "was that initially her body language was sort of hostile, but that she became more convinced of my points as the meeting went on." Later that afternoon he met with the service General Counsel to the Army, Steve Morello, and of the Air Force, Mary Walker, who was not popular with the Air Force JAGs because she was seen to be in Rumsfeld's pocket. Also attending were senior Judge Advocates General. This meeting had also been arranged by Haynes, and Haynes called Mora later to say that he had briefed Rumsfeld and that modifications were in the offing.

But over the weekend and in the first days of the week that followed no news came. Mora spoke with Dan Dell'Orto, Haynes's deputy. Nothing was said to indicate that any changes had occurred. Mora woke up on the morning of Wednesday, January 15, determined to do something. He prepared a draft memorandum to Haynes and Jane Dalton, making three simple points: 1. The majority of the Category II and III techniques violated domestic and international law and constituted, at a minimum, cruel and unusual treatment and, at worst, torture; 2. the legal analysis by Diane Beaver had to be rejected; and 3. he "strongly non-concurred" with these violative interrogation techniques. In the hierarchical, well-ordered world of the U.S. military that was tough language. Putting it in writing was the nuclear option. His conclusion was unequivocal: even "the misperception that the U.S. Government authorizes or condones detention or interrogation practices that do not comply with our domestic and international legal obligations . . . probably will cause significant harm to our national legal, political, military and diplomatic interests."

He delivered the draft memo to Haynes's office and followed up with a telephone call to say he would sign off on the memo late that afternoon. Mora knew that Haynes didn't like tracks and would want to avoid a paper trail. Haynes later told one colleague that he had no recollection of receiving a threatening memo by Mora.

Over the next few hours Mora sat in his room and waited.

INTERROGATION LOG OF DETAINEE 063
Day 37, December 29 2002

0015: Whenever detainee appeared too comfortable, lead instructed him to stand up and sit down several times. . . .

0200: Detainee offered water—refused, so lead poured it over detainee's head. . . .

0330: Detainee offered water—refused, so lead poured bottle over detainee's head. . . .

0530: Detainee awaked and offered water—refused, so lead poured bottle over detainee's head. Approach continued. . . .

1430: Interrogator instructed MPs to unshackle the detainee except for his legs to let him feel what it was like and gave the detainee a chance to make a decision to talk. Detainee refused and was reshackled. . . .

17

Two years after these events, Alberto Gonzales, Jim Haynes and Dan Dell'Orto told the press that Haynes went to see Rumsfeld on Sunday, January 12 to discuss the new interrogation techniques. They described how Rumsfeld picked up the phone, called General Hill and suspended the use of all the techniques approved the previous month, with the exception of the two Category I techniques of yelling and deception.[1] They also said that three days later, on January 15, Rumsfeld followed up with a written directive to General Hill to rescind the Haynes memo, except for the Category I techniques, indicating that the aggressive interrogation of al-Qahtani had ended on January 12, 2003. The publicly available interrogation log showed Saturday, January 11, 2003 as the last day.

The difficulty was this timeline didn't square with Mora's account of events on Wednesday, January 15. After waiting a few hours, Mora had returned to Haynes's office later in the afternoon. "It was January 15th, a Wednesday, about three in the afternoon," he told me. "We sat at the circular desk in his office. He had the manila envelope with my draft memo in it, the flap was open. He pushed the envelope over to me. He said: 'I don't know what you are trying to do with this.' I almost went for his throat, because the implications were ugly to me, I'd had more than two hours in the two meetings with him setting out my concerns, they were virtual monologues, and now he was saying he didn't know what my concerns were." As Mora shared this with me he became visibly agitated, unlike his the usual calm, matter-of-fact demeanor.

Mora described how the gorge rose up in his throat. "Jim said, 'Surely you must know what impact your words have had on me.' I said, 'I have no idea what your views are.' He chuckled. 'Yeah, I guess I am kind of silent.' We looked at each other. He must have been worried about how I was interpreting that, because then he said 'Well, you will be pleased to know that the Secretary is considering rescinding the authorisations.' I hesitated, didn't say anything. Jim hesitated a few seconds. He must have thought I was thinking that wasn't good enough, so he said 'I know, I know, let me talk to the Secretary and I'll call you back.'" Two hours later, at about 5 P. M. on January 15, Haynes called Mora. "I'm pleased to tell you the Secretary has rescinded the authorization. We'll set up an interrogation group and do this proper."

So when did the interrogation stop? On January 12, as the Administration claimed, or on January 15? If Rumsfeld had already suspended the interrogation techniques three days before Mora went to see Haynes on January 15, why had Haynes not made that clear? Why did Haynes wait until the end of the day on the 15th to call Mora to tell him that Rumsfeld had suspended? There were two possibilities. Either Mora got the date wrong, or the three lawyers got their dates wrong. If Gonzales, Haynes and Dell'Orto were wrong, then al-Qahtani's aggressive interrogation continued for three extra days and they would have seriously misled the press.

When I went back to see Mora he was adamant that he had the dates correct. Diane Beaver was unable to help. "The interrogation stopped when General Hill's command came down," she told me, but she couldn't remember the precise date. Doug Feith recalled the background but not the date. He described how Jim Haynes showed up one day at the round table for the morning staff meeting, and said something like "Mr. Secretary, I've got a problem." That was a good way to get Rumsfeld's attention, because one of his standard lines was that "bad news does not get better with time" and he wanted bad news brought to him as soon as it was heard. The bad news concerned the Haynes memo, said Feith, there were lawyers in the services who were "raising legal questions about these new interrogation techniques." Feith recalled for me the "impressive promptness" with which Rumsfeld did not say, "Who are those bastards?" or "Screw them." "What he says," Feith reported, "was 'stop what we're doing, stop any new thing that we're doing, get all the relevant lawyers together, get this thing reviewed and we will not use any new techniques until it gets reviewed again.'" Feith was impressed. "I sat there and I said, boy, I'm proud to be an associate of this," he explained. "I believe that if the leading civil libertarians in America watched that meeting they would have had no problem with either Haynes or Rumsfeld."

This account of Rumsfeld's impressively prompt reaction didn't seem accurate, or in character. Rumsfeld once attended a news conference with General Peter Pace, following the discovery of a secret prison in Iraq where Iraqi security forces were allegedly torturing detainees. General Pace said that U.S. troops had to stop abuse when they saw it. "But I don't think you mean they have an obligation to physically stop it," Rumsfeld interjected, "it's to report it." General Pace stood firm and overrode Rumsfeld. "If they are physically present when inhumane treatment is taking place, sir, they have an obligation to try to stop it."[2]

So what happened between January 12 and January 15? I discovered the answer to that question from General Hill. In October 2005 he gave testimony to an army investigation into alleged abuses at Guantánamo. He was asked why the special interrogation of al-Qahtani had stopped in mid-January.[3] "The Secretary told me to stop it," he answered. Rumsfeld had called him on the weekend, a Saturday or Sunday (which would have been the 11th or 12th of January). They discussed the interrogation, as someone had come to him and suggested that it needed to be looked at. "What do you think?" Rumsfeld asked. "Why don't you let me call General Miller," Hill replied, "I'll talk to him about it, I'll call you back."

Hill called Miller and they discussed the "on-going interrogations." "General Miller said to me I've personally been looking at it. Al-Qahtani is gaining weight. We think we're right on the verge of making a breakthrough. We ought to continue it." So Hill called Rumsfeld back and said that his best recommendation was that the people on the ground said that there was valuable intelligence. Hill described what he said to Rumsfeld: "We're just about to get there. We're not doing anything wrong. We're taking care of business. We got him under hospital—you know, doctor's care. He's gaining weight. He's not under any duress. We think we're going to get this. The Secretary said fine." A few days later they were directed to stop the interrogation. Hill thought it was a couple of days later. "He obviously had greater discussions on it the first couple of days of the week," Hill explained, "and decided no, we're going to stop this and we're going to do a 'real' formal review. . . ." Hill was relieved. "My attitude on that was, 'Great!' . . . all I'm trying to do is what you want us to do in the first place and doing it the right way."

Hill's account was consistent with Mora's. General Miller told an army investigation that the interrogation was stopped on January 15.[4] The interrogation had lasted fifty-four days, with the last three days unaccounted for at the end of al-Qahtani's interrogation log. Gonzales, Haynes and Dell'Orto were not accurate in the account they gave on June 22, 2004.

INTERROGATION LOG OF DETAINEE 063
Day 41, January 2 2003

0100: Detainee was shown the Bin Laden shrine and told that he could only pray to Bin Laden. Detainee was subject to loud music and yelling. . . .

18

What information did al-Qahtani give up? War crimes or grave breaches of Geneva, as well as violations of the Torture Convention, cannot be justified on the grounds that they have produced useful material. Nevertheless, the Administration made the claim that fifty-four days of aggressive interrogation had produced such information and it needed to be considered. In June 2004, Gonzales, Haynes and Dell'Orto told the assembled media that the new techniques had worked and that the aggressive interrogations made America a safer place. According to Dell'Orto, al-Qahtani had admitted he had met Osama bin Laden, that he knew one of the 9/11 pilots, and had been sent to the United States by Khalid Sheikh Mohammed.[1] It was also claimed that he had provided detailed information about a number of key people, including José Padilla, the dirty bomber, and Richard Reid, the British shoe bomber. No details were given to support these assertions, and none of the claims could be checked.

On the face of it, al-Qahtani's interrogation log provided little support for any of these claims. The only apparent connection between the log and the assertions was in respect of the claim that al-Qahtani knew one of the 9/11 pilots. On December 30 the log stated that "the first name of his best friend (he stopped before he would tell the last name) matches the name of the pilot of the fourth hijacked airliner on 9/11." That falls well short of the claim, and given that the name Ziad (the pilot of flight 93, the fourth airliner, was alleged to be Ziad Jarrah) is widely used and popular in the Arab world it was hardly conclusive evidence. The interrogation log had al-Qahtani giving up some names of people he knew in Saudi Arabia, the United Arab Emirates and Afghanistan, but there was no reference to any Briton (Richard Reid)

or American (José Padilla). The log recorded that al-Qahtani was questioned about his cover story as a car dealer, and that 'all personalities
were checked against known terrorists and all the names matched the
names of known terrorists." But the only detailed information in the
log concerned the provenance of his visa and related money issues for
his trip to the United States.

I asked people who were present during the interrogations whether
they had really produced anything useful. Nobody I spoke with was able to
confirm the far-reaching claims. When I asked Mike Dunlavey whether he
thought the new techniques worked he gave no answer.

Diane Beaver told me she would occasionally arrive unannounced and
observe al-Qahtani's interrogations, as would members of her staff. Most
of the interrogations took place in a small room. Al-Qahtani didn't face
the door, so she could enter the room and stand behind him, unnoticed.
Her job was to make sure that the standards set out in the Haynes memo
were being respected. She never saw those standards violated, and so ac-
cordingly there was no abuse in her eyes. She thought he did "remarkably
well." Had she felt uncomfortable watching the interrogation? "It was an
interrogation, not a chit-chat," she replied, so that observing this would
make you uncomfortable. The prospect of getting information out of him
excited her. What information, I asked? "Information on money and
visas." That was all Diane Beaver came up with. She couldn't remember
anything. And when al-Qahtani did give information, she volunteered, it
was because his ego was threatened, not for any other reason.

In June 2004 General Hill was asked whether al-Qahtani had provided any actionable intelligence or whether he just resisted. "He gave us
some pretty good stuff and continues to do so," he replied, without giving
any detail. Did Hill attribute that to the eighteen techniques? "Yes," came
the clipped answer.[2] The following year an army investigator asked him
whether al-Qahtani's "special interrogation" produced useful intelligence.
"To my recollection the answer to that is yes," he said, "there were sources
and methods that did lead to some good intelligence."[3]

A year later Lieutenant General Randall Schmidt led an investigation
into abuses at Guántanamo. Asked about the quality of the intelligence obtained from al-Qahtani, Schmidt replied: "I don't know that all of it was
very factual."[4]

I was unable to find support for the claims of Gonzales and Haynes,
but wanted to be sure so looked elsewhere. Since the Defense Intelligence
Agency's DHS was involved in running al-Qahtani's interrogations, I

thought someone there might know. I was directed to Cal Temple, who hit the spot. A forty-something intelligence expert who was as bright and thoughtful as anyone I met on this trail. Temple started his career with infantry in the Army before moving to the FBI, eventually joining the intelligence section (J2) of the Joint Staff, where he worked on the bombing of the USS *Cole*. As with Mike Gelles, that incident was a key moment; a warship was attacked, no one could be arrested, the erosion of the criminal law enforcement model began.

Temple started working on detainee issues soon after September 11. By January 2002 he was actively engaged as the detainee numbers in Afghanistan grew. That was when they started asking: how do you break the detainees? With that question in mind he shifted over to the Defense Intelligence Agency's Joint Intelligence Task Force for Combating Terrorism (JITF-CT), the DoD's intelligence fusion center in the long-term, global campaign against terrorism. At JITF-CT he had numerous roles, including the identification of targets, assessment and recruiting, and analytic support of intelligence. In early 2002 an Exploitation Team was created at JITF-CT to support interrogations at Guantánamo. By the time al-Qahtani's aggressive interrogation began in November, Temple was in charge of it. He ran a staff of about 200, some of whom were down at Guantánamo playing a support role to the interrogators, but not directly involved in the interrogations. He was frequently over at the Pentagon and well-placed to know what was going on.

His team's supporting role in the interrogation dealt with surrounding material: al-Qahtani's personal background, his family and friends and associates, and baseline psychological factors that could help in directing the interrogation and understanding the quality of information obtained. The role of the Exploitation Team was to maximize the intelligence potential of the detainee. It was a dynamic process, reacting in real time to information coming from al-Qahtani. As the interrogations were underway, his responses would be fed locally and directly up to Washington where Temple was based. Here the material would be immediately analyzed. If al-Qahtani gave information about a particular street or building in Riyadh or Khost (Afghanistan), the Exploitation Team could check its accuracy and provide follow-up material for the interrogators. Similarly, if he gave them names they could be checked instantly, and they were.

The Exploitation Team was certainly aware of the context in which the interrogations took place, and the use of new techniques. Temple was at pains to point out their behind-the-scenes role. "We had little visibility," he told me, "we weren't in the booth for al-Qahtani, although we were for Slahi." The distance was important. Some of the Exploitation Team analysts wanted to be in the booth, but it was important to keep them separate. Getting too close could limit their role; they needed to keep a certain distance.

When I asked Temple about the treatment of al-Qahtani I sensed a slight hardening, a modest defensiveness. "My analysts periodically were being dragged into difficult processes, like transporting the detainees, and that wasn't their role," he said of those on the ground, pointing out that "mostly this was the result of resource constraints." Everyone was there to help, but getting too close wasn't appropriate. The chief of the Exploitation Team set out guidelines on conduct. There was to be no handling of detainees, no involvement in the interrogations unless there was a unique situation in which direct information was at issue, and any interrogation activity that members of the Exploitation Team felt had violated the law or that was fundamentally disturbing had to be reported.

In this context then, Temple seemed generally comfortable with al-Qahtani's interrogation. Like others, he pointed out that he was bound by the Secretary of Defense's guidance. Rumsfeld had signed off on the use of the techniques, and that was the end of the matter so long as the interrogation came within that guidance, Questioning Rumsfeld's authorization would have been insubordination. "The techniques were there for a reason," he said, "I was comfortable that this individual might have had information." It wasn't Temple's role—or his expertise—to determine whether the techniques used on al-Qahtani were justifiable under international law. "There was a climate of concern at that time," he added, "if the techniques were appropriate for anyone, he was the person." That was consistent with what Mike Dunlavey, Diane Beaver and Mike Gelles described, the constant pressure to get information from the detainees, some of it coming right from the top, directly from the Secretary of Defense, through the Joint Staff and down to the Combatant Command.

Temple didn't object to aggressive interrogation as such, provided it was done under careful conditions. "I believe that we need a set of conditions in which, on a high threshold and in the most limited of circumstances, and on the highest level of approval, officers of the U.S. government can have the ability to use aggressive techniques." The obvious issues were how limited these conditions should be, and how to determine whether they were met. I wondered whether al-Qahtani met them. Temple had obviously thought about these conditions carefully. The need would have to be time sensitive. The threat would have to be catastrophic. The interrogations must be overt, not carried out offshore on an out-of-sight island. The harsh techniques should be limited in duration, and they had to be subject to clear lines of authorization, with threats of serious punishment if repeated elsewhere.

Did al-Qahtani meet these criteria? Temple thought not. The crucial moment for an interrogation was the moment of capture. "Immediately after you have captured someone you have a window of opportunity." An effective interrogation had to be done in the first 48 hours after detention. You put the detainee in a room with somebody who would shock him into delivering what he had, or you put him on a roof or in a helicopter and threaten to push him from a great height. Months later wasn't timely and wouldn't work. Waterboarding wouldn't work. Yet the interrogation of al-Qahtani did come months after he'd been detained, giving him time to settle down. "You need to get the guy's attention, you can't give him time to retrench, it can be done without physically injuring him." Others described this to me as a "shock and awe" tactic. "The hardest nut," said Temple, "is the one who is mentally rebalanced and centered." All of which suggested that there had been no adequate, prior assessment of the implications of the new techniques. That view was consistent with the conclusions of a DIA-supported study published in late 2006 by the National Defense Intelligence College, which found that there was almost no scientific evidence to back up use of controversial interrogation techniques in the fight against terrorism, with some experts believing that aggressive approaches could hinder the ability to get good information. The Chairman of the study, Robert A. Fein, suggested that the shortfall in "advanced, research-based interrogation methods . . . may have contributed significantly to the unfortunate cases of abuse that have recently come to light."[5]

By the time al-Qahtani was interrogated aggressively he had been in detention for nearly a year. He had time to rebalance and center himself. Had the pressure from the Pentagon produced anything useful? A measured and thoughtful man, Temple chose his words with care. "There was a lot of data of interest," he said. "It was contextual in nature, confirming in nature. Did it help us catch Osama bin Laden? No."

I took that as a no. There seemed to be little to back up the bullish overstatements made by the Administration's lawyers in June 2004.

INTERROGATION LOG OF DETAINEE 063

Day 42, January 3 2002

0700: taken to cell at X-Ray and offered MRE and water—refused. Interrogators poured the bottle of water over his head and took his food away. . . .

1945: Detainee shown graphic victim photos. . . .

19

The assertions from the Administration's lawyers looked increasingly empty. The aggressive interrogation of al-Qahtani hadn't finished on January 12, as claimed, but, in the face of a conscious decision that further cruelty might break him, three days later. And, it seemed that al-Qahtani hadn't provided the useful information the lawyers had professed.

There was another purpose to the Gonzales and Haynes double act in June 2004. The lawyers went to great lengths to make the point that concerns about aggressive interrogation ended with the decision on January 15 to rescind the Category II and III techniques listed in the Haynes memo. They sought to crush any suggestion of a connection between Guantánamo and Abu Ghraib. Gonzales "categorically" rejected the link on the grounds that there were "two separate legal regimes" that governed those two places.[1] Abu Ghraib had nothing to do with any of the policies discussed in the Guantánamo memos, he said, a point to which Dan Dell'Orto returned, telling journalists that "I want to make sure that I keep Guantánamo distinct from Iraq and Abu Ghraib."[2]

The facts, however, suggest that there was a link between the two places, and that the Haynes memo had a malign influence over time and distance. The facts spoke for themselves. One army investigator compared the treatment of al-Qahtani with that displayed so graphically in the Abu Ghraib photos. "Here's this guy manacled, chained down, dogs brought in, put [in] his face, told to growl, show teeth, and that kind of stuff," he said of al-Qahtani, "if you had a camera and snapped that picture, you'd be back to Abu Ghraib."[3]

To be sure, certain actions to restore some semblance of lawfulness were taken after January 15. Donald Rumsfeld set up a working group to look into the development of new interrogation techniques and on April 4, 2003 the group published its report, evaluating and proposing thirty-five interrogation techniques.[4] Two weeks later, with Jim Haynes's support, Rumsfeld approved twenty-four of those thirty-five techniques for use on unlawful combatants at Guantánamo.[5] Haynes later told the Senate Judiciary Committee that seventeen of the twenty-four techniques were based on procedures taken from *FM 34–52*, and the remaining seven were "highly regulated."[6] Yet the fundamental rules didn't change. The working group followed the "reasoning" of the Bybee/Yoo memo of August 1, 2002, which remained in effect for over a year until the Abu Ghraib scandal caused it to be suspended, together with another memo that Yoo wrote in March 2003 that adopted the same arguments.[7] Congress didn't legislate to prohibit cruel, inhuman and degrading treatment of Guantánamo detainees until December 2005, when all DoD interrogations were required to comply with *FM 34–52*.[8] The restoration of the detainees' rights under Common Article 3 had to wait even longer.

Needless to say, reports of the death of the Haynes memo were premature. In August 2003 General Miller made a trip from Guantánamo, where he was Commander, to Baghdad. He was accompanied by Diane Beaver. His mission was to help get the most out of human intelligence operations in Iraq. "We had learned a great deal in Guantánamo," said General Keith Alexander as he stood alongside Gonzales and Haynes in the Eisenhower Executive Office Building on June 22, 2004, "and we wanted to ensure that the lessons that we had in Guantánamo were also in Iraq."[9] The question is—which lessons?

General Miller and Diane Beaver visited Abu Ghraib and found shocking conditions of near lawlessness. Miller made recommendations to General Ricardo Sanchez, the Commander of Coalition Ground Forces in Iraq, to codify and develop proper interrogation techniques. Within two weeks, on September 14, 2003, General Sanchez signed a memorandum authorizing new techniques.[10] They were vetted by his Staff Judge Advocate, Colonel Marc Warren, who later told the Senate Armed Services Committee that in preparing the memorandum they had taken account of operating procedures and policies "in use in Guantánamo Bay."[11] Unlike at Guantánamo, however, the Geneva rules were being treated as applicable because of the nature of the conflict in Iraq. This should have marked a major difference. Yet that didn't stop General Sanchez from authorizing techniques that were not listed in *FM 34–52*, that plainly violated Geneva, and that were included in the Haynes memo, including environmental manipulation (temperature adjustment), the presence of military dogs, sleep management (four hours sleep per twenty-four hour period), and stress

positions.[12] These would have been very familiar to al-Qahtani. The pho-
tographic evidence showed abuse beginning at Abu Ghraib on October
17—one month later.

Mike Gelles explained to me his fears that the techniques used at
Guantánamo could migrate, that once limits to interrogation were raised
in one part of the military they could be raised elsewhere, that abusive interrogation in one place would lead to abuses elsewhere. The migration
theory has been controversial, partly because, if established, it could extend
the responsibility of those who contributed to the implementation of the
techniques at Guantánamo to abuses that occurred elsewhere. After leaving government John Yoo described the migration theory as "an exercise in
hyperbole and partisan smear."[13]

Yet various Army and DoD investigations have rejected Yoo's view.[14] In
August 2004 the Fay-Jones report on detainee abuse at Abu Ghraib concluded that the Pentagon's multiple policies on interrogation techniques for
use in different operations "confused Army and civilian interrogators at
Abu Ghraib."[15] The interrogation training team that General Miller took
from Guantánamo to Abu Ghraib lacked understanding of approved interrogation policies for Guantánamo and this "inadvertently validated restricted interrogation techniques," such as nudity.[16] General Paul Kern was
picked by Rumsfeld as the appointing authority for the Fay-Jones report,
and he made the point bluntly: "We found in computers in Abu Ghraib
SECDEF memos that were written for Guantánamo, not for Abu Ghraib.
And that caused confusion."[17] Confusion then opened the door to abuse.

Soon afterward, a report written by former Defense Secretary James
R. Schlesinger also concluded that techniques intended only for Guantánamo had migrated. The "augmented techniques for Guantánamo migrated to Afghanistan and Iraq where they were neither limited nor
safeguarded," his report concluded rather definitively.[18] It also found that
abuses resulted from "confusion about what interrogation techniques were
permitted by law," a result of the failure to distinguish between permitted
interrogation techniques from Guantánamo and other environments, on
the one hand, and Iraq, on the other.[19] Jim Haynes was one of the individuals interviewed by the authors of the Schlesinger Report, although what
he said was not recorded.

In August 2006, the Pentagon Inspector General released his own
deeply damning report. This concluded unequivocally that interrogation
techniques had migrated to Iraq because operations personnel believed
that traditional techniques were no longer effective for all detainees.[20]

General Miller's assessment team visited Iraq and proposed the use of harsher counter-resistance techniques. While these were not endorsed by the Iraq Survey Group, the combined Joint Task Force for Iraq (CJTF–7) incorporated some of the techniques into its policies and procedures, on September 14, including "sleep management."[21]

The clear conclusions from these reports—three in three years—reinforced what Mike Gelles told me about "force drift," the situation where interrogators come to believe that if some force is good then more will be even better. "If you let slip the dogs, they will run," was the way a former DoD official put it. The drift was not limited only to the interpretation of the techniques, but also to their geographic reach. The dogs ran.

In this way, the Haynes memo eventually reached Matrix Chambers in London, the barristers chambers of which I am a member. Tim Owen QC was asked to act for a British soldier who was charged with allowing the abuse of Iraqi detainees in Basra, in September 2003. The detainees there had been subjected to conditioning processes to prepare them for interrogation, involving "maintaining a stress position and deprivation of sleep whilst hooded and cuffed."[22] One of the detainees died. Eventually seven British soldiers were charged, the most senior being Colonel Jorge Mendonca, Commanding Officer of the Queen's Lancashire Regiment. Six of the defendants were acquitted, the seventh (Corporal Donald Payne) pleaded guilty to the charge of "inhumane treatment of persons" and was jailed for one year. Mendonca was charged for an offense at Basra, Iraq, "between the 13th day of September 2003 and the 16th day of September 2003." As Commanding Officer of the Queen's Lancashire Regiment, he negligently performed his duty by failing to take reasonable steps to ensure that Iraqi civilians being held at the temporary holding facility were not ill-treated.

The fact that the events occurred on those days in September was a remarkable coincidence, given that they involved at least one of the techniques (sleep deprivation) approved by General Sanchez for Coalition Force for Iraq on September 14, just days after General Miller's visit. In his defense, Colonel Mendonca argued that he was advised that sleep deprivation, stress positions and other conditioning processes (to prepare the detains for interrogation) had been cleared by the chain of command and the army legal adviser, Major Russell Clifton. The Court Martial Board accepted this defense on the basis of the available evidence and dismissed the charges, on the grounds that Mendonca was following approved procedures. There was also evidence before the court that the British army lawyers had been in contact with U.S. military lawyers before they gave their approval of the practices.

One of the witnesses was Brigadier Ewan Duncan, a Staff Officer responsible for British HUMINT operations. Under cross-examination he stated that the United States thought the British "were not getting as much information and intelligence out of the prisoners" as they should.[23] There was a significant UK contribution to the Iraq Survey Group in Baghdad, including interrogations, and some members of the British intelligence community agreed with U.S. concerns. Asked whether the United States wanted the British to take a tougher line, Brigadier Duncan said that he wouldn't put it that way. "I would say," he explained, "that the United States felt we should get more out of the detainees that we held than we did." And would that be "by adopting a rather tougher interrogation technique?" "Perhaps, yes," he replied. Did that mean that Duncan believed that if hooding ended they would get less out of the interrogations? "I do not think it is as clear cut as that," he answered, "but it would contribute to a process that might end up in that situation." So, in the face of American pressure to adopt firmer techniques of interrogation the idea of adopting less vigorous techniques was not one that appealed? "Correct," Brigadier Duncan answered. I took the exchange as confirmation that American pressure caused the British to change their practices.

I thought back to Doug Feith's excitement about his role in the Geneva decision, how his little speech became a memo and then a policy decision, and how in turn new interrogation rules emerged that ultimately resulted in torture at Guantánamo. Now the line could be taken even further, from Guantánamo to Abu Ghraib and then south to Basra and westward back to a barristers' chambers in London.

INTERROGATION LOG OF DETAINEE 063
Day 50, January 11 2003

0230: Source received haircut. Detainee did not resist until the beard was cut. Detainee stated he would talk about anything if his beard was left alone. Interrogator asked detainee if he would be honest about himself. Detainee replied "if God wills." Beard was shaven. A little water was poured over the detainee's head to reinforce control and wash the hair off. Interrogator continued the futility approach. The detainee began to cry when talking.

RESPONSIBILITY

20

January 15, 2003 was the last day of aggressive interrogation for al-Qahtani. By then he'd been segregated from the other detainees and kept in isolation for 160 days. "I went down and looked at him and he looks like hell," said an army investigator who saw him just as he was coming out of the period of aggressive interrogation; "he has got black coals for eyes."[1]

Five years after the end of al-Qahtani's aggressive interrogation, the man described by Donald Rumsfeld as "a very bad person, a person who clearly had information about attacks against the United States" remained in detention with no end in sight.[2] Despite the certainty of the claim that he came to the United States to participate in the September 11 attacks, he was not charged with any criminal offense. The 9/11 Commission Report referred to him as a "muscle" hijacker, but he was not charged, even as an accomplice.

Information about al-Qahtani emerged in the summer of 2004 as the Administration struggled to respond to the Abu Ghraib scandal. The Secretary of Defense and other leading officials singled him out as an example of the new kind of terrorist whose treatment required a different approach to the international rules. That same month, June 2004, the U.S. Supreme Court decided in *Rasul v. Bush* that detainees like al-Qahtani, and other non-U.S. nationals held at Guantánamo, could bring challenges before the U.S. courts.[3] With that decision, the detainees finally gained access to lawyers and could establish some connection with the outside world.

Until then the Bush Administration had been determined to prevent detainees from getting legal assistance. Vice Admiral Lowell Jacoby explained why. As Director of the DoD's Defense Intelligence Agency, Jacoby ran the group that contributed to al-Qahtani's interrogations at Guantánamo, and the detention and interrogation of other detainees, including José Padilla, the alleged dirty bomber. As al-Qahtani was entering the seventh week of aggressive interrogation, in January 2003, Jacoby provided a declaration to the U.S. District Court for the Southern District of New York in a case brought by José Padilla against the U.S. Government, seeking access to counsel and various remedies. As an American citizen, Padilla was able to claim rights not available to foreigners. Nevertheless, Jacoby supported the Administration in denying him access to a lawyer.[4] "Providing Padilla access to counsel," wrote Jacoby, "risks loss of a critical intelligence resource, resulting in a grave and direct threat to national security." Jim Haynes had made the very same argument three months before Jacoby, in a letter to the President of the American Bar Association.[5]

The way that Jacoby set out the reasons also explained the approach to al-Qahtani. The DIA interrogations aimed to establish an atmosphere of dependency between the interrogator and the detainee, and achieving that atmosphere took time. Anything that threatened that dependent relationship undermined the value of interrogation as an intelligence-gathering tool. "Even seemingly minor interruptions," wrote Jacoby "can have a profound psychological impact on the delicate subject-interrogator relationship." This led him to his key point: "Any insertion of counsel into the interrogator relationship can undo months of work and may permanently shut down the interrogator process."

But this was not the only reason to restrict access to legal advice. "The United States is now engaged in a robust program of interrogating individuals who have been identified as enemy combatants in the War on Terrorism," Jacoby wrote, as Alberto Mora was lobbying Jim Haynes to suspend the eighteen techniques. Jacoby believed it was vital to prevent al-Qaeda from learning about these techniques: releasing such information could compromise national security. Access to detainees could "unwittingly provide information to the detainee, or be used by the detainee as a communication tool."

Jacoby's declaration explained why the Administration wanted to keep the interrogations secret and shed light on the rationale for the new techniques—total isolation of the detainee—and the overwhelming fear of publicity. The difficulty was that Padilla was an American national, and the U.S. Constitution guaranteed his right of access to counsel. Jacoby got around this by resorting to the necessity principle, which gave priority to principles of national security.

But *Rasul v. Bush* did away with Jacoby's claim that Padilla was not entitled to access to a lawyer. Padilla received the help of a civilian lawyer because he was American. Eventually al-Qahtani did too, although that took longer.

In October 2005, Gita Gutierrez was assigned to al-Qahtani. She worked for the Center for Constitutional Rights (CCR), a campaigning organization based in New York City. I met Gutierrez in December 2006 in Washington D.C., the day after Doug Feith explained how the Geneva decision was taken. We talked about her background and her client's story, although on al-Qahtani she was circumspect and discreet.

Gutierrez grew up in Kentucky. She is Hindu and half Indian. She studied law at Cornell Law School and has a strong background in civil rights and public international law. After law school she clerked on the Second Circuit with Judge Guido Calabresi, a renowned federal appeals court judge, who taught at Yale before going to the bench. On September 11 she was with Calabresi in New Haven, Connecticut, watching the smoke drift over Long Island Sound. As Guantánamo was being conjured up she was back at Cornell and became a member of the New York Bar: Guantánamo coincided with her "coming of age" as a lawyer.

She spent the summer of 2002 looking at the legal and policy issues thrown up by Guantánamo. She didn't know—no one outside of a small group did—that new techniques of interrogation were being developed. The issue on which she focused was whether the response to terror should be situated within the criminal law, or the law of war, or both. This was the same issue that divided al-Qahtani's interrogators. In 2003 she began to work pro bono for CCR in New York City with Joseph Margulies, a leading civil rights lawyer and one of the first to address the position of the detainees at Guantánamo. She moved to a public interest law fellowship to work with Gibbons, Del Deo, a law firm in Newark, New Jersey, and her mentor there was John J. Gibbons, former chief judge of the Court of Appeal of the Third U.S. Circuit, who had a strong commitment to public interest law. Judge Gibbons argued and won *Rasul v. Bush* before the Supreme Court.

Gutierrez began by representing two British detainees, Feroz Abbassi and Moazzam Begg, and was one of the first habeas corpus lawyers to be involved. She told me she was the very first lawyer to visit Guantánamo, in July 2004, an experience she found grueling. The place was difficult to get to, there were a great many administrative obstacles, and she was even subjected to full body searches. She worked with CCR to recruit a wider group of lawyers to represent individual detainees and in August 2005 was hired full-time by CCR. Three months later al-Qahtani Mohammed became her client.

In early 2005 one of the law firms that provided free representation for detainees visited Bahrain and invited anyone who knew any of the detainees at Guantánamo to provide information. Man-Ae al-Qahtani, Mohammed al-Qahtani's father, made the journey to Bahrain from his home in Riyadh in Saudi Arabia. He had a few Red Cross letters from his son, which he brought with him, and eventually these heavily censored letters made their way to New York, to CCR's office and finally to Gutierrez's desk. "The first time the original Red Cross letters arrived in my office in Manhattan I cried," she said. In the summer of 2005 al-Qahtani's father agreed that he should be represented.

Gutierrez realized that al-Qahtani was in a special category. Although the father had almost nothing by way of information, the son was frequently in the news. A U.S. Department of Defense press release made far-reaching and firm claims about him. "He is an al-Qaeda operative with strong ties to senior al-Qaeda leadership, including Osama bin Laden," the DoD asserted; they claimed he had trained at terrorist camps in Afghanistan.[6] The DoD also claimed that the new interrogation techniques had produced results, with al-Qahtani admitting that he was sent to the United States by Khalid Sheikh Mohammed, an alleged lead architect of the 9/11 attacks. A law firm was chosen to represent him; then, in the summer of 2005, an article appeared in *Time* magazine providing more information about his alleged role and the circumstances of his interrogation.[7] The law firm bailed out. Gutierrez needed no persuading to take on his case. She went to Gibbons, Del Deo and said they should take him on. They did and the case was assigned to her. A few months later al-Qahtani's interrogation log was published in *Time* magazine. The contents of the log strengthened her commitment to work on his case.

By the time I met Gutierrez she had spent considerable time with al-Qahtani. She went down to Guantánamo to see him, on average, every other month and on the visits she spent about five hours a day with him, one on one. He was now in Camp Echo. In her presence he was always shackled, and she assumed their conversations were monitored. Not surprisingly, he wasn't in good shape. He knew of CCR's work, and according to Gutierrez, never questioned her role as his lawyer: with her South Asian background she didn't look too American, she reminded me, and in his presence she wore the hijab.

Like any lawyer acting for a client, one issue into which Gutierrez would not be drawn were the merits of his case—what he had or had not done, what his background was. We did touch on the DoD claims that under interrogation he admitted various facts: meeting Osama bin Laden on several occasions, being trained as a terrorist at two al-Qaeda camps, and having contact with many senior al-Qaeda leaders. "More importantly," claimed the DoD, "he provided valuable intelligence information helping the United States to understand the recruitment of terrorist operatives, logistics, and other planning aspects of the 9/11 terrorist attacks." None of that was in the interrogation log. The DoD also asserted that he had provided specific information on José Padilla and Richard Reid (the shoe bomber), on al-Qaeda's infiltration routes and methods used to cross borders undetected and on the way in which Osama bin Laden had evaded capture by U.S. forces. He also "provided detailed information about 30 of Osama bin Laden's bodyguards who are also held at Guantánamo."

How did Gutierrez react to these claims? She spoke carefully. "He says that he has never given any information that they haven't given him first." It was true, I recalled, that these admissions did not appear in the interrogation logs that had been made public, although the logs might not have been complete. Moreover, there were important days missing from the log, between January 11 and 15, the days when Major General Miller, General Hill and Secretary Rumsfeld decided to carry on with the interrogation in the hope that he might break. Later al-Qahtani had a Combatant Status Review Tribunal (CSRT) hearing to determine whether he had been correctly classified as an enemy combatant, but initially he declined to participate in it. He finally participated in 2006 in an effort to defend himself and has now been through an Administrative Review Board, the process established to determine whether he still represents a threat and should continue to be detained. He made a statement in 2006 that has not yet been made public. In his statement he said he was "a business man, a peaceful man," without any connection to terrorism, violence or fighters. He described his treatment as amounting to physical and psychological torture and inhuman treatment, and said that it was only during that period that he was "forced to make false statements and fabricate a story." He said that the characterization of him as a person with high intelligence value "was exaggerated to justify the torture." "Interrogators provided me with this information and details and under pressure and coercion forced me to adopt the story that the interrogators wanted to hear," he said, adding that what he provided "was information I only got from them during interrogation sessions."

It was impossible for me to form a view as to what al-Qahtani had or had not done in the period before and after he was turned back from Orlando in August 2001. There were a great number of al-Qahtanis, Gutierrez said, and many Mohammed al-Qahtanis. Did I know that there were several al-Qahtanis even at Guantánamo? I asked whether he tried to get into the Orlando airport. Gutierrez confirmed that he did. But, she said, it wasn't clear whether he was the same person who was said to be the falcon trader who was spotted in Afghanistan. He had arrived in the United States saying that he wanted to buy used cars and denied any link with falcon traders. The account he gave in the interrogation log was too inconsistent to allow a clear view to be reached about who he was and what he did.

Gutierrez talked about his health and state of mind. His levels of distrust and paranoia were more heightened than for her other clients at Guantánamo. "He constantly articulates that he has no point of reference," she said. His mind returned again and again to the same topics, and he proceeded on the basis that he had been so lied to, so deceived, and so abused that he had given up all hope. Did he trust her? When she first met him her appearance (maybe the hijab helped) caught him off-guard for a split second, allowing her to start talking. Trust was growing, she said, and now he talked a great deal. There were difficult moments, especially when she talked about his family, the newborn nephews and nieces he hadn't met.

The subject of the aggressive interrogations was difficult, very difficult. Gutierrez visited the facility where al-Qahtani had been interrogated. He knew about the *Time* magazine material and about the interrogation logs. He recognized the particular intensity of that period in November and December 2002, although he could not date it exactly. Gutierrez said it was difficult to talk to him about that period. "He is still reconstructing his narrative." She wanted to emphasize that the abuse began well before November 23 and directed me to an FBI document released in December 2004, under a freedom of information request. It was a letter dated July 14, 2004, written by T. J. Harrington, the FBI's Deputy Assistant Director of the Counter Terrorism Division, to the criminal investigation division of the Army. Harrington's letter described what FBI agents had observed during the course of what they had described as "highly aggressive interrogations." "Look at the third paragraph of that letter," said Gutierrez, "it refers to al-Qahtani's treatment in the period before the aggressive interrogation began." I tracked down the letter. The third paragraph contained the following observation:

In September or October of 2002 FBI Agents observed that a canine was used in an aggressive manner to intimidate Detainee [█████████] and, in November 2002, FBI Agents observed Detainee [████████] after he had been subject to intense isolation for over three months. During that time period, [████████] was totally isolated (with the exception of occasional interrogations) in a cell that was always flooded with light. By late November the detainee was evidencing behavior consistent with extreme psychological trauma (talking to non-existent people, reporting hearing voices, crouching in a corner of the cell covered with a sheet for hours on end). It is unknown whether such extended isolation was approved by appropriate DoD authorities.[8]

It was clear from this that serious concerns were expressed even before the aggressive interrogation began on November 23. By then the FBI agents saw al-Qahtani in a state of "extreme psychological trauma." Gita Gutierrez described the interrogation over the next fifty-four days as torture. She asked me if I thought he had been tortured, I said I hadn't yet formed a clear view: there were issues of law and of fact, the test was "severe pain or suffering, whether physical or mental." I needed to speak to an independent expert to reach a more definitive view.

21

The independent expert I was recommended to speak to was Dr. Abigail Seltzer, a London-based doctor who had been a consultant psychiatrist for eleven years. She divides her time between Britain's National Health Service, where she works extensively with asylum seekers and other refugees, and the Medical Foundation for the Care of Victims of Torture.

I prepared myself for what became a lengthy and far-reaching conversation by reading various reports prepared by the U.S.-based Physicians for Human Rights, and articles by Dr. Steven Miles, a professor of medicine at the University of Minnesota.[1] I wanted someone who would come to the interrogation log with a fresh set of eyes and a couple of weeks before we met, I sent Dr. Seltzer a copy of al-Qahtani's log, together with the list of eighteen techniques. I also shared with her the definitions of torture in the Torture Convention and in U.S. law.

We met on an early summer's day, in London. She struck me as a cautious person, not prone to excess or hyperbole. All my questions—and there were many over several hours—were answered after careful reflection. I wanted a thoughtful interlocutor, someone who could adopt a more conservative approach, and was pleased to have found her. She stressed that in order to form a definitive view she would need more information than an interrogation log—ideally, access to al-Qahtani himself. But given the circumstances of his interrogation and continued detention that wasn't an option.

Seltzer had worked with traumatized refugees for about a decade. In the course of this work, she had heard hundreds of stories of ill treatment, and therefore had ample material with which to compare the interrogation log. Her clinical training equipped her to spot inconsistencies and anomalies in a story, and she explained to me how diagnosis was essentially an exercise in pattern recognition. She had not treated any of the British

Guantánamo detainees, although she was familiar with some of their case histories, but she had treated—and was treating—many victims of torture or organized violence, individuals from all over the world. She knew about the issues and the techniques but had no predisposition one way or the other as to whether al-Qahtani had been abused or tortured.

Early on I asked for her initial reaction to the list of eighteen techniques and the interrogation log. "I have come across all of these techniques before," she replied, "although what makes them different from most is the lack of overt physical violence." She was struck by the apparently highly organized way in which the techniques were applied, assuming that the interrogation log accurately reflected what had happened.

She also wanted me to understand her ground rules. There was no such thing as a medical definition of torture: clinicians and lawyers approached the subject from different angles. From a medical perspective, doctors look for pathology, in other words abnormal functioning of the body or mind. A doctor cannot say from examining someone whether they have been tortured, but can only describe physical or psychological injuries, and from their knowledge of the body's workings, what might have caused them. Depending on the nature and extent of the injuries, a doctor may be able to conclude that they are consistent with a story of cruel treatment, but there is no definitive "medical test" for torture. This is not to say that doctors can or should turn a blind eye to torture—their ethical codes oblige them to refuse to participate in it and to do whatever they can to prevent it. However, they cannot "diagnose" it.

Given this explanation, Dr. Seltzer told me how she had approached the materials I had given her. On the table she laid out a marked-up copy of the interrogation log, which she had gone through carefully, page by page. She had used four different colors to highlight words that struck her as relevant: words marked in yellow indicated abusive treatment; pink showed where the detainee's rights were respected, where he was fed or given a break, or allowed a nap or sleep; green singled out the many examples of medical involvement, where al-Qahtani was given an enema or an intravenous feed, or where he had been taken to the hospital; and finally blue, which identified what Dr. Seltzer called "expressions of distress." She later took me through each one as we tried to assess the extent and severity of al-Qahtani's "pain and suffering," the test set by the Torture Convention. Every page had at least one color other than pink, and many pages had every color. This was certainly true for the first thirty or so days. The latter days seemed to reflect a change of style, which she thought reflected a more chaotic approach. Or, Dr. Seltzer pondered, it could just be that events weren't recorded as systematically.

She pointed out signs of al-Qahtani's resistance: his efforts not to take food or water, his attempts to remove the IV, his struggles and silences. These efforts meant he needed medical care, in particular for dehydration. There was nothing in the log to indicate that he ever came close to death, although the hospitalization in early December apparently indicated concerns about hypothermia. The medical care described by the log appeared to be of a decent standard. But, she added, the care that he'd been offered appeared to be intended to prepare him for further interrogation. In her view, preparing a detainee for fitness for interrogation raised serious issues of medical ethics, and possible complicity in abuse.

We turned to the list of techniques. "In terms of their effects, I suspect that the individual techniques are less important," she said, "than the fact that they were used over an extended period of time, that several appear to be used together: in other words, the cumulative effect."

The interrogation log as a whole showed a consistent approach over time. It was obvious that it was carefully thought through. Do you know what happened to him before November 23, she asked, before they started to use these techniques on him? I explained that I had little information on that, although there was some evidence that he had been through a pretty tough period in the previous two months, including extended periods of isolation. I told her about the two FBI emails, which described his treatment during October and November and said that by late November he was "evidencing behavior consistent with extreme psychological trauma." "It would be significant to know what prior sensory deprivation he had been subjected to, that would confirm whether or not his coping abilities were already compromised," said Dr. Seltzer. It seemed likely that those "coping abilities" had already been seriously compromised.

Her marking of the interrogation log was helpful and reflected a series of consistent themes. There was systematic sleep deprivation, in which al-Qahtani was allowed no more than four hours of sleep in any twenty-four-hour-period. It was not clear whether he had actually been able to sleep during those periods. "Given that he had no consistent rhythm, he may well not have slept." If his circadian rhythm were interrupted, that is likely to have impaired his ability to sleep (the circadian rhythm is a roughly twenty-four-hour cycle in the physiological processes of living beings, the disruption of which can have significant adverse health consequences). The use of water droplets—and then bottles of water—being poured on the detainee was also associated with the sleep deprivation technique and was more invasive.

I understood that a disturbed sleep pattern would have significant consequences, all the more so over such extended periods of time. Concentration becomes reduced and reaction time slows; cognitive abilities are compromised. Assuming al-Qahtani was a reasonably average person, one would expect some slowing that would undermine the reliability of his responses. The most significant effect, however, would have been to reduce his resilience and his capacity to cope with what was happening to him. This would raise serious doubts about the reliability of anything he said in response to the interrogation.

Dr. Seltzer explained that she would not necessarily expect sleep deprivation alone to cause any long-lasting damage. In large part the effect would depend on his pre-morbid personality—the kind of person he was before his detention. Nevertheless, combined with the other techniques it could certainly contribute to a state of severe mental anguish or distress while it was being used.

Another aspect that drew Dr. Seltzer's attention was the degree and manner of his physical restraint. The important point was how much movement was restricted and over what periods of time. This wasn't clear from the log, although she understood, based on the information I gave her, that he was shackled and cuffed. Again, on its own this might not be problematic, but coupled with other techniques it could cause significant distress. What was striking to her, and what tipped over into real concern, was the nature of the physical restraint over time, coupled with the other techniques.

The third aspect she commented on was the use of systematic techniques of humiliation, together with other forms of psychological testing, that ran throughout the period of interrogation, the entire fifty-four days. The humiliation seemed to have increased over time, probably intended to break down barriers and make al-Qahtani ever more dependent on his interrogators. She thought that the use of photos—of 9/11 victims—seemed weird, but was plainly intended to humiliate. The use of photographs of scantily clad models would have been deeply humiliating and offensive for a Muslim man. The manipulation of cultural and religious beliefs was deliberately designed to achieve psychological humiliation. The invasion of al-Qahtani's space by a female would have been clearly humiliating, which was why even light physical contact could produce a severe adverse reaction when it was performed by a female. What looked unproblematic on paper could therefore cause severe mental anguish in practice. The hinted threats to his family—of which there were several—would have added to al-Qahtani's sense of helplessness. Forced nudity, shaving, and grooming would all have contributed to an extreme sense of humiliation and degradation.

What would have been the effect of psychological humiliation, I asked. "Psychological humiliation is a powerful stressor, because it attacks a person's sense of self," she replied. The actual effect would have depended on al-Qahtani's personal history, his past, his strengths, his weaknesses, his beliefs. Even so, assuming some prior sensory deprivation, subjecting an individual to two months of such humiliation, followed by four and a half years of continued detention with no end in sight, could very well lead to "long-lasting psychological changes."

Other techniques also caught her eye, for example, the apparent presence of dogs. I recalled the account of a psychiatrist who had witnessed the use of dogs with al-Qahtani, including one named Zeus: "Dogs were used to intimidate the detainee by getting the dogs close to him and then having the dogs bark or act aggressively on command."[2] Regarding the regular and persistent use of white noise, Dr. Seltzer couldn't say what the effect would have been on him without interviewing him personally. At the very least, the noise would be an irritating and persistent stimulus if he couldn't blot it out. The same would go for the use of loud noise, which also seemed to be a regular feature over the entire period of the interrogation.

She also spotted throughout the interrogation log signs that suggested the use of temperature variations. Dr. Seltzer pointed out one example, on December 22, at 1400 hours: "The interrogator removed the blanket and turned the air conditioner back up." But there were other examples, for instance December 6, at 1600 hours: "Detainee asked for air conditioner to be turned off and asked for blanket." It wasn't clear from the log how consistently this had been done. "This would cause physical stress, even if it didn't lead to damage on its own. Think what it's like when you are very cold, you are unable to get warm, make yourself warmer. You can't control getting warmer, that is the difficulty." The fact that enforced nudity had also been used would have compounded his sense of total loss of control, humiliation, and greater dependence. In this state, refusing a request to pray would also remove whatever vestiges of control al-Qahtani had left.

I asked about the medical treatment. Dr. Seltzer thought dehydration was the likely cause of the log's reference to his swollen feet. This had necessitated the use of intravenous drips and, on December 7 and 8, hospitalization. It was clear that by then he was probably significantly underweight, having dropped from 160 pounds to less than 120.

Dr. Seltzer said that some of the medical procedures had been physically intrusive and as a consequence could be expected to be subjectively unpleasant. They would most likely have caused a degree of physical suffering. She directed me to one example that had troubled her, November 25 at 0445:

> Corpsman tried several times to get IV into the detainee without success. The corpsman stated that the detainee's dehydration was causing his veins to roll in his arm. The corpsman succeeded in getting an IV in the top of the hand but the IV stopped flowing. The corpsman retried the IV in the hand but was unsuccessful. The doctor was called to make a trip to perform an assessment.

A couple of hours later, at 0645, the doctor "attempted to put in an IV and was unsuccessful." At 0730 the doctor "ran an IV by putting in a temporary shunt to allow continuous IV." At 0745 the detainee "bent over and bit the IV tube completely in two. The guard strapped him to a stretcher and the corpsman attached a new IV. The detainee struggled through the entire process, but could no longer reach the IV."

This was obviously an extremely unpleasant procedure that would most likely have caused significant distress. Further example was on December 1 at 0745: "Corpsman administers IV. Detainee's head is restrained by MP to prevent detainee from biting IV."

Dr. Seltzer was greatly concerned about the involvement of the medical profession in al-Qahtani's interrogation. Diane Beaver had thought it fine, mentioning that a CAT scan was performed as precaution. Captain Albert J. Shimkus Jr. was the Commanding Officer of the U.S. Naval Hospital at GTMO. "He would stop something cold if there was a problem," Beaver had told me. However Dr. Seltzer wasn't as sanguine. She took me back to the log entry on December 6 at 2030. "The Medical Representative checked the detainee's blood pressure and weight. She cleared the detainee for further investigation." "She seems to be checking that the detainee is fit enough to undergo further interrogation," Dr. Seltzer suggested. Later I found the guidelines governing the role of doctors in interrogations, which stated clearly that a doctor "shall not countenance, condone or participate in the practice of torture or other forms of cruel, inhuman or degrading treatment," or provide any premises, instruments, substances or knowledge to facilitate such practices.³ She also directed me to the World Medical Association's International Code of Medical Ethics, in particular the statement that "a physician shall respect a competent patient's right to accept or refuse treatment." It was clear to her that if the doctors had refused to treat the detainee the interrogation should have been stopped.

The application of the plan over fifty-four days revealed a "sophisticated jig-saw." It didn't include crude beatings, but "in many ways the totality may be worse than any individual, sensational aspects," Dr. Seltzer explained. It seemed that the techniques were part of a sophisticated plan and hadn't been invented on the spot.

After going through the interrogation log methodically we eventually got to the main question: did this constitute torture? Others had already expressed their views on this question. Lieutenant General Schmidt, the army investigator, had responded: "At what point do you say it's mildly annoying, to where it's abusive, and what point do you actually say it's torture?"⁴ Schmidt's conclusion was that the "creative, aggressive and persistent" interrogation of al-Qahtani was "degrading and abusive treatment," an echelon above inhumane but below torture.⁵ However that still made it a breach of Geneva, and punishable as a war crime.

Alberto Mora had been unimpressed by the Schmidt-Furlow report, which he called "a disgrace." He thought that what had been done to al Qahtani "could be torture, it was borderline, but I thought it could be."

I looked at the Torture Convention again with Dr. Seltzer. In the definition of torture, three elements had to be satisfied: the act must intentionally inflict "severe pain or suffering, whether physical or mental"; it must be intended to obtain from the detainee or third person information or a confession; and it must be inflicted by, or at the instigation of, or with the consent or acquiescence of, a public official. It was clear that the interrogation of al-Qahtani was the product of an extensive organizational infrastructure. The element of intent was certainly present. It was clear on the face of the log that the interrogation was intended to produce information or a confession—that had been admitted by the Administration. It was also clear that the acts had been inflicted by public officials, interrogators, lawyers and doctors, all of whom were employed by the U.S. government.

That left physical or mental pain or suffering, and the severity of it. The language of the Torture Convention suggested that the pain or suffering could be felt at the time the acts had been inflicted. It did not require any demonstration that mental suffering would be prolonged over time, or that there would necessarily be severe, long-term psychological damage.

The UN's Committee Against Torture is charged with interpreting the Convention, and it has confirmed this was the correct approach.[6] The question was: what did the detainee experience? Coupled with her professional experience in dealing with these kinds of cases, Dr. Seltzer's knowledge of the consequences of these and similar techniques led her to form a reasonably clear view. She went further than Schmidt, who had neither medical nor legal training and was singularly unqualified to form any sort of a view.

Mental pain or suffering was not a medical concept, she reminded me again. What she had looked for in the interrogation log were signs of severe distress on the part of the detainee. She had assumed that only the most significant examples would have been included in the log, and that the authors may have exercised some degree of self-censorship. "That said, over the period of fifty-four days there is enough evidence of distress to indicate that it would be very surprising indeed if it had not reached the threshold of severe mental pain." She had marked specific examples in blue on the interrogation log. We looked at December 1, 1800 hours: "Detainee stated that his treatment was making him forget things." She explained why this had caught her eye. "When stressed, people cannot concentrate, and when they cannot concentrate they cannot recall things with ease. He could be faking, but this is equally consistent with being severely stressed." Going through the blue marked parts that showed where she had identified expressions of distress, it was striking how many examples there were. In reading the log by myself I had not focused on this aspect. Like most lay people I was more interested in the nature of the technique used, and its frequency. Now looking at it through Dr. Seltzer's eyes, al-Qahtani's reactions jumped off the page.

> Detainee began to cry. Visibly shaken. Very emotional. Detainee cried. Disturbed. Detainee began to cry. Detainee butted SGT R in the eye. Detainee bit the IV tube completely in two. Started moaning. Uncomfortable. Moaning. Turned his head from left to right. Began crying hard spontaneously. Crying and praying. Began to cry. Claimed to have been pressured into making a confession. Falling asleep. Very uncomfortable. On the verge of breaking. Angry. Detainee struggled. Detainee asked for prayer. Very agitated. Yelled. Agitated and violent. Detainee spat. Detainee proclaimed his innocence. Whining. Pushed guard. Dizzy. Headache. Near tears. Forgetting things. Angry. Upset. Complained of dizziness. Tired. Agitated. Yelled for Allah. Started making faces. Near crying. Irritated. Annoyed. Detainee attempted to injure two guards.

It went on and on.

> Became very violent and irate. Attempted to liberate himself. Struggled. Made several attempts to stand up. Screamed. Woke up on his own. Emotional problems. Began to cry. Very annoyed. Urinated on himself. Began to cry. Began to cry. Complained of being dizzy. Very angry. Began to cry. Pains in kidneys. Incoherent. Broke down crying. Asked God for forgiveness. Cried. Cried. Became violent. Began to cry. Broke down and cried. Began to pray and openly cried. Began to cry. Began to cry and sob out loud. Cried quietly under the towel. Began to cry and sob loudly. Appeared to be crying. Cried out to Allah several times. Trembled uncontrollably. Yelled. Cold. Said death had been entering his mind. Broke out in tears. Cried for half an hour. Began to cry. Tried to cry again. Crying. Began to cry when talking.

The blue highlights produced a striking effect: the conclusion was inescapable. "If you put twelve clinicians in a room and asked them about this interrogation log, you might get different views about the effects and long-term consequences of these interrogation techniques," Dr. Seltzer told me. "But I doubt that any one of them would claim that this individual had not suffered severe mental distress at the time of his interrogation, and possibly also severe physical distress."

Why had she used the word "distress," rather than "pain" and "suffering" that was used in the Torture Convention? None of these words were clinical terms, nor indeed was "distress." "Distress" was used as a blanket term to describe the behavior displayed by the detainee at the time of his interrogation. "What I look for is a pattern of symptoms and signs which conform to a recognized disorder, a psychological pathology if you like. It is not possible to determine from a description of someone's behavior alone, even a detailed description such as this, whether someone has a psychological disorder. However, the log contains clear behavioral descriptors of stress, or, if you prefer, distress. From a medical perspective those descriptors are consistent with what the drafters of the Torture Convention might have had in mind when they used the terms 'pain' and 'suffering.'" The interrogation log did not contain much on the detainee's symptoms, but what it indicated very clearly—tiredness, confusion, crying—were signs that were present each day and that reflected significant emotional responses.

Dr. Seltzer was careful to point out she was not expressing a legal view, which was outside her expertise. Nevertheless, her conclusions struck me as clear and rational.

"It certainly seems that there was an intent to cause harm, for example the humiliation," she said. She reminded me that torture wasn't a unified phenomenon with a single, predictable outcome. Few are likely to be unchanged by the experience, and while there is significant long-term physical and mental morbidity associated with torture, it does not invariably leave a legacy of irreparable physical or mental injury. That said, the interrogation log suggested a very high level of psychological morbidity, as well as the physical morbidity occasioned by his dehydration. It was also clear to her that the interrogation log tracked directly back to the Haynes memo. "They were implementing the techniques listed in the memo, there is no question about that." We went through the techniques one by one. Of the fifteen that were recommended for approval by Haynes, and signed off on by Rumsfeld, I noted that every single one had been used.

There was one other issue that I wanted to ask her about. The OLC legal memos had argued that the definition of torture was not the one in the Convention, but the one that had been applied in U.S. domestic law. I showed her that definition, which limited mental pain or suffering to "*prolonged mental harm* caused by or resulting from . . . the administration or application . . . of mind altering substances or other procedures calculated to disrupt profoundly the senses or the personality." The State Department had confirmed that this interpretation was not intended to limit the scope of Article 1 of the 1984 Torture Convention.[7]

Dr. Seltzer was again careful not to express a view on the law. As a medical matter, however, she considered that distress over a period of fifty-four days was likely to be considered as "prolonged." It appeared that the sleep deprivation, humiliation and application of techniques had been calculated to profoundly disrupt al-Qahtani's senses or personality.

With this, our conversation came to an end and I was left in no doubt that Common Article 3 had been violated. Al-Qahtani had been humiliated and degraded. Outrages were inflicted on his personal dignity. He was treated cruelly. Dr. Seltzer's medical conclusions went further, pointing to torture and giving rise to a violation of the Torture Convention. It looked clear to me that the trail from the OLC legal memos through to the Haynes memo and on to the application of the techniques was direct and unbroken, crossing the line that crucially separated bad advice from advice authorizing a criminal act.

22

In June 2006, two years after the *Rasul v. Bush* judgment, the Supreme Court took another big step and overturned President Bush's decision on Geneva, ruling it to be unlawful. The judgment was a judicial cluster bomb, spreading detritus far and wide, creating a calamity for the Administration. The blank pages of Diane Beaver's rulebook were filled once again. The labyrinthine logic of Doug Feith's legal brain blew a fuse and General Hill's greatest concerns were realized. General Myers's belief that Geneva had been applied all along ran into a brick wall. Last but not least, the curtain that had shielded John Yoo, Jay Bybee and Jim Haynes was lifted.

The Supreme Court confirmed that Common Article 3 applied to *all* Guantánamo detainees. It was as simple as that. Whether they were Taliban or al-Qaeda, every one of the detainees had rights under Common Article 3, and that included Mohammed al-Qahtani. Someone having lunch with Jim Haynes on the day of the judgment described him as looking "shocked" as the news sunk in. "He just went pale," I was told, and the lunch was brought to an early end.

The Court's decision was reached in the case of *Hamdan v. Rumsfeld* (2006).[1] It was not about interrogations, but rather revolved around the system of military commissions designed for the Guantánamo detainees. Salim Ahmed Hamdan from Yemen was said to be Osama bin Laden's personal driver and bodyguard. He argued that the rules governing military commissions did not meet the requirements of Common Article 3, which raised the issue of detainee rights under that provision. A majority of five to three ruled that Common Article 3 had been violated. Of the eight justices, only two—Clarence Thomas and Samuel Alito—agreed with the Administration's argument that Common Article 3 wasn't applicable at all: the majority ruled that Common Article 3 established "requirements" that the United States was bound to follow and all the Guantánamo detainees could rely upon it as a right.

The majority opinion was written by Justice John Paul Stevens. "Common Article 3," he wrote, "affords some minimal protection, falling short of full protection under the Conventions, to individuals who are involved in a conflict in the territory of a signatory." This conclusion had been reached by looking at the official commentaries to the Geneva Conventions, which confirmed its wide scope. They invoked the U.S. Army's *Law of War Handbook,* which described Common Article 3 as "a minimum yardstick of protection in all conflicts, not just internal armed conflicts." They also relied on decisions of the International Court of Justice and the International Criminal Tribunal for the former Yugoslavia, decisions that were ignored by Gonzales and Haynes because they were inconvenient.

One of the Justices went even further. Common Article 3 was part of the law of war and of a treaty that the United States had ratified and accepted as binding law. "By Act of Congress," Justice Anthony Kennedy wrote pointedly, "violations of Common Article 3 are considered 'war crimes,' punishable as federal offenses, when committed by or against United States nationals and military personnel." War crimes may be punishable before the courts of other parties to Geneva, a commitment to the principle that there is to be no impunity.

Justice Kennedy's remark put the issue of war crimes on the American political agenda. Individuals who had contributed to a violation of Common Article 3 would know that they were at risk of criminal investigation and, if a case was shown, prosecution. That concentrated minds. The mind of Jack Goldsmith, for example, Haynes's former Special Counsel, who described the ruling as "ominous," since it made the War Crimes Act applicable to "many elements of the administration's treatment of detainees."[2] Even more ominously, it underscored the risk for those involved to be investigated outside the United States.

On July 7, 2006, a few days after the Court's judgment, Deputy Secretary of Defense Gordon England signed a memorandum on behalf of Rumsfeld giving effect to the judgment and determining that all DoD personnel must adhere to the standards of Common Article 3.[3] A few days later Jim Haynes appeared before the Senate Judiciary Committee in a judicial confirmation hearing. Senator Leahy reminded him that in 2003 he had said that there was "no way" that Geneva could apply to the Afghan conflict and the war on terror. "Do you now accept that you were mistaken in your legal and policy determinations on the issues of military tribunals?"

Leahy asked him. Haynes avoided answering the question. He said only that he was bound by the Supreme Court's decision.[4]

Shortly after, the U.S. Senate Armed Services Committee held a hearing on the Geneva Conventions.[5] The Judge Advocate General for each of the four services attended: Major General Scott Black of the Army, Rear Admiral James McPherson of the Navy, Major General Jack Rives of the Air Force and Brigadier General Kevin Sandkuhler of the Marine Corps. They were also joined by General John Hutson, former Navy Judge Advocate General, and General Tom Romig, former Army Judge Advocate General (the same General Romig who had helped Diane Beaver get to Guantánamo). "Would you agree that some of the techniques that we have authorized clearly violate Common Article 3?" Senator Lindsay Graham asked Major General Rives. Rives barely paused. "Some of the techniques that have been authorized and used in the past have violated Common Article 3," he answered. "Does everyone agree with that statement?" Senator Graham asked the other five. There was a common murmur, a positive murmur. The transcript for the hearing recorded: "Affirmative response by all concerned."

Jack Rives knew what he was talking about. In February 2003, after Rumsfeld had rescinded the authorization of the eighteen techniques and as new proposals were being prepared, Rives cautioned against a return to aggressive interrogation. He warned Mary Walker, the Air Force General Counsel, that interrogations that violated international laws put "the interrogators and the chain of command at risk of criminal accusation abroad, either in foreign domestic courts or in international fora, to include the [International Criminal Court]."[6] His views were shared by others. Kevin Sandkuhler of the Marines told Walker that aggressive counter-resistance techniques would have an adverse impact, in particular the risk of criminal and civil liability before domestic, foreign and international courts.[7] Tom Romig also concurred. He had "serious concerns" about any proposals for aggressive interrogations. "These concerns center around the potential DoD sanctioning of detainee interrogation techniques that may appear to violate international law, domestic law, or both." He disagreed with "several pivotal aspects" of the Bybee/Yoo memo, which could not form the legal basis for interrogation techniques. He objected to the necessity argument, and questioned whether it would prevail in any courts. The United States would expose itself to criticism that it was "a law unto itself."[8]

These important voices were silent in October and November 2002, as the eighteen techniques were being considered. They were silent because they had no idea what Rumsfeld and Haynes were doing; they had no idea about the eighteen techniques. "They just cut the Services out," Romig told me. "Someone overheard Addington say 'Don't bring the TJAGs into the process, they aren't reliable.'" Romig first heard of the eighteen techniques when they were in a meeting with Jim Haynes and Alberto Mora raised it. "We weren't aware of it," he said, "There was shock in the room." Now the military lawyers raised real and serious concerns that international crimes might have been committed.

By these international legal standards the consequences of the interrogation of al-Qahtani seemed clear. War crime violations of Common Article 3 had occurred. Further, Dr. Seltzer's analysis indicated that the acts also violated the Torture Convention.

Like anyone else I find it hard to know where to draw the line between inhumane and degrading treatment, on the one hand, and torture, on the other. I focused intensely on this issue in 2005, as part of a team preparing a case before the House of Lords on the admissibility of evidence that might have been obtained by torture. In England, torture has long been prohibited and its by-products may not be relied on in a court of law. "Once torture has become acclimatized in a legal system," wrote Sir William Searle Holdsworth, author of the definitive twelve-volume *A History of English Law,* "it spreads like an infectious disease."9

One of the judges sitting on the case was Lord Hope. A year earlier he had written a law review article entitled "Torture,"10 which endeavored to determine the dividing line. He recalled the interrogation techniques used on IRA suspects by the British security forces in Northern Ireland: standing for long periods in a stress position against a wall, hooding, continuous noise, sleep deprivation, and deprivation of food and drink. They were strikingly similar to the eighteen techniques used at Guantánamo. A divided European Court of Human Rights had ruled in the case of the IRA suspects that the techniques were inhuman and degrading but did not cross the line to torture.11 Diane Beaver had referred to that ruling in her short legal opinion. But that judgment had been thirty years earlier, and in any case the decision was controversial. Recent decisions of the European Court had pointed to stricter standards. "It seems likely," Lord Hope wrote, "that the mixture of physical and psychological pressures that were used in the case of the IRA suspects would now be regarded as torture within the meaning of Article 3 of the [European] Convention." He added that in his view, "Any inhuman and degrading treatment which is used for the purpose of extracting information or a confession will constitute torture," but said nothing about the eighteen techniques or about Guantánamo or other places. He wasn't in a position to know, he wrote, although silence bred suspicion. "We can assume that whatever has been and is being done to the prisoners has and is being done with the cold and ruthless efficiency that characterizes the actions of officials who are determined to obtain results and whose actions are not subject to international inspection or to the control of any independent and impartial judicial authority."

Others were less circumspect. The Red Cross reportedly concluded that the construction of the Guantánamo system, the stated purpose of which is the production of intelligence, "cannot be considered other than an intentional system of cruel, unusual and degrading treatment and a form of torture."[12] The UN Committee Against Torture called for the closure of the detention facility at Guantánamo and an end to the use of techniques such as search humiliation (internal examinations), "short shackling" (chained to the floor on short chains) and the use of dogs, "that constitute torture or cruel inhuman or degrading treatment."[13] The UN Human Rights Commission concluded that the use of some of the techniques—nudity, dogs, exposure to extreme temperatures—could give rise to extreme psychological suffering so as to amount to torture.[14]

As with the Geneva Conventions, the parties to the Torture Convention are required to investigate any person who is alleged to have committed torture. If appropriate they must then prosecute, or extradite the person to a place where he will be prosecuted. The Torture Convention is also more explicit than Geneva in that it criminalizes any act that constitutes complicity or participation in torture. Complicity or participation could certainly be extended to the lawyers involved in the condoning of the eighteen techniques. The scheme applied to al-Qahtani was devised by lawyers, reviewed by lawyers, overseen by lawyers. "This is not torture outside the law but, ostensibly, under it," wrote Professor Jose Alvarez of Columbia Law School, a leading American international law scholar and a former State Department attorney, about the memos.[15] At the top of the legal edifice in the Pentagon sat Jim Haynes. He had knowledge of dubious legal advice from John Yoo and Jay Bybee at the Justice Department that was later rescinded. He had relied on determinations made by President Bush's personal counsel, Alberto Gonzales, and David Addington, Cheney's lawyer. And down at the bottom of the pile, in Guantánamo, was Diane Beaver, "sitting in the dirt," as she put it, under the authority of Judge Mike Dunlavey. She had observed the interrogations and signed off on the application of the techniques. And of course she had authored a short legal opinion, the only advice which Jim Haynes identified as one he had relied on.

23

"In situations like this you don't call in the tough guys; you call in the lawyers." George Tenet made this point crystal clear in his memoir.[1] The former Director of the CIA might have added that you should also make sure you call the right lawyers, the ones who'll give you the answer you want, irrespective of what the law actually says. In March 2002 Abu Zubaydah, a high-ranking al-Qaeda official, was captured in Faisalabad, Pakistan. Tenet's team wanted an aggressive interrogation, but that had to await the completion of legal opinions, a task assigned to Jay Bybee and John Yoo by Alberto Gonzales. "It took until August to get clear guidance on what Agency officers could legally do," wrote Tenet. "Clear guidance" was given on August 1, 2002 and it came in the same Bybee/Yoo memos that I was told Jim Haynes was able to rely on as he signed off on the Haynes memo, and in the opinion that John Rizzo of the CIA had asked for on specific techniques.

The lawyers you choose can be crucial. Jim Haynes made clear to the Senate Judiciary Committee that he had decided not to go the TJAGs or to Jane Dalton. It was blindingly obvious why—they would not have given the answers he—and, more significantly, his client—had already decided they wanted. So the legal advices did not come from career lawyers with an interest in the long-term well-being of the United States military; instead, they came from a tight group of political appointees, a group of men who could be relied upon to give the right advice.

However, all lawyers, even political appointees, work within two sets of constraints. The first is the ethical rules of professional responsibility that bind all practicing lawyers. Since June 2004, when the legal advices and the Haynes memo were made public, there has been a lively debate in the United States on whether the lawyers who drafted the various legal advices on interrogation complied with their ethical responsibilities. At the heart of the debate were requirements like those of the District of Columbia Rules of Professional Conduct, which set out the parameters for lawyers in the government service who gave legal advice. Two of these rules were particularly relevant. Rule 1.4(b) states that: "A lawyer shall explain a matter to the extent reasonably necessary to permit the client to make informed decisions regarding the representation." And Rule 2.1 requires a lawyer to render "candid advice." This would not prevent a client from consulting a lawyer to confirm his own preconceptions rather than to seek genuine advice, and the lawyer could be tempted to play sycophant to such a client. However, Rule 2.1 prohibits such an approach: the lawyer has to exercise judgment that is "independent and professional."[2]

The practical implications were summarized in an article by Kathleen Clark, a law professor at the Washington University School of Law. "In advising a client," she wrote, "the lawyer's role is not simply to spin out creative legal arguments. It is to offer her assessment of the law as objectively as possible."[3] As Clark put it, this meant that the lawyer not only had to tell the client what he wanted to hear, but "must tell the client her best assessment of what the law requires or allows." So a lawyer could give advice that wasn't supported by the majority of legal authority, sometimes referred to as "forward-leaning" advice. But in those circumstances the lawyer had a responsibility to make it clear that the weight of authority was contrary to that advice and that others—including courts or tribunals—may come to the opposite conclusion. The point was put simply by Professor Clark: "A lawyer who fails to warn a client about the possible illegality of proposed conduct has violated her professional obligations."

Clark took this standard and applied it to the memos. She concluded that the authors of the Bybee/Yoo memos had violated their professional obligations in purporting to give legal advice: they had failed to give candid advice and they had failed to inform their client about the state of the law of torture. Clark considered that their assertions about the law were "so inaccurate that they seem to be arguments about what the authors (or intended recipients) wanted the law to be rather than assessments of what the law actually is."[4] She identified some major inaccuracies in Bybee's memo of August 1. The reference to the level of pain associated with organ failure was lifted from a Medicare statute that had nothing to do with torture. The discussion of a potential defense of necessity available to those who might be prosecuted flew in the face of the Torture Convention's exclusion of any such defense, a point on which the Bybee/Yoo memo was silent (the UN Committee Against Torture has confirmed that "no doctrine under domestic law impedes the full criminal responsibility of perpetrators of acts of torture").[5] Clark concluded that the legal analysis in the memorandum was "so indefensible that it could not—and did not—withstand public scrutiny."[6]

The memorandum did not even withstand the scrutiny of the man who commissioned it, Alberto Gonzales. He disavowed it the day he made it public, on the grounds that it set "the limits of the legal landscape" and included discussion that was "irrelevant and unnecessary." He also claimed that the memo did "not reflect the policies that the Administration ultimately adopted"—which explained why Haynes could not tell the Judiciary Committee that he had relied on the memo in recommending the eighteen techniques. Such an admission would have undermined Gonzales's claim.

Clark's view also has more widespread support. Professor Stephen Gillers teaches at New York University and is renowned as one of the country's leading authorities on the ethical responsibilities of lawyers. "In our system the lawyers are the gatekeepers of legality and constitutionality," he told me, echoing Spike Bowman's view. "I was offended by the legal ethics aspects of all those legal memoranda." He was familiar with all the advices that were in the public domain. "I knew enough to know that this was not advice, these were advocacy documents that used the form of legal methodology and academic methodology to advance the advocacy of governmental positions."

I've known Gillers for many years. He is a mild-mannered man of considerable restraint and caution who had taken care to assess the issues from competing perspectives. This made his critique of what happened in 2002 all the more remarkable. Sitting in his office he passed me a copy of an article he'd written in July 2004, shortly after Gonzales and Haynes had presented the Administration's "bottom-up" narrative. His article focused on an earlier memo, sent by John Yoo and Robert Delahunty to Jim Haynes on January 9, 2002 (though it was only made public in draft form, a point Gillers was careful to note). The memo was the first to advise that Common Article 3 (and Geneva generally) should not be available to al-Qaeda and Taliban detainees in Afghanistan. The authors of this memo had to accept "moral responsibility for the abuse to which acceptance of their position led," wrote Gillers.[7] The memo effectively cast Geneva aside. But it was picked up by Doug Feith who ran with it to hoodwink the Chairman of the Joint Chiefs into believing that Geneva was being applied when it wasn't. There were subsequent failures of commission and omission. "Perhaps . . . someone high in government explained that complete and balanced advice was not the client's wish, that the client instead wanted arguments to support decisions already made," Gillers suggested. "If this is what happened, then the lawyers might claim that they simply did their client's bidding and, so long as their advice had some merit, they cannot be blamed for the consequences."

Even so Gillers thought the lawyers bore some responsibility. "If the [January 9, 2002] memo was meant to legitimate the client's predetermined end, the lawyers are still to blame because they would have chosen to give the client the advice it wanted when the dangers of doing so—of consigning prisoners to a lawless state—were obvious." Gillers is a quintessentially fair man and was concerned that I should also familiarize myself with the counter-arguments. He directed me to various other articles, including a response to his article, written by Jeffrey Shapiro and Lee Casey, lawyers who served in the Office of Legal Counsel at the Justice Department in the Administrations of the first President Bush and then President Clinton.[8] Shapiro and Casey took issue with Gillers for making personal attacks and, in effect, encouraging OLC lawyers to give advice on moral and policy choices, as well as the law. That certainly wasn't how I had read Gillers's article. For Shapiro and Casey, what mattered at the end of the day was the nature and quality of the legal advice. In their view the President's decision on Geneva was "sensible and nuanced" and showed "how the system should work." Yet it seemed they were unaware of the direct consequences of the legal advice on the President's decision, to the effect that Common Article 3 was cast asunder.

The President's decision was essentially based on the reasoning set out in the January 9, 2002 memorandum, as developed by Doug Feith. Four years later, in the *Hamdan v. Rumsfeld* case, the U.S. Supreme Court decisively rejected that reasoning, with Clarence Thomas penning an alternative view (an apparent aficionado, with Justice Antonin Scalia,[9] of the television series 24 and the Justice with whom John Yoo had served, coincidentally no doubt, as a law clerk back in 1994). For the military lawyers, however, the President's erroneous decision on Common Article 3 was a *fait accompli*: it was not endorsed by those most directly affected, the senior military lawyers who protected the interests of servicemen and women, because they were given no opportunity to comment.

I couldn't see much merit in the criticism by Shapiro and Casey that Gillers had failed to demonstrate how the OLC's legal memoranda had contributed to the alleged abuses. Cause and effect are never easy to establish. But in this case the line from the OLC memo to the President's decision on Geneva and onward to the eighteen techniques was direct and unbroken. My own conversations with some of the architects of the policy of aggressive interrogation had confirmed the intentions. The removal of Geneva's constraints on interrogation was neither a likely nor intended consequence of the President's decision and the advice, it was the desired intention. When I asked Doug Feith straight out whether the President's decision on Geneva was intended to avoid constraints on interrogation he replied: "Absolutely," without hesitation. It was reasonable to assume that the Undersecretary of Defense for Policy knew why decisions were taken.

The line that divides erroneous legal advice from unethical advice is often a difficult one to draw. In this case, however, the difficulties are not pronounced: it was plain that in the period after 9/11 public officials felt themselves under tremendous pressure to do everything possible to prevent further attacks. Shapiro and Casey made the point in their critique of Gillers. Instead of wasting time unfairly maligning OLC lawyers, they wrote, "we should be doing everything possible, within the law, to stop these fanatics before they do us more harm."[10] Of course, the crucial words in that sentence are "within the law": they cannot be over emphasized. For there is another line that may not be crossed, and that is the line that separates unethical advice or actions from illegal advice or actions. The law operates as a further constraint on what lawyers do. A lawyer has the same responsibility as any other government servant or agent to comply with international rules. If anything, the responsibility of the lawyer, as gatekeeper of legality, is even greater. If lawyers cross that line they may become complicit in the commission of a crime, willing accomplices in actions that are internationally outlawed. "Violations of Common Article 3 are considered 'war crimes,'" wrote Justice Anthony Kennedy.

The complicity of the lawyers began to be pointed to with the publication of the Abu Ghraib photographs and the legal memos, as some observers sought to draw a link between the legal advice and the abuse. New York attorney Scott Horton was one of the first to connect the arguments in the OLC's legal memoranda and those made six decades earlier by senior officials and lawyers in another era, in Nazi Germany.[11] He came across one parallel that was particularly striking. In the 1940s, one of the justifications for ignoring the predecessor to the Geneva Conventions was the claim that it was "obsolete," unsuited to the new kind of ideological warfare that Germany faced. The statement bore an uncanny resemblance to a claim made in a memo signed by Alberto Gonzales, but largely written by David Addington, of January 25, 2002. It recommended that President Bush should not apply Geneva, noting that the war against terrorism was a new kind of war. "This new paradigm renders obsolete Geneva's strict limitations on questioning of enemy prisoners and renders quaint some of its provisions. . . ."

Like many, Horton was careful not to draw strict parallels between atrocities divided by more than sixty years. He focused on the analogy, if any, between the legal arguments, and in this he was not alone. Speaking at a conference at Case Western Reserve Law School on October 7, 2005, Columbia Law School Professor Jose Alvarez[12] argued that many of the arguments presented in the OLC memo in support of the President's Geneva decision and aggressive interrogation techniques were so extremely at odds with the actual law they purported to be interpreting that they amounted to an "extreme perversion of the law."[13] Professor Alvarez became President of the American Society of International Law and previously served as an attorney in the State Department: he had nothing to gain by adopting a tone of hyperbole or excess. For him the legal opinions were a "paper trail of apparent complicity in torture."[14]

Alvarez concluded that the memoranda, taken together with the public statements of officials of the Bush Administration, suggested a "conscious reinterpretation of existing law, both national and international, intended to respond to alleged 'new' circumstances faced by the United States in its new 'war.'" His far-reaching critique of the memos and various statements is difficult to dismiss. They misconstrued various U.S. treaty obligations prohibiting torture or ignored them altogether; they ignored the plain meaning of Common Article 3 and turned the Convention *Against* Torture into the convention *for* certain kinds of torture when it came to actions outside the United States, turning a blind eye to the absolute nature of the ban on torture. They selectively chose non-U.S. judicial authorities to reflect conclusions concerning the severity of pain needed to constitute torture and dismissed customary law in a way that was cavalier and reckless. They devoted almost no attention to the possibility of criminal liability under international law, and, most pertinently for present purposes, they failed to address "the potential criminal liability of government lawyers such as the memoranda writers themselves."[15]

Alvarez understood the frustration of the lawyers who had produced memos under great pressure only to have conclusions that were never intended to be made public being scrutinized by law professors with the luxury of time and research assistants. "Yet," wrote Alvarez, citing the judgment in the 1946 *Altstötter* case at Nuremberg, "that was the basis for the film *Judgment at Nuremberg*." "the notorious history of Nazi lawyers who 'prostitut[ed] . . . a judicial system for the accomplishment of criminal ends' hangs over us all." He did not pull his punches: "As the *Altstötter* case demonstrates, when government lawyers torture the rule of law as gravely as they have done here, international as well as national crimes may have been committed, including by the lawyers themselves."

In October 2005 I was unaware of what Alvarez had said. But as he spoke, I was preparing comments for a panel discussion with John Yoo at the World Affairs Council in San Francisco. I'd seen Scott Horton's piece, which had alerted me to the *Altstötter* case. John Yoo's advice on aggressive interrogation was already public, however, I'd not yet made the connection between the memos he wrote with Jay Bybee and the memo that Jim Haynes had written on November 27, 2002. Nor was I then aware that the special interrogation plan developed for Mohammed al-Qahtani had been based on the eighteen techniques and, more distantly, Yoo's advices. These connections only emerged in later conversations with Beaver, Dunlavey, Feith and Myers.

John Yoo and I spent an hour in conversation before a full house at the World Affairs Council. He wanted to talk about Iraq. I wanted to talk about detainees. I mentioned my experience of sitting in hearings in London on the Pinochet case, back in 1998, my conversations with Pinochet's advisers, who had never imagined that the Torture Convention would come back to haunt the former Chilean head of state; after all it was that which caused him to lose his claim to immunity. "The Torture Convention will come back to haunt those associated with the Administration's interrogation policy," I now told the audience in San Francisco: I read out Article 4 and made the point about complicity. Its provisions were clear, and there was also international authority from Nuremberg, in the case of *Altstötter,* which suggested "that legal advisers who prepare legal advice that is so erroneous as to give rise to an international crime are themselves subject to the rules of international criminality." I proceeded gently since I was relying on Scott Horton's piece rather than the full judgment and pleadings, which were not available in London (I would later visit the Holocaust Museum in Washington to track down all the pleadings in that case). "Individuals who are associated with the policy of torture are likely to find themselves facing the very same tap on the shoulder that Senator Pinochet got so unexpectedly on October 16, 1998."

Yoo declined to take the bait. He was all charm and humor and unctuousness in the face of an audience that was hostile to his approach, and generally quite measured in his responses. However that changed when we got on to the quality of the advices he had given. There was the odd put-down ("I cannot match Professor Sands, with his florid rhetoric that can only be learnt on fields of schools like Eton and the other schools that you all go to!") but generally we stuck to substance. His arguments were predictable and the message mirrored the defenses offered by Addington, Gonzales and Haynes. The world had changed. The greatest threat was from terrorist organizations like al-Qaeda, and rogue and failed states.

The United States was right to try to change international legal rules that were outdated and relevant to another age. The Geneva rules had not been written in anticipation of this new situation and they didn't apply to al-Qaeda, which hadn't signed up to them. All these points were made six months before the Supreme Court gave its ruling in the *Hamdan* case. The closest Yoo got to discussing the crucial point about the *Altstötter* case was on the abuses at Abu Ghraib, involving renegade actors. He accepted that it was necessary "to follow the chain, go up the chain no matter how high it goes and make sure that those responsible for the policy are investigated and punished." But Guantánamo was different: "The Geneva Conventions's rules do not apply there," he said with great assurance.

"The problem is not renegade actors," I countered during the discussion, perhaps a little too harshly, "but renegade lawyers like John Yoo." They had attempted to redefine torture, and had done so with no proper basis and in a way that other countries would not accept. The whole rationale for international rules was to set minimum standards below which no state could fall. If each state adopted its own definition you might as well do away with the international rule. That point was accepted by senior career military lawyers at the highest levels. I took my cue from them. I invited Yoo to stick to the rules of international law when he gave legal advice in future.

Yoo blinked first. "First off, Mr. Sands, I could sit here and call you names and call you a silly person and I have not," he said, snappishly. "You can certainly engage in *ad hominem* criticisms, but I choose not to." Now his true agenda was revealed in its full glory. The U.S. Constitution did not allow international law to trump American domestic law. "What the United States has been doing is interpreting domestic law," said Yoo, "and I think it's quite fair to say that even if international law requires the United States not to engage in inhumane or degrading treatment the U.S. view is that that rule does not apply in the war against terrorism and against members of al-Qaeda."

Yoo on the law and Yoo on policy were happily convergent: there was no distinction, it seemed. There were no international constraints on the exercise of presidential power. National Security was all. The Administration believed that the war on terrorism was a very different kind of war. "The need for information to stop other terrorist attacks is much higher than in other kinds of conflicts," Yoo said, "so the Administration wants to retain the kind of flexibility to do more than simply ask questions of people who are captured, who are al-Qaeda leaders and who may have knowledge of future plans to attack the United States."

A few months later the Supreme Court gave its judgment in *Hamdan v. Rumsfeld*. Yoo's views on Common Article 3 were brusquely rejected (although not by his mentor Clarence Thomas). Not surprisingly Yoo thought the Court's decision to be a mistake. "Weak, selective and ahistorical" was the way he characterized the majority's ruling.[16] The Court had failed to come to grips with the Geneva Conventions and the decision on Common Article 3 was wrong. "The Court chose to reinvent this area of law out of whole cloth." In doing so it had "made the legal system part of the problem, rather than part of the solution."[17]

These must have been difficult times for John Yoo. Aside from the Supreme Court decision, the memo he wrote with Jay Bybee was rejected and then withdrawn. "The Justice Department bowed to Administration critics and withdrew the leaked 2002 opinion," Yoo later wrote in his book. "I thought this a terrible precedent. It showed that Justice Department judgments on the law had become just one more political target open to partisan attack and political negotiation."[18] Yoo believed that Attorney General John Ashcroft had taken a political decision to reject his memo, and it was on him that his anger was focused. He understood the pressures that Ashcroft and others were under, but he objected to the pretence that back in 2002 the Attorney General was out of the loop. That was wrong. "No opinion of that significance could ever issue from the Justice Department without the review of the Attorney General's staff, in particular that of his counselor, or without the Attorney General's personal approval." As the ship sank, Yoo was going to make sure that others went down with him.

To compound the sense of grievance, not only was Yoo's advice withdrawn and rejected and its underlying argument trashed by the Supreme Court, but now new officials at the Justice Department launched an ethics investigation into the circumstances in which his memo was prepared. "These individuals decided they needed to go to extraordinary lengths to discredit the first opinion," wrote Yoo. They opened an investigation into all those who worked on it (the outcome of which I was unable to ascertain), from the career attorneys to the head of the office, "to determine whether we had violated our professional responsibilities in preparing legal advice."[19] This made him really angry, so angry in fact that he left his readers unaware of the outcome of that investigation. "It is fair to disagree with our conclusions on the merits," he wrote, but "to claim ethical violations is unfounded and unfair." That view was not shared by Kathleen Clark or Stephen Gillers.

24

John Yoo had declined my invitation to discuss the *Altstötter* case but I had a slightly more willing response from Doug Feith, although our conversation was far from easy. It had the great merit, however, of teasing out the main issues.

"These were Nazi lawyers you are talking about," Feith said sharply. I was well aware of that, I replied, but they were also university academics, highly educated professionals who trained at the very best law schools and had then entered government service. In these positions of power they had committed crimes in exercise of their professional activities.

I hesitated to draw analogies. This was not about comparing atrocities, which were plainly on a vastly different character and scale. I was interested in the issue of principle: what did a lawyer have to do to cross a line into illegality? The only international cases that had ever dealt with that issue were at Nuremberg—the *Altstötter* case and the other *Justice* cases. I was interested in knowing how Telford Taylor, the chief prosecutor, had come up with the idea of identifying and then prosecuting lawyers. And, I reminded Feith (recalling Scott Horton's article and the arguments I had put to John Yoo), there was an analogy in the legal reasoning: domestic law and national security needs trump everything, international rules are obsolete, a new paradigm exists.

Feith was not persuaded. His voice was edgy. "The difference between the domestic constitution of the Nazi government, which was a lawless government, and the U.S. constitution, there's failure of perspective here that's really serious." This was not an unreasonable point. "I don't think they're analogies, I think you are wrong."

"What's the difference," I responded, "between a lawyer in the Justice Department who says, the President can do anything he wants, he can commit torture, he can carry out a genocide . . ." Feith broke in: "He did not say he can carry out a genocide." "What's the difference?" I asked again. "The difference is the entire context," he replied. "With the United States you're dealing with a democratic government in a country founded on respect for individual rights." He paused again, and reflected. This conversation clearly bothered him; it had taken an unexpected turn. "I would object to any comment of mine being in your book, if you plan to start your book with this as the analogy and then you're asking me to explain."

He shifted tack. "Let me just give you the picture of who's around the table working on these things as I see it, and what attitudes people bring to this. I have the sense that everybody around the table loves the Constitution, respects the founding fathers, gets teary-eyed at the principles on which our Revolution was fought, believes in the dignity of man and the individual rights that, you know, underline all the principles on which our government is built, because they're all deeply rooted in philosophical ideas about man's relation to God, man's relation to the state and man's relation to other men and—these are deep, important things. These are good Americans that are interested in human rights and individual rights and constitution principles and everything else."

"Do you think something went wrong?" I asked. "Hang on now," he replied, "so you start off with the idea that you are not dealing with Nazis. It's a big difference whether you are dealing with Nazis, OK?" I nodded. There was indeed a difference. Having dealt with the individuals, he proceeded to the next strand of his argument, the context.

"Here we are, we've been attacked, we're concerned about the next attack. The only way to fight this war is to get the intelligence about what the enemy is doing. During the Cold War we could get that from satellites looking at armoured formations. In this war the intelligence is all in people's heads. So interrogation is as important as our eyes in the skies during the Cold War. You cannot overstate, you appreciate that, you were saying it, you cannot overstate the importance of interrogation because intelligence that we need to fight this war, defend the country, protect possibly millions of people from attacks by smallpox or anthrax, that intelligence is in the heads of these people. We need to extract it."

How far are we allowed to go to extract it? I inquired of the man who had spent four years developing policy on precisely these issues. "Well, I don't know," he said, "I haven't made a whole study of this thing." Another short pause for reflection. "We are a country of laws, so make sure you're doing it lawfully."

Could the interrogation techniques that Feith approved of be used on U.S. nationals? John Walker Lindh and Jose Padilla had not been subjected to aggressive interrogations. Feith left open the possibility that they could be, although not by U.S. personnel. Rumsfeld was making decisions every day concerning U.S. military personnel who were acting in ways that stripped them of their entitlement to protection and subjected them to the risk of being shot. The idea of reciprocity was, in any event, theoretical. "You are not really in the same world as the rest of us if you are worried about reciprocity from al-Qaeda," he said pointedly.

Feith then shifted the conversation back to ground on which he was more comfortable. He wished that people would recognize that the Administration was dealing with a really difficult problem. The United States had been attacked; they were simply trying to head off the next attack. They were trying to fight vigorously, effectively, successfully and decently. "They are grappling with hard issues . . . they are grappling with gigantic, large, constitutional issues that are a brooding omnipresence over this whole subject."

Did he agree that moral authority was important, and working within the rules provided support for that authority? "When you talk about moral authority," Feith replied, "I make the distinction between whether we're entitled to it and whether we have it." He paused for dramatic effect. He was almost quivering. "We're entitled to it." And, he added, the officials who had taken those decisions were entitled to be treated as having moral authority—and that included the lawyers. He never for a moment thought that they behaved immorally. He may have disagreed with them on some issues, but it was not right to say that "they lack the moral authority that a decent official is entitled to."

Or, I inquired, to suggest that they have crossed the line into criminality? He agreed enthusiastically. To make charges like that was "to attack the moral authority of one of the few governments that actually is entitled to moral authority." My approach did not raise levels of morality around the world; all it did was take officials who were dealing with difficult questions involving serious ethical issues and legal and operational judgements and subject them to "a simple outsider's critical position, crapping on all of them from a position of non-responsibility and moral superiority." The only effect would be "to persuade people that nobody respects the law, not even these Americans, that the law is shit in everybody's view. . . ."

Ultimately, the Americans' violations of Geneva at Guantánamo were brought to an end by the decisions of the courts. In *Hamdan v. Rumsfeld* the

Supreme Court decided that Common Article 3 applied to all detainees at Guantánamo. Feith's own arguments were rejected, as the legal system rejected them. In Feith's view it would be useful for me to write a book that said "the system works, people made arguments that ultimately didn't prevail and shouldn't prevail, but the people who made those arguments were not bad people." In seeking to protect the decision-makers he was also protecting himself. "They do not deserve even to be distinguished from Nazis, that's the thing that really galls me." That was not what I was trying to do, I suggested, but he was on a roll: "I would not consider it a triumph that you've compared them to Nazis and distinguished them."

And then he offered some advice. "The service that you could do, the most powerful thing you could say is: 'I have looked at what these lawyers have done and I think it's incorrect.' And you can say: 'I don't believe they're criminals, I don't believe they're stupid, I don't believe they're ill-motivated, I don't believe they're unpatriotic, I don't believe they are totalitarian, I don't think they are brutal and inhumane, I simply think that they made an incorrect judgment.'" He thought there was more I could say. "That the American system ultimately decided it was incorrect—it went through a process—but what is evident is you had a whole bunch of people all of whom agreed on basic admirable humane principles, the principles embodied in the U.S. Constitution. They were all grappling with this extremely difficult problem of how do you defend the system against enemies of this kind, and some people came up with some ideas that were a little over-enthusiastic and some of these ideas have nothing to do with the war on terrorism, they have everything to do with these broader points about presidential power and all the rest of it, and at the end of the day it got sorted out."

This could certainly be one interpretation of the events I was exploring.

Doug Feith went some way in persuading me that the *Altstötter* case wasn't exactly comparable and that further inquiry would cause offense in some quarters at least. The difficulty was that *Altstötter* was the only international precedent available and it was being referred to by others with increasing frequency. So, with some trepidation, I decided to lift the lid on that obscure decision, and find out a bit more about it.

25

"The dagger of the assassin was concealed beneath the robe of the jurist."
These words came at the beginning of Lord Wright's foreword to the
heavy tome that is volume VI of the forbiddingly titled *Law Reports of Trials of War Criminals,* the official law reports of the Nuremberg trials, prepared by the United Nations War Crimes Commission. As Chairman of
the Commission, Lord Wright explained in his foreword the significance
of the report on the trial of *Josef Altstötter and Others,* the *Justice Cases* later
made into the film *Judgment at Nuremberg.* He said that the case was intended to set an example, to show that government lawyers and judges
had special responsibilities—and it remains the only example of an international court establishing the guilt of lawyers for participating in
governmentally organized cruelty and injustice by the violation of the
laws of war and humanity.

Sixteen lawyers appeared as defendants before a U.S. military tribunal,
charged with war crimes, crimes against humanity and membership of
criminal organizations. Josef Altstötter had the alphabetical misfortune to
be lead defendant because of his name, although he was certainly not the
most important or notorious of the sixteen. Others, like Franz Schlegelberger, the Acting Minister of Justice, and Herbert Klemm, State Secretary
at the Ministry, were more sinister. Both these men were sentenced to life
imprisonment, as was Oswald Rothaug, the Senior Public Prosecutor of
the People's Court, and Rudolf Oeschey, the lawyer who had succeeded
Rothaug as Chief Justice and who was singled out for his "sadistic attitude
and conduct." Of the sixteen, four were acquitted and one committed sui-
cide before the trial ended.

There were no compelling reasons for me to focus on Josef Altstötter,
except that his name was associated with the case that was drawing some
attention. The judgment of December 1947 set out his background as a

well-regarded member of society and a high-ranking lawyer. Before the war he had worked for various government departments, and from 1939 to 1943 he served in a judicial capacity with the Wehrmacht, the armed forces of Nazi Germany. In 1943 he joined the Reich Ministry of Justice, where he served as Chief of the Civil Law and Procedure Division, holding the title of Ministerialdirektor until Germany's surrender. Before the rise of the Nazis he had been a member of the Stahlhelm, the largest and most nationalistic of the paramilitary organizations of the Weimar Republic. When the Stahlhelm was absorbed into the Nazi structure he automatically became a member of the Sturmabteilung (SA), the brownshirts. In 1937 he became a member of the Schutzstaffel (SS). By May 1944 he had risen to the rank of Oberführer in that organization, the Senior Colonel rank that allowed the officer to wear two oak leaves as a distinguishing mark on his uniform collar.

Altstötter was found guilty of membership of a criminal organization, the SS, with knowledge of its illegal activities, but acquitted of other crimes. He served a full five-year prison sentence. With his membership of the SS established, the law report identified the central factual issue on which he was convicted: "The remaining fact to be decided," said the Tribunal, "was whether he had knowledge of the criminal activities of the SS."[1] The prosecution had to prove that Altstötter knew about the SS's criminal activities, and as a first step they invoked his professional background and his rank to conclude that "no person of the defendant's intelligence, and one who had received the rank of Oberführer in the SS, could have been unaware of its illegal activities."[2]

The Tribunal had to go further, however, and look at Altstötter's actual activities, his professional functions as a lawyer. They noted his job and contacts with high-ranking officials of the SS, and his attendance at conferences of the department chiefs and officials in the Ministry of Justice, "including those in charge of penal matters." That alone was not sufficient, so they examined documents which showed that he "knew of the evacuation of Jews in Austria and had correspondence with the Chief of the Security Police and Security Service regarding witnesses for the Hereditary Biological Courts." As a member of the SS at the time of the November 1938 pogroms, such as *Kristallnacht,* he must "surely" have known of the part played by an organization of which he was an officer, even if he took no part in the slaughter or did not approve.

"As a lawyer," concluded the Tribunal, "he certainly knew that . . . the Jews were turned over to the police and so finally deprived of the scanty legal protection they had heretofore had." He must also have known of the sinister provisions for police confiscation of property on the death of the Jewish owners. Yet despite all this, the Tribunal continued, he maintained friendly relations with the leaders of the SS, including Heinrich Himmler, Ernst Kaltenbrunner and Karl Gebhardt. "He refers to Himmler," the Tribunal noted, "one of the most sinister figures in the Third Reich, as his 'old and trusty friend.'" Altstötter had accepted and retained membership in the SS— its insignia, its rank, its honors, and its contacts with the high figures of the Nazi regime. "Conceding that the defendant did not know of the ultimate mass murders in the concentration camps and by the Einsatzgruppen, he knew the policies of the SS and, in part, its crimes." In the end, the Tribunal established guilt on the basis of his eminent role as a lawyer. "For that price he gave his name as a soldier and a jurist of note and so helped cloak the shameful deed of that organization from the eyes of the German people."

This law report graphically illustrated the extent of the horror perpetrated by the Nazi regime and the extent to which the entire German legal system had been subverted. It also demonstrated the gulf between events in Germany in the 1930s and the prosecution of the war on terror. Drawing analogies between the facts would be absurd, as the U.S. Supreme Court's decision in *Hamdan* showed. Though many observers thought the Supreme Court judgment weak, it showed that the system worked, with an independent judiciary bringing to an end the refusal of rights under the Geneva Conventions for detainees at Guantánamo.

Nevertheless, there were aspects of the reasoning in the *Altstötter* case that still seemed pertinent here, which was why it was being cited to rein in the Administration's lawyers. The law report was thin on detail, so it wasn't easy to understand precisely how the Tribunal had relied on Altstötter's professional role as a government lawyer to conclude that he had actual knowledge of international crimes. It was there—his attendance at meetings, the writing and receiving of correspondence, lending his name as "a jurist of note"—but not spelled out in any detail. I wanted to see the actual pleadings in the case, which were not available in London. I tracked the material to the library of the Holocaust Museum in Washington, D.C. and, with assistance from the helpful librarians, I made my way through thousands of pages of microfiche. The opening and closing arguments were quite full, yet still shorter than I would have imagined. By contrast, modern international criminal trials, like those of Slobodan Milošević or Charles Taylor (the Liberian leader), were deluged with evidence and legal arguments.

But there was interesting material, and two things especially caught my eye. Both concerned responsibility for the *Nacht und Nebel (Night and Fog)* trials, which arose as a result of a directive adopted in 1941 for the abduction and disappearance of thousands of political activists from France, Belgium and the Netherlands and other Nazi-occupied territories. Secret trials had been held before Special Courts and the People's Courts in plain violation of the Hague Conventions and other principles of international law that predated Geneva. Negotiations for the program were commenced between the Justice Ministry and the German High Command (Oberkommando der Wehrmacht [OKW]). The Justice Ministry assumed responsibility for trying the *Nacht und Nebel* cases, after the military's General Rudolf Lehmann objected to the trials on the grounds that they were not justified by military necessity and the secrecy was abhorrent. "For manifold reasons—for reasons of international law, for reasons of justice, and policy of justice, and primarily," Lehmann said, because "the administration of justice should never do anything secretly."[3] "What kind of suspicion would have to arise against our administration of justice," Lehmann asked the representative from the Justice Ministry, "if these people, inhabitants of other countries, brought to Germany, would disappear without a trace?" His lawyers in the military agreed. Lehmann was later convicted in the *High Command Case* (the last of twelve trials for war crimes—of the General of Wehrmacht—for violating international law in a way that gave rise to other international crimes. But on this matter the arguments he put reflected exactly the same concerns that the TJAGs—Rives and Romig—had put to Jim Haynes sixty years later.

The Tribunal rejected the prosecution's claim that Altstötter had knowledge of the crimes associated with *Nacht und Nebel*: without such knowledge he could not have participated. On the other hand, they found that he did have knowledge of the international crimes carried out by the SS, of which he was a member. For that knowledge, and presumably for turning a blind eye, Josef Alstötter was convicted and spent five years in prison, until 1950. He died in 1979.

I wanted to discover more about the evidence relied upon by the Tribunal to establish his knowledge. The trial records show that one of Altstötter's advisers was Dr. Ludwig Altstötter, and a retired lawyer of that name still lived in Nuremberg. I contacted him through a partner at his old law firm and received a letter from Ludwig Altstötter, Josef's son. The older Dr. Ludwig Altstötter had been Josef's younger brother, a Notary Public in Bamberg, who had worked with his father's main counsel, Dr. Hermann

Orth. In his letter the younger Ludwig said that he had copies of all the Tribunal documents, and his father's correspondence. These materials contained much that was private but he would welcome a visit if I would undertake to treat the materials objectively and fairly. "The reason for this condition," he wrote, "is that the [Tribunal's] judgment is a misjudgment from my point of view and from the point of view of everybody who is familiar with the case of my father, as [it] violates basic principles of a constitutional legal system." In his letter he drew a parallel with the proposed military tribunals for the Guantánamo detainees, which, he wrote, "seem increasingly to violate the basic principles of a constitutional legal system." He was unaware that the Supreme Court had agreed with him, in the *Hamdan* judgment, and ended on a cautious note. "I am aware that I will not be heard or maybe even will be attacked as I am the son of a 'culprit.'"

A few weeks later I flew to Nuremberg, and made my way to Ludwig Altstötter's office, with Mirja Trilsch, a doctoral student from Berlin who had agreed to serve as my interpreter. Ludwig Altstötter greeted me with a big smile. He had a cherubic, rosy face and a great deal of white hair for a man in his mid-seventies. He looked like a man who enjoyed life.

On a table he'd set out several piles of documents: transcripts, orders, correspondence, newspaper articles, and photographs of the trial. One showed his father in the famous Nuremberg courtroom, suited and bespectacled, seated amongst a group of seven noted jurists. He sat in the second row of the defendant's dock, attentive, his head turned as Franz Schlegelberger addressed the tribunal. His hands were folded before him, resting on a book on his lap. He looked serene.

Ludwig Altstötter recalled the father he knew: his distinguished academic record, his success at university exams at the law faculties in Munich and Erlangen, awards of a stipend, a great honor in those days. He had served in the First World War, then had worked as a sole practitioner before becoming a judge. He had started in the higher local courts and briefly worked in the prosecutor's office. As a professional he was a prestigious and senior figure in society.

Ludwig was born in 1934. His father was frequently away from home during his early childhood, first as a soldier on the front from 1939, then in Berlin at the Justice Ministry from 1943, then in War Criminal Prison No. 1 in Landsberg, Bavaria. Ludwig saw him rarely and only once visited him in Berlin. Had he been curious about what his father was doing? He didn't remember any conversation with his father about his professional activities. Just before the end of the war the young Ludwig started high school in

Leipzig, where they lived. After the war ended his father came home on a bicycle, since there was no other means of transport from Berlin, some 300 kilometers away. Shortly afterward his father was arrested by the Americans. "He was arrested in the family home, I was present," he said without emotion. It was no surprise. His father had suspected he would face trouble, having filled out a questionnaire on all positions he held. "It was rather clear in the family because, you know, he held that position in the Ministry of Justice as a Director, and he had also provided the information in the questionnaire that he was a member of the SS." "The common SS," Ludwig took pains to point out, "not the Waffen SS." He returned to this distinction frequently during our conversation. The family wasn't shocked by the arrest. They were children of the war; they'd lived through the air bombardments of Leipzig. "We were not that sensitive any more to catastrophes." After his arrest the family moved down to Landshut, Bavaria, to live with Ludwig's uncle, about 180 kilometers southeast of Nuremberg.

The trial remained vivid for Ludwig, although he never attended any of the hearings. "It lasted all the way through to 1947, and the hearing against my father took place in September 1947." The family was convinced that Josef would be found not guilty. "My mother kept writing letters to my father saying, you haven't done anything, so I'm waiting here for you, I know you are going to be back soon, you haven't done anything. We expected him to be free after the trial." When the judgment finally came in December 1947 the family was unable to comprehend what had happened. Sixty years later, Ludwig was convinced his father had done no wrong. He was a lawyer doing his job, he had never been actively involved with the SS. Ludwig was familiar with all the details of the judgment: there had been a clear miscarriage of justice. "My father was a person full of integrity and honesty and he would have never succumbed to those kind of . . ." His voice trailed off.

Ludwig visited his father only once while he was in jail, with his mother, for an hour. "When I entered I saw my father cleaning the hallway with the broom. It was unusual to see my father doing household chores. At home he didn't even know where to find the salt." After his father was released he went through the process of denazification, which was necessary to rejoin the bar. The family returned to Nuremberg, and Altstötter joined the law office of Dr. Orth, his defense lawyer, where he worked for the rest of his life. They rarely talked about the trial. "Every once in a while it would become an issue at home, and basically what was said was that five years of his life were stolen." Ludwig had pressed his father to do something about the judgment—but he never did.

Josef Altstötter, Circa 1945–46

Our conversation focused largely on the one count on which Altstötter was convicted, namely membership of the "common SS." "There was not sufficient evidence for the other points," Ludwig explained. "In the Ministry he worked on private law matters, not on criminal law matters, so he was not involved in making those laws that would persecute people."

Six decades on, Ludwig was still perplexed about how someone's professional position could, in itself, give rise to criminal responsibility. As far as he was concerned the two departments in the Justice Ministry—private law and criminal law—worked independently and separately of each other. "Political decisions were channeled toward the criminal law department, and my father was never involved in that," Ludwig insisted. "He didn't have any knowledge, there were affidavits saying he did not have knowledge of all those groups and acts." Ludwig handed me one of the trial documents. It was a chart showing the organization of Section VI of the Justice Ministry in 1944.[4] At the top of the tree sat Dr Altstötter, the Ministerialdirektor. The directorates for which he was responsible included Subdepartment B, which was concerned with Family Law and Racial Law (Rasserecht). One of the Units under that subdepartment dealt with legislation for the protection of the German blood. During his trial Altstötter had claimed that the term "race" was a general term and did not specifically refer to Jews.[5]

The Tribunal decided otherwise, but Ludwig thought they had got the evidence wrong. "The judges say they know this, but where from?" He referred to his father's affidavits, as well as the affidavits of others that had been tendered on his behalf. One, he said, was from a Jewish lady in Berlin who said he was a fine man who, like her, did not know about the camps. "My father did not have knowledge." He was shocked when he learned about the concentration camps. "He always stressed that he did not know about that."

Ludwig was exercised by factual errors in the Tribunal's judgment. They said he was given the golden pin of the SS, which was not true. He did receive an award during the war, and it happened to be golden, but it was not what it was said to be in the judgment. And the silver medal he was awarded came not from the Nazi party or the SS, but was a medal he had received for having served twenty-five years as a civil servant for the state. Of course I was not in a position to identify the truth in these points of detail; all I could do was listen and note Ludwig's passionate insistence.

The conversation shifted direction, to his father's attitude. Had he ever expressed regret at being a member of the SS? Ludwig didn't really answer the question. His father told him that membership was basically thrown at him, he hadn't sought it out. But did he express any regret for his membership in the SS, or his involvement in the Ministry of Justice, or anything else? "He didn't feel that he had done anything wrong," came the answer, "he didn't feel guilty for anything." I wondered if he had expressed regret about what others who were close to him had done. Ludwig was reluctant even to address this question. "Those contacts were completely innocent," he replied. The judgment had said that his father knew Himmler, that they were close friends. "The fact is that Himmler and my father came from the same city, which was Landshut, and that's how they knew each other, but they'd seen each other maybe three times and it was all completely innocent."

I understood that he was unhappy with the judgment, but was there not some part of him, the lawyer in him, that raised the question: how could my father, an educated and honorable man, a religious man, serve as one of the most senior legal advisers in a government that was so obviously discriminating and acting in ways that were widely known and notorious? "Until 1943 my father was a soldier," he replied, "he was at the frontline, in Russia, so he was probably not informed about what was going on." He paused. "In the 1930s people knew what was going on, people knew what Hitler was doing," I said quietly. "I didn't know what my father's position on that was, because he was a civil law judge, and I wouldn't know how far he considered it, knew and thought about that. You are bringing me back to what my father knew," said Ludwig. "My father was a religious person and he, in every way, adhered to the law. He was very correct in everything he did and very, you know, rightful." Adhering to the law in Nazi Germany meant doing things that today would not be acceptable. "There was a system," he replied. "If we would go that far, then 80 or 90 percent of Germans would have ended up in prison, because it was common knowledge that discriminatory laws existed."

I suggested we look more closely at the judgment. I read out the most striking passage. "He gave his name as a soldier and a jurist of note and helped to cloak the shameful deeds of that organization from the eyes of the German people." Ludwig listened. "In order to help you must know that you are helping something," he suggested, "and if you don't know what's happening, how can you be helping?" It was not right to draw conclusions from somebody's position. If you believed in the rule of law you needed evidence for somebody's guilt, proper evidence. In finding him guilty on a single charge, the Tribunal had referred to some correspondence. I had not been able to find copies, and Ludwig now went through the piles and produced the three letters, the originals, in German. Mirja helped me with the translations.

The first was a letter dated May 3, 1944.[6] It came from the Chief of the Security Police and the Sicherheitsdienst (SD), the intelligence service of the SS. Requests had been received from the Regional Court of Vienna concerning the whereabouts of certain Jews who had initiated legal proceedings for the purposes of "hereditary examination" to establish that they weren't Jews. The Vienna Court wanted them to appear as witnesses. However, wrote the Chief, these people had been "evacuated to the East or sent to Theresienstadt." The Regional Court of Vienna had been repeatedly advised that these requests could not be met for "security reasons"; nevertheless, they persisted in making the request. "The Jews had the time and the opportunity to clarify the circumstances of their descent, the procedures for descent verification brought forward by the Jews generally and from experience only serve to conceal their descent in order to defy the measures planned or executed against them by the Security Police." So the Chief of the SD wrote to Altstötter to "request that the Regional Court of Vienna be asked to refrain from making such requests in the future," on grounds of security and "in the interest of the urgent handling of war-related matters."

A month later, on June 3, came Josef Altstötter's response to the President of the Higher Regional Court in Vienna.[7] "For security reasons, these requests cannot be granted," he wrote, "even if the interrogation of these Jews may often help to thwart concealment tactics." He told the Court's President that he was intending to make further dispositions about the handling of the descent cases of Jews and half-Jews in a Reich Decree. Altstötter then set out his decision: "For Jews who have been deported to Theresienstadt or other locations, the questioning as a witness or a hereditary examination is not possible for security reasons, because accompanying personnel and means of transportation are not available. Therefore, if the registration office or any other police department provides the information that a Jew has been deported, all other inquiries about his whereabouts as well as about his appearance, interrogation or examination, are redundant. Rather, it is to be assumed that the Jew is not available for the taking of evidence."

As Mirja read this last part she looked at me and I looked at her. We said nothing.

The Court was therefore instructed not to direct any questions to police departments about the whereabouts of deported Jews. "Should there be a public interest in individual cases that the taking of evidence be made possible through the exceptional employment of accompanying personnel and means of transportation," wrote Altstötter, "I request to report to me and to demonstrate the importance of the case." The lot of the evacuated Jews looked pretty unambiguous, as did the interference with the functioning of an independent court. But perhaps that was only with the benefit of hindsight. "He did not know that," said Ludwig, returning to the fate of the Jews. He picked up the letters. The correspondence had been misunderstood by the Tribunal. "From the correspondence you can only tell that Jews were deported from Vienna for reasons of security, but these Jews could at the request of the Ministry of Justice be interrogated as witnesses, so basically that [Tribunal's] statement is incomplete." His father had appealed on that point, but the application failed. "The letter said that the Jews could be interrogated as witnesses, that indicated for my father that nothing inhuman was going to happen to them, so it was a normal procedure for him." That could be one reading, I thought, but not the obvious one.

We moved to the third and final letter, which had been written three days later. It was from Altstötter to SS-Group Leader General Lieutenant of the Waffen, Professor Dr. Karl Gebhardt. "I read in the press that the Führer has awarded you with the *Ritterkreuz zum Kriegsverdienstkreuz mit Schwerten* [Knight's Cross to the War Cross of Merit with Swords]," he wrote. This was an award that was bestowed on only a few "especially eminent men." "I am particularly pleased about your award," Altstötter continued, "because I see it as a recognition of your great war achievements not only as a doctor and a surgeon, but also as a scientist and an organizer, that has been intended for my old and trusty friend."[8]

The Tribunal relied on this letter as evidence of Altstötter's knowledge. "He refers to Himmler, one of the most sinister figures in the Third Reich, as his 'old and trusty friend,'" wrote the judges. Ludwig cited this as an example of the Tribunal's error: his father's letter had referred to Gebhardt in those terms, not Himmler, but that oversight ceased to be so significant as I learned more about Karl Gebhardt. One-time President of the German Red Cross and personal physician to Himmler, he was hanged on June 2, 1948 in Landsberg prison, where Josef Altstötter was serving his sentence. Gebhardt had been the doctor who led the medical experiments on inmates at Ravensbrück and Auschwitz concentration camps.

Altstötter had made various appeals, all of which failed. In 1948 Dr. Orth wrote to Charles LaFollette, who led the American prosecution team, asking him to intercede in a pardon application. Dr. Orth cited the inadequacy of the evidence on which the Tribunal had relied. "I cannot agree with your interpretation of the evidence," LaFollette responded. "I state to you very frankly that if I were asked to approve a request for pardon for Herr Altstötter I would not do so." LaFollette took this position as a lawyer, he added, evaluating the evidence. "He was simply convicted on evidence which I consider justified his conviction and, by my standards, that ends the matter."[9]

A few months after we met Ludwig sent me a lengthy, handwritten letter, setting out his father's virtues in over forty pages. Like many other Germans, Ludwig believed his father was a "follower" without criminal intentions; he was convicted by a military tribunal that lacked legitimacy. The situation was fundamentally different from that relating to Guantánamo. The American lawyers were "well informed about the undertakings of the Bush regime and could base their decisions on that information, whereas my father knew nothing about the actions of the Nazi regime." He concluded by expressing the hope that I would "do his father's personality and aspirations justice."

This left me in a slightly difficult position. Although it was plain to me that Ludwig was genuine and honest in his belief, I could do no more than lay out the material, and leave it to speak for itself. It was clear that in one, important sense Doug Feith was right. What had happened in Washington in 2002 bore no comparison with what had occurred sixty years earlier in

Nuremberg. Yet it wasn't quite that simple. In both cases the lawyers had carried out their functions, boxed in by the immediacies of the situation and political imperatives. Security was the principle invoked by Alberto Gonzales, Jay Bybee, John Yoo and Jim Haynes; for Josef Altstötter, in his correspondence with the Viennese court, it was "security reasons."

The trawl through the *Altstötter* case had shed some light, however. It had identified the standard applied by the U.S. military tribunal where the application or enforcement of a rule had resulted in the violation of an international criminal law. What had to be shown to establish wrongdoing was that the lawyer had participated in the development, application or enforcement of a rule, and had done so in the knowledge that it would violate international law, or at least that he had proceeded recklessly. Knowledge was the key, necessity was the trap.

26

The *Altstötter* case prompted me to consider how a case debating the role of the lawyer would be treated today. To answer that question I needed to speak to a prosecutor.

The idea of talking to a judge and a prosecutor came to me as I read a web blog written by Lawrence Wilkerson, who was Colin Powell's Chief of Staff at the State Department in 2002, at the time that the Haynes memo was being drafted. He and Powell were cut out of the decision-making on the new interrogation techniques, but he had strong views, especially on the role of the lawyers. Wilkerson thought there was insufficient evidence to walk into an American courtroom and win a legal case on war crimes, but an international courtroom "might feel differently." "There is enough evidence for a soldier of long service, someone like me with 31 years in the Army," he wrote "to know that what started with John Yoo, David Addington, Alberto Gonzales, William Haynes at the Pentagon, and several others, all under the watchful and willing eye of the Vice President, went down through the Secretary of Defense to the commanders in the field," resulting in the violation of longstanding practice and law.[1] I traveled to the capital of a European country, a NATO member, for a meeting with a judge experienced in international criminal cases. We were joined by a prosecutor. As both asked me to keep their identities confidential, I will refer to them as the Judge and the Prosecutor.

Now, spread out on a table before me and the Judge and the Prosecutor were the key documents that Wilkerson might have had in mind: Common Article 3 of the Geneva Conventions, the key provisions of the Torture Convention, President Bush's decision on Geneva, the Haynes's memo, signed by Donald Rumsfeld with his "why is standing limited to 4 hours?" question, and the list of eighteen techniques. In addition, we had Mike Dunlavey's request, Diane Beaver's legal advice, the OLC legal

memos written by John Yoo and Jay Bybee, Mohammed al-Qahtani's interrogation log and Dr. Seltzer's medical conclusions pointing to torture.
The judgment in the *Altstötter* case and a photograph of Dr. Altstötter sitting in the dock in the famous Nuremberg courtroom completed our
dossiers. Of the mug shot of Dr. Altstötter, the judge observed, "He looks
like Mr. Rumsfeld."

The premise for our conversation was that al-Qahtani's interrogation
violated the requirements of Common Article 3, that he was subjected to
cruel treatment and torture, as well as "outrages upon personal dignity."
Those responsible for these actions had violated the Geneva Conventions,
an international crime, and would be subject to investigation and, if appropriate, penal sanctions. I wanted to know from the Judge and the Prosecutor whether the lawyers who had authorized these actions could be subject
to criminal investigation. Would they be at risk of prosecution if they traveled internationally, to face the same fate as Senator Pinochet?

The Judge picked up the Haynes memo and examined it closely. Who
exactly is William J. Haynes II, he asked, pointing to the name of the author of the memo. What does it mean to be General Counsel? I explained
that he was the most senior lawyer in the Pentagon, the person who gave
legal advice directly to the Secretary of Defense. As a matter of practice
within the Pentagon, asked the Judge, was he the one who approved the
techniques of interrogation as being lawful? He was, I answered. And how
had he concluded, asked the Judge, that the application of these techniques
was not an "outrage upon personal dignity," or "cruel," or even "torture,"
within the meaning of Common Article 3? I explained that President Bush
had decided that Common Article 3 could not be invoked by the Guantánamo detainees, and hence Mr. Haynes had felt no need to ask himself the
question.

The Prosecutor intervened. Was Mr. Haynes involved in the President's decision on Common Article 3? He was, I replied. Did he support
that decision? My understanding was that he did, I responded. The Prosecutor looked at the Judge, the Judge looked at me, I looked at the Haynes
memo. There was silence as they reflected.

Then the Judge spoke. "My point of view," he said, "is that when you
take the application of the prohibitions on torture and other acts in the
Torture Convention and the Geneva Conventions, then it is clear that the
lawyer who advises has a positive obligation to denounce the abusive acts
and take steps to ensure the proper treatment of the victim." He proceeded
to explain that the whole thrust of the human rights norms that had been

adopted after the Second World War, and the emergence of the doctrine of universal jurisdiction, which meant that there would be no refuge for the torturer or the international criminal, was to impose duties on every person who was involved in the decision-making process.

I took them to Article 4 of the Torture Convention. It criminalizes an act by any person that constitutes "complicity or participation" in torture. Was it their opinion that the giving of legal advice, or signing off on the legality of techniques that the lawyer knew would be used on a particular detainee, would amount to complicity or participation? I asked the question because the Geneva Conventions had no equivalent provision. The Prosecutor got out of her chair, went to the bookshelf, lifted a volume and brought it back to where we were sitting. She had a copy of her country's criminal code. She took me me to the relevant provision and read it out loud. "It is quite clear," she said, "that the lawyer who gives such legal advice is not treated as an accomplice, it is as though he is the author of the act." So in theory he could be criminally responsible under your country's application of Geneva or the Torture Convention, I inquired. I explained that under English law the fact that a criminal statute was silent on accomplices or accessories was not likely to be relevant, since that kind of responsibility would be read into the law. "Not in theory," she responded, "but in reality, because the lawyer has the same responsibility as the interrogator." The Judge agreed. The lawyer had a responsibility—the same responsibility—because he acted with the decision-maker. This was a long-established principle, it went back to Roman law.

Would this principle ensnare the authors of the OLC legal memos, like John Yoo and Jay Bybee, and the author of the Haynes memo? They didn't see why not. If the legal advices they wrote had opened the door to abuse or even torture and the use of techniques of interrogation on specific individuals, then in theory the responsibility would go back to the author of the legal advice on which the General Counsel and the decision-maker had relied.

Did it make any difference that these facts were limited to a single detainee over a period of fifty-four days, rather than to many detainees over many years? It didn't matter at all, said the Judge. Assuming the facts were established, assuming the interrogation was abusive and violated Common Article 3 or the Torture Convention, it made no difference that only one victim was involved. An international crime was an international crime; if the evidence was there it had to be investigated and, depending on the facts, prosecuted.

So would the Judge investigate, and the Prosecutor prosecute, in a case such as this? There would be some prerequisites, said the Judge. For crimes of universal jurisdiction, which may include war crimes under Geneva, they would not investigate or prosecute until the country in which the crime occurred had had a chance to exercise jurisdiction. They would prefer to wait and see if the United States investigated or prosecuted, since all the lawyers involved were based in the United States.

There had been a number of investigations of the alleged abuses at Guantánamo, but I thought them rather half-hearted. The Pentagon had commissioned a report from vice Admiral Albert Church. In March 2005 a summary was published[2] but the full report has never been made public. The Church report assumed that FM 34–52 was "inadequate," that the techniques recommended by the Haynes memo were not abusive. Church had no mandate to consider compatibility with Common Article 3 or the Torture Convention, and he concluded that the interrogations were "sufficiently aggressive" to highlight the difficult question of "precisely defining the boundaries of humane treatment of detainees,"[3] but there was no suggestion that al-Qahtani's interrogation had crossed that line. Church reported that DoD officials and senior military commanders responsible for interrogation policy "evidenced the intent to treat detainees humanely" and that this was inconsistent with abuse being permissible.[4] The Guantánamo interrogators "closely adhered" to the new interrogation policies, and in only a small number of cases of abuse did the interrogators exceed the bounds of approved policy.[5] Since the interrogation log wasn't public when Church's report was published, people couldn't form their own view.

Three months later, in June 2005, the Army published a report by Lieutenant General Randall M. Schmidt and Brigadier General John T. Furlow on specific FBI allegations of abuse at Guantánamo, including in respect of Detainee 063.[6] The report took "DoD guidance" (in other words, the Haynes memo on the eighteen techniques) as the standard against which the review would be carried out. The Schmidt-Furlow report did not "review the legal validity of the various interrogation techniques . . . approved by the Secretary of Defense." The use of a dog was fine because it had been approved,[7] so was straddling and invasion of the detainee's space by a female interrogator.[8] Yelling and loud music were authorized, and Detainee 063's sleep deprivation required no action because it was "an authorized interrogation technique approved by SECDEF." Even temperature adjustment by use of the air conditioner required no action. The Schmidt-Furlow report found no evidence that

Detainee 063 was physically assaulted, and rejected a number of factual allegations. There was no corroborated evidence to show that he was forced to stand for extended periods or that he was threatened with homosexual rape. If water was regularly poured on his head it was done "as a control measure only." There was no evidence that showed humiliation intentionally directed at his religion, although he may have interpreted many of the techniques this way. Therefore they found no torture.

The Schmidt-Furlow report identified facts that did raise concerns, however. On December 6 al-Qahtani was forced to wear a woman's bra and had a thong placed on his head. On December 17 he was told that his mother and sister were whores and that he was a homosexual and other detainees knew about these tendencies. On December 20 a leash was tied to his chains and he was led around the room and forced to perform a series of dog tricks. He was also forced to dance with a male interrogator. Also in December he was strip-searched and, on one occasion, forced to stand naked for five minutes with females present. On three occasions he was prevented from praying during interrogation. On another occasion two copies of the Koran were put on a TV, and at another time an interrogator "unintentionally" squatted over his Koran. On seventeen occasions interrogators poured water over his head.

The report found that many of these techniques were used in an effort to establish complete control over Detainee 063, to create "the perception of futility and reduce his resistance to interrogation." Schmidt and Furlow found that the interrogators "believed that they were acting within existing guidance" and that every technique employed against Detainee 063 was "legally permissible."[9] Nevertheless, Schmidt and Furlow concluded that a line was crossed, that the coercive, aggressive and persistent interrogation "resulted in the cumulative effect being degrading and abusive treatment." The authors were troubled by "the combined impact of the 160 days of segregation from other detainees, 48 of 54 consecutive days of 18- to 20-hour interrogations, and the creative application of authorized interrogation techniques." In this context, the use of a leash, thong and bra, the insults to the detainee's mother and sister, and being strip-searched and forced to stand naked in front of a female interrogator was "abusive and degrading," even if it did not rise to the level of prohibited "inhumane treatment." They found that the Commander of JTF-GTMO, Major General Geoffrey Miller, had failed to monitor and supervise the interrogation of al-Qahtani and this allowed subordinates "to make creative decisions in an environment requiring extremely tight controls."

In their report, Schmidt and Furlow also recommended that Miller should be held accountable and admonished.[10] On their way to see Donald Rumsfeld they met for an hour and a half with General Bantz J. Craddock, who had succeeded General Hill as Commander of SOUTHCOM. "We went in and General Craddock . . . told me that he disagreed with my recommendations and finding on General Miller," Schmidt said, "and he said we agree to disagree."[11] Craddock had been Rumsfeld's Senior Military Assistant when Rumsfeld had signed the Haynes memo. Craddock later told the Armed Services Committee that he had rejected Schmidt's recommendation because al-Qahtani's interrogation "did not result in any violation of a U.S. law or policy."[12] He was, in effect, protecting himself and his old boss. No further action was taken.

I was in good company in feeling that this inquiry was inadequate. One of the strongest critics of Craddock's decision to reject Schmidt's recommendation was Senator John McCain. "I hold no brief for the prisoners," he said, "but I do hold a brief for the reputation of the United States of America as to adhering to certain standards of treatment of people, no matter how evil or terrible they might be.[13]

The investigations were a whitewash.

Beyond that, as I explained to the Judge and the Prosecutor, in November 2006 President Bush signed the Military Commissions Act, which created a new defense to alleged breaches of Common Article 3 for government employees where the misconduct concerned the "detention and interrogation of aliens" between September 11, 2001 and December 30, 2005. "So it created an immunity?" asked the Prosecutor. In effect, I replied. "That is very stupid," she added ominously.

Both the Judge and the Prosecutor said that made matters ominously clearer. Legislation creating such an immunity would allow the crime to be covered up: it was almost an admission that a crime had occurred. The Judge leaned over and took the piece of paper on which I was writing. He wrote out two words: *"pactum scaelaris,"* meaning an "evil pact." Referring again to the Criminal Code, to that part which showed that contributing to the avoidance of an investigation of a crime could itself give rise to complicity, he said. "If the facts are as you say then I have an obligation to intervene in this case."

So, I asked, if Mr. Haynes visited your country, would he face any risk of investigation or prosecution? "I can act on my own initiative," said the Judge, "it is possible that I can intervene, but it is not necessary that I do so, since always it depends on the facts." And of course, he added, if I issue a warrant it is effective all over the world. Then he smiled and looked at me. "Except in the United States."

The politics were difficult: the Haynes memo and its consequences involved senior people at the upper echelons of government in the most powerful country in the world. We had now crossed the line from law into realpolitik. We talked about cases in which investigations had been commenced but no one had yet been arrested. In 2004 and 2005, arrest warrants were issued in Italy for twenty-two alleged CIA operatives said to be involved in abducting an Egyptian cleric off the streets of Milan, while in Spain arrest warrants were issued against three American soldiers alleged to have been involved in the killing of a Spanish journalist.15

The Judge and the Prosecutor were already examining the issue of extraordinary rendition, although at this stage, only in relation to the potential criminal responsibility of nationals of their own country, not Americans.

"It's a matter of time," said the Judge, "these things take time." I gathered the papers. "And then something unexpected happens, when one of these lawyers travels to the wrong place."

27

The name of the lawyer that kept cropping up—literally with everyone I met—was that of Jim Haynes. While he didn't seem to be the legal genius behind the aggressive interrogation, an accolade most likely claimed by David Addington, he was a constant presence. Early on I wrote to request a meeting. I didn't expect a positive response, having been told that he was of the "David Addington School," which I understood to mean no tracks and no interviews. The big difference of course was that in Haynes's case there was a rather deep track in the form of his memo. A few weeks after my first request I received a letter from Colonel Kelly Wheaton, a Judge Advocate and Hayne's Senior Military Assistant: Mr. Haynes was too busy to meet with me.

I left it there, assuming there was no point in trying again, until General Myers told me he'd seen Haynes shortly before we met and told him of our meeting. "I've recommended Jim talk to you," Myers said, "call his office, ask him." So I wrote again, in hope rather than expectation, to offer "a further opportunity" to consider whether he might meet with me to share his perspectives. A month later a more promising email arrived from Colonel Wheaton. Mr. Haynes had not forgotten about my request but hadn't yet decided whether to make himself available. A few days later, Wheaton followed up with a request that I provide "a better idea" of what I'd like to talk about, including a list of questions. I provided seven, the last one asking whether there were any aspects of his involvement in the eighteen techniques in which he felt particular pride or regret.

Two weeks passed. Then, during my meeting with Dr. Seltzer, an email arrived from the Pentagon. "Mr. Haynes has agreed to meet with you," wrote the press office, "during the last week of June." Another email arrived. "Thanks for your patience," wrote Colonel Wheaton, "looking forward to meeting you." He seemed very decent.

Cynthia Smith in the Pentagon press office wanted to discuss and agree on ground rules for the interview, which we did. She followed up with an email. "Off the record interview. No tape recording. Quotes may be used if authorized by GC prior to publication." I understood and wrote back to accept. "What type of book are you writing?" she asked. "A good and serious book, I hope," I replied, "it's about lawyers and the war on terror."

I had a couple of weeks to prepare for the meeting and tried to find out as much as I could, wanting to be as fair as possible. My meetings with Diane Beaver had changed my impression of her and of her role. But Haynes had written almost nothing and given few published speeches, although he'd appeared before various Senate committees. So I was left with the notes of my interviews with others, in which he had made frequent appearances. I also spoke with several people who worked closely with him.

Haynes had followed a well-trodden path. He was born in Waco, Texas, in 1958 and attended Davidson College, a small liberal arts school in North Carolina with a strong Presbyterian tradition. Like Diane Beaver, he had paid his way through college with an ROTC Scholarship. He graduated from Harvard Law School in 1983, and then returned to North Carolina to clerk for Judge James McMillan, a federal judge appointed by President Johnson in 1968. Judge McMillan was probably a tad too liberal for Haynes, but Haynes learned much from him, including aphorisms he liked to wheel out. "Never attribute to malice that which can be attributed to stupidity" was one. "Government has no rights, only responsibilities" was another.[1] Someone who knew him well told me he thought of himself as an idealistic kind of person. Another who worked closely with him in the Bush Administration said he was "not a deep thinker" and had "no reputation as an intellectual." Yet another thought he rather liked the responsibilities of an office that made him the "chief legal officer of a large corporation." The extent of his dependence on David Addington was a constant theme.

From 1984 to 1989 he was in the Army, rising to the rank of captain, and spent time working at the Pentagon. In 1989 George H. W. Bush was elected President and Haynes became politically active. Bush senior appointed him General Counsel to the Army, where he remained until 1993. At this time Dick Cheney was Secretary of Defense and David Addington was his Special Assistant and then General Counsel. During the Clinton years, Haynes worked for General Dynamics Corporation, a major defense contractor, and as a partner in the law firm of Jenner & Block. A lawyer who had dealings with people around Haynes at that time told me he'd heard that he wouldn't have made partner at Jenner & Block "but for his very impressive political connections." "He is not someone who engages deeply," I was told, "his orientation is to furnish his client with what his client wants." An associate lawyer who was at the firm with him described him to me as "fairly light" as a lawyer but a "nice and moderate guy." Courteous, polite and friendly were descriptions used by almost everyone I spoke with. "I like him personally," a former JAG said, "a person that is one on one a decent individual, I just don't know what drove him, whether it was ambition or weakness or whether there was an ideological part to it, given his association with the Federalist Society." When Mike Gelles met him, which was much later, he was "respectful, polite, corporate, listened." Several people told me he was deeply religious, a born-again Christian.

Haynes became DoD General Counsel in 2001. "Haynes was chosen by Rumsfeld to help transform the military," said John Yoo, who worked closely with him after 9/11. According to Yoo, Haynes saw his mission as "preserving the Defense Department's legal and policy options and the prerogatives of his boss, Secretary Donald Rumsfeld."[2] Haynes advised Rumsfeld, who wouldn't let "modern day shibboleths stand in the way of vital national security goals."[3] Rumsfeld knew he was the kind of lawyer who would help his client, not put up obstacles. And, of course, Haynes was a protégé of David Addington, who had helped secure that powerful position for him.[4] In the 1990s, when Haynes was General Counsel to the Army, Addington was Secretary of Defense Dick Cheney's General Counsel. Rumsfeld would have known about Haynes's track record during that time, seeking to rein in the military lawyers, and trying, as former Army TJAG General Romig told me, to "subordinate the Army TJAG to the General Counsel of the Army." Haynes was reliable, a logical choice, a safe pair of hands, who would seek to concentrate legal power in the service of his client. His confirmation hearings raised no real issues.

Haynes spent most of September 11 at Rumsfeld's side and in the days that followed he was intimately involved in many of the most important decisions on President Bush's war on terror. They asked themselves what they would do if they started capturing al-Qaeda personnel. In October 2002 he gave a speech to the Federalist Society, in which he described October 7, 2001 as a key day on which important decisions were made, "the beginning of the United States' kinetic response to the treacherous attacks of 9/11." That day they had posed for a photographer around Rumsfeld's famous stand-up desk. "Not a one of us is sitting down in *any* of the pictures," Haynes assured his audience; in fact the Pentagon's staff did "very little sitting down." "Why is standing limited to 4 hours," Rumsfeld had scrawled on the Haynes memo, a few weeks later. What is it with the standing thing, I wondered?

In his speech to the Federalist Society, Haynes focused on the detention of al-Qaeda operatives, a subject that concentrated his mind. Although he said nothing about interrogations in that speech, there were some clues to his approach in the days before Dunlavey's request reached his desk. He echoed the contents of the notorious statement that Admiral Jacoby had prepared for the Padilla case three months later, making it clear that detainees should have no access to lawyers. This would threaten national security by interfering with "ongoing efforts to gather and evaluate intelligence about the enemy." He invoked al-Qaeda's Manchester training manual, a "chilling document" that should be read by every American.[5]

Before September 11, Haynes had joined Rumsfeld and Wolfowitz in pushing for streamlined legal advice, making the military lawyers subordinate to an all-powerful General Counsel. General Myers had resisted that effort, but he could not prevent the post-September 11 changes in which Haynes played a leading role. In the days after the attacks Haynes's mentor David Addington dominated early discussions, concluding that the criminal justice system couldn't handle the new paradigm of terrorism, so a warfare model was needed.[6] One participant at a White House Situation Room meeting a few days after September 11th recalled that "if you favored international law, you were in danger of being called 'soft on terrorism' by Addington." Haynes, too, supported that approach and had no time for interrogations being unduly constrained by international rules. The war paradigm did away with a criminal law approach and gave the President "the authority to detain enemy combatants until the war is over," Haynes told the Federalist Society, and the policy of detention was justified "to collect information about the enemy."[7] Detention became a means to an end, whatever Geneva said.

Haynes understood Common Article 3 would limit the methods used to collect information. He followed the "good work" being done at his alma mater on "highly coercive interrogations" and spoke approvingly of the work of Professor Philip Heymann of Harvard Law School.[8] "Military necessity can sometimes allow . . . warfare to be conducted in ways that might infringe on the otherwise applicable articles of the convention," Haynes said of Geneva, speaking in June 2004. He provided no support for that claim, and he could not. In effect, he created out of thin air a new rule that might allow cruelty or torture where none previously existed.⁹

From all I had picked up it was clear that Haynes stood four-square behind the treatment of al-Qahtani. I looked for material that pointed the other way, that might indicate he had tried to put the brakes on, but found none. Haynes wanted Geneva out of the picture, and in January and February 2002 he played a key role in fashioning the President's decision on the Geneva Conventions. Doug Feith told me that Haynes had agreed on his approach to Geneva, that it shouldn't be available to any Guantánamo detainees. Shortly afterward, Haynes interviewed Mike Dunlavey for the position of head of military interrogations at Guantánamo, revealing himself to Dunlavey as a man of limited questions or curiosity.

A few weeks later, Colin Powell's lawyer Will Taft wrote a lengthy memorandum to Haynes, setting out the State Department's view that even if Common Article 3 didn't apply as such, that provision reflected customary international law binding on the United States. "I hope the memorandum will be useful to you," wrote Taft.¹⁰ It wasn't. "You can't send this out," Haynes told Taft, who told me that the real reasons for refusing clearance "may be connected to the fact, unknown to us until much later, that DoJ was developing its own advice on the law without our involvement." Taft's memo obviously made little impression on Haynes. He was however, more sympathetic to other colleagues. The Office of Legal Counsel at the Justice Department was then headed by Haynes's friend Jay Bybee, who in August 2002 wrote the key memos with John Yoo. "If OLC says it's OK then it must be OK," was his approach, General Romig told me, "Jim was tied at the hip with Jay Bybee; he would quote him the whole time."

Alberto Mora the U.S. Navy General Counsel, believed that Haynes "wanted to concentrate all the legal power in his office." In the 1990s he had failed in his effort to make the Army TJAG subordinate to the Army General Counsel. Now he wanted to appoint the Chairman of the Joint Chiefs of Staff's legal adviser, or at least approve the choice, and take complete control over all legal advice. "That would have altered the custom at the Pentagon, in which the Chairman gets independent legal advice," said Mora, "but on that issue General Myers held his ground." DIA Director Vice Admiral Jacoby told me that Jim Haynes had been very focused on intelligence issues and "wanted to control the provision of legal advice on that subject." Keeping close control over legal advice was the modus operandi for Haynes and the other members of the "War Council," so that no one could challenge the failure to provide the normal analysis of counter-arguments and counter-interpretations. At the OLC, Bybee and Yoo not only refused to engage in consultation with State Department and other lawyers with more expertise, they cut them out altogether. At the DoD, on the key interrogation issues Haynes made sure he was always involved and in control, over and above George Pierce, the DIA's General Counsel. "Duplicitous" was one former JAG's characterization of Haynes on this issue. "He tried to buddy up to the military, and while commending them he'd be trying to rein in the TJAGs."

In September 2002, Haynes visited Guantánamo, accompanied by Addington, Gonzales and Rizzo. There he met Mike Dunlavey and Diane Beaver, who described herself as "scared" when she first met him, even if he seemed a "very nice man." It was clear to her that Addington was in charge. Interrogations were discussed, and the visiting lawyers observed at least one. They were particularly interested in al-Qahtani. "They wanted to know what we were doing to get to this guy," Dunlavey told me.

The OLC memos from Bybee and Yoo went to Gonzales and Rizzo, but Haynes knew what they said. John Yoo confirmed that implicitly. He said he thought that only the CIA should be involved in aggressive interrogations, but that "people at the White House and at DoD felt differently," apparently referring to Addington, Gonzales and Haynes. Others were more explicit. Doug Feith said that the decision to proceed on the eighteen techniques "was a thoroughly interagency piece of work for the lawyers, as far as I understood, from day one." General Hill had asked expressly for DoJ approval, and Haynes had told Rumsfeld that "the lawyers who need to review this have reviewed this." General Myers concurred about Haynes's knowledge. "He would be the one who would have known about the Justice effort," he said, referring to an "intrigue" that "was probably occurring between Jim Haynes, White House General Counsel and Justice." Alberto Mora was certain that Haynes was "in the loop" because the detainees were in DoD custody.

By October, Dunlavey's request had reached the Pentagon and Haynes was fully engaged. General Myers's "main interaction" on this subject was with Jane Dalton, General Hill, Rumsfeld and Jim Haynes. He went over the eighteen techniques with Haynes and believed that all the techniques "came out of the book, there weren't any techniques invented." Haynes as General Counsel didn't disabuse him. Doug Feith said that during the key period the authorization of the eighteen techniques were mainly issues for Haynes and Stephen Cambone.

On November 23, Rumsfeld gave the verbal command allowing the aggressive interrogation of al-Qahtani. The go-ahead would not have been given without the support of Haynes, who was preparing his memo at that time, and four days later the memo was sent. He didn't include the caveat that Diane Beaver had recommended, that all proposed interrogations had to undergo legal, medical, behavioral science and intelligence reviews "prior to their commencement." He also concluded that "all Category III techniques may be legally available," including waterboarding. None were ruled out.

In early December, Spike Bowman of the FBI called him to raise concerns about the interrogation of al-Qahtani. "Jim basically blew me off," said Bowman, "he did not want to talk about it at all." Bowman believed that Haynes had sought to control what the lawyers were doing and didn't know whether he listened to anybody else. Bowman didn't think Haynes "was of a mind to say 'no' about anything." You can't unread anything once you've read it, Haynes had said to him on an earlier occasion.

Twice in mid-December, Alberto Mora confronted Haynes with further concerns about detainee abuse. On both occasions Mora found Haynes to be impassive and the aggressive interrogation of al-Qahtani continued for four more weeks. In the middle of January, Mora returned to Haynes and told him that he would send a written memo raising concerns unless Rumsfeld suspended the authorization of al-Qahtani's interrogation. Only after that did Haynes buckle.

In August 2005, Deputy Secretary of Defense Gordon England called a meeting of over thirty senior Pentagon officials to try to agree on a return to Common Article 3. Jim Haynes was reported to be one of only two participants who objected[II]; the other was Stephen Cambone. A former White House official summarized for me the basis of Haynes's objections, to the extent they could be understood. He was worried about the "creep" of international law and believed that a world with fewer legal constraints was generally a good thing, particularly at a time of unpredictable threat when options should be kept open. Haynes was also worried about the vagueness of Common Article 3, and its capacity to give rise to war crimes claims.

When David Addington heard about this initiative, he sided with his protégé and the initiative was killed off. News articles described how Matthew Waxman, who served as Deputy Assistant Secretary of Defense for Detainee Affairs from August 2004 to December 2005 and then moved to the State Department, tried to champion Common Article 3 but that Addington "just ate him for lunch."[12] Addington told Waxman that the vagueness of Common Article 3 would leave U.S. troops timid in the face of unpredictable legal risk and that the President's decision could not be overridden.[13] According to one former Administration official, Addington waved the February 2002 decision on Geneva about and pointed to the President's signature.

Time and again I was told that Addington was the central player in objecting to Common Article 3, strongly supported by a deferential Jim Haynes. A former Administration official explained that Addington and Haynes took "a theological view, which posits that the best way to maximize American power is to increase the flexibility and freedom of movement of the President, so that more latitude means more freedoms." "They fail to appreciate that binding oneself can sometimes strengthen you," the official observed ruefully. It took a judgment of the Supreme Court to override the President and stop Addington and Haynes in their tracks. In June 2006, the Court overturned the Geneva decision and confirmed that all detainees at Guantánamo were entitled to rely on Common Article 3. Haynes was attending a luncheon at the time: another guest reported to me that when he was told the news he went pale, and the lunch ended early. Haynes told a former DoD colleague that the Court's ruling was "a big surprise." The decision had clear implications for Haynes personally, as he knew.

A couple of weeks after the Supreme Court's decision, Haynes appeared before the Senate Judiciary Committee, in hearings on his nomination to be a Court of Appeals judge on the Fourth Circuit. He had an opportunity to set the record straight and move on from his earlier role, but he failed to take it, misjudging the mood. Twenty retired military leaders, including several former Judge Advocate Generals, wrote to the Judiciary Committee to express "profound concern" about the nomination and his role in interrogation policies that had led to the abuse of detainees and "a dangerous abrogation of the military's long-standing commitment to the rule of law." The abandonment of Geneva was a central concern. While Haynes did not bear sole responsibility for the decisions, they wrote, he was "arguably in the strongest position of any other senior government official to sound the alarm" because he had heard the concerns of the uniformed Judge Advocates General. Instead, he "muted these concerns, rather than amplify them."[14]

Another group of retired senior military leaders wrote to the Senate Committee to object to this letter, taking issue with a number of points.[15] In their experience, Haynes had provided thoughtful, rigorous advice on some difficult issues faced by the United States. "He approaches each issue dispassionately, logically, and collegially." A third group joined in to support Haynes, including his former Special Counsel. Jack Goldsmith had frequently come to Haynes's defense, including in a recent book that described his time as a lawyer in government service but which, curiously enough given that the two worked closely at that time, glossed over Jim Haynes's role in the weeks before and after the Haynes memo was written and approved and, even more surprisingly, made no mention of Alberto Mora's approach to law and judgment or Mohammed al-Qahtani.[16]

It may be that Goldsmith was wholly unaware of what was going on, even as Haynes provided him with "an endless stream of fascinating legal problems" to deal with, including the Guantánamo detentions. But to some that will seem improbable, since Goldsmith accompanied members of the "War Council" to Guantánamo in September 2002 and was not shy in defending Jim Haynes before the Judiciary Committee. When aggressive interrogation techniques were first requested in 2002, Goldsmith and others wrote, Haynes recommended "a more limited set than those that had been approved by military lawyers below him." This was a generous interpretation, since Haynes had not rejected any of the techniques, but had merely said of three techniques that "they may be legally available" but blanket approval was not warranted "at this time," for policy reasons. The consequence was that these other techniques, including waterboarding, remained legally available for future use. Interestingly, Goldsmith had an open mind on these techniques, seeing no *a priori* reason to exclude waterboarding or other equally aggressive techniques that were listed in the Bybee II memo. "I didn't affirmatively believe they were illegal," he wrote, "or else I would have stopped them. I just didn't yet know."[17] This same group of supporters also claimed that Haynes had deserved credit for bringing others' concerns to Rumsfeld.[18] Given Alberto Mora's compelling account of events this interpretation is rather unpersuasive.

Haynes had other supporters, and listed some distinguished references. I wrote to a couple to ask whether I might have a copy of their letters. Paula Boggs, the General Counsel of Starbucks, responded with a friendly email saying she'd known Jim Haynes for a long time but had never submitted any written materials on behalf of his nomination. Ruth Wedgwood, Professor of International Law at Johns Hopkins University, also sent a friendly response, after some prodding. "Answer to most everything," she wrote, "is OLC, OLC, OLC, OLC." But what, I thought, of those who were willing to buy into the arguments of the OLC, like Jim Haynes.

Views were obviously divided. I didn't attend the hearing but, like many members of his staff in the General Counsel's office, watched it on C-SPAN, It was an uneasy experience for them. I recognized John Yoo's description of the 'charming, athletic man' who had been compared to James Bond in a legal magazine.[19] He was well turned out in a light grey suit and striped blue tie, his dark hair neatly combed, glasses parked halfway down his nose. The only mannerism I detected was a regular tapping of the right hand on the table. Behind him sat his wife and two of their three children: the experience cannot have been comfortable for them. Early on a woman in the audience started heckling and was removed. The family's dignified manner was admirable.

The session lasted about an hour and a half and most of it was devoted to the Haynes memo. While some senators defended him, the majority engaged in a frenzied attack led by Senator Ted Kennedy and Senator Lindsay Graham who, although a Republican, had been a JAG lawyer and knew all about Geneva. The encounter was bloody and unpleasant, although it did make for gripping television.

Haynes's strategy looked familiar; it was the same as that adopted at the post–Abu Ghraib press conference. The difficulty he faced was that the world had moved on, even if he hadn't. The request to use new techniques came from Guantánamo, he said, from an "aggressive Major General." It was "accompanied by legal review by the Staff Judge Advocate at Guantánamo." They had concluded that the use of stress positions and other techniques was "legal under the circumstances." He didn't seek any other legal advices and none were given. "I do not recall an opinion on this matter from the Legal Counsel for the Chairman of the Joint Chiefs of Staff," Haynes said.[20] He didn't consult with any of the JAGs before signing off. Dunlavey's request was an operational issue concerning interrogation of combatants during war. "I did not believe that it was necessary to coordinate with the TJAGs,"[21] he said.

What about the OLC's Justice Department memos? "No, I did not seek a written opinion from the Department of Justice," he retorted, avoiding the key issue of whether he had knowledge of the contents of the Bybee and Yoo memos before he wrote and then sent his memo. Haynes became nervous: his hands fidgeted anxiously, the glasses slipped further away from the forehead, his responses became ever more terse. "The August 1, 2002 Memorandum was addressed to the then-White House Counsel Alberto Gonzales," he told Senator Arlen Specter. "I did not have a copy of it and I did not shape its legal analysis." No one then posed the logical follow-up question: had he read it or was he otherwise aware of its contents? When we met this would be my central question, and I would be sure to give him every opportunity to answer. But the answer was blindingly clear: given every opportunity to say he didn't know what was in those opinions when he wrote his memo, he failed to do so.

The more persistent the questions on the OLC memos, the more Haynes dodged and weaved, and the more defensive he looked. Senator Graham asked whether Haynes was part of the "architecture team" that came up with the Bybee/Yoo memo. It was not addressed to him, he responded, he did not have a copy and he did not "shape its legal analysis." But not once did he say that he didn't know what was in it at that time. He couldn't admit to knowing the contents of the Bybee/Yoo memo before 27 November because that would make it clear that the OLC's legal advice was relied on in support of the eighteen techniques. The claim that the request came from the bottom up rather than top down would collapse, because the OLC memos predated the request. And Alberto Gonzales's assertion that the memos were "not relied upon by decision-makers" would be shown for what many supposed it to be: a lie. The finger of responsibility for the eighteen techniques would not point to Dunlavey and Beaver, but to Haynes and Rumsfeld, to Addington and Cheney, to Gonzales and Bush, to Bybee and Yoo.

Jim Haynes never admitted to the Committee that he was aware of the contents of the Bybee/Yoo memo. "Yes, he had access to the opinion," Diane Beaver had told me, and "anybody who had a copy of that opinion had to pull it." At one point during his investigation Vice Admiral Church had asked to see it—he wasn't allowed to have a copy. And what about the second Bybee memo the one that signed off on specific techniques, for the CIA? "It was in the office," Beaver told me, "it was kept in the safe." She knew because she had prepared talking points for Jim Haynes. Although she didn't see it herself, even when she worked there, she told me that "if I'd have asked they would have let me read it, but I never asked."

At the hearing meanwhile, Jim Haynes was no less evasive on the other issues.

He declined to consign the Bybee/Yoo memo and its defenses of necessity and self-defense to the rubbish heap. Gonzales would end up agreeing with Goldsmith that the OLC memos "really were as bad as you said."[22] But in front of the senators Haynes was unwilling to go that far. The memo "should not have been requested," was all he said. "It was unnecessary and invited speculation about hypotheticals that need not have been requested."[23] Apparently he had had no immediate difficulty with the memo's legal reasoning, which was adopted more or less verbatim in a later March 2003 memo written by Yoo. Goldsmith later described Haynes's reaction to the decision that the memo should no longer be relied upon: "There was a long silence. "OK, Jack," Haynes eventually replied. "After another silence," Goldsmith wrote, "he asked quite fairly, what was wrong with the opinion."[24]

Before the Judiciary Committee, Haynes dissembled on the Bybee II memo, which had given the green light to the CIA to use specific interrogation techniques. He was not asked whether he was aware of the existence of an opinion from the OLC on specific techniques of interrogation. To answer that question would have been difficult, since Diane Beaver had told me that he had been aware of such a document and that a solitary copy was in the safe in his office when she worked there. No one else was allowed to have a copy.

He waffled on whether any of the interrogation techniques he recommended were "cruel, inhuman or degrading." "I do not believe so," Haynes replied, "certainly not at the time."[25] But what about now? Silence.

He spun on Common Article 3. "The individuals held at Guantánamo are treated in a manner that exceeds the requirements of Common Article 3," he told Senator Leahy.[26] But what about back in December 2002? Silence.

He fudged when he told Senator Feinstein that he did "not believe that the techniques authorized by the Secretary, properly administered, constituted cruel, inhuman and degrading treatment."[27] The caveat was "properly administered."

He misled the committee on waterboarding and other techniques. "In my November 27, 2002 memorandum," he said, "I recommended against the proposed use of a wet towel."[28] In fact he recommended against blanket approval, which was not warranted "at this time." He didn't tell Rumsfeld it was unlawful.

He shafted the "aggressive" Mike Dunlavey, who, he claimed, had "concluded that all of the techniques that he requested do not violate U.S. or international laws."[29] And in so doing he undermined Diane Beaver, who had signed off on Dunlavey's techniques, and who was by now a member of his own staff.

He was inaccurate when he told the Committee that "only a few of the reduced number of techniques approved by the Secretary were actually employed with the twentieth hijacker, Qahtani."[30] I had been through the interrogation log with Dr. Seltzer: all fifteen were used.

He obfuscated over the use of dogs, saying that his understanding was that in "the brief period during which this technique was authorized, the animals were to be merely present, walking security, with muzzles."[31] Had he not read the interrogation log? And if not why not?

And then, finally, a crack appeared. Asked about stress positions and Common Article 3, Haynes said that he didn't have to decide whether they were consistent since that provision didn't apply to members of al-Qaeda or the Taliban.[32] Were stress positions consistent with *FM 34–52?* They were not specifically authorized by the *U.S. Army Field Manual,* said Haynes, so "such a technique would not be permissible." Could forcing an individual to stand, sit or kneel in abnormal positions for prolonged periods of time be physical torture? Yes, he replied, referring to the Conventions, depending on the facts that "constitute physical torture."[33]

There was much more that could have been said. The Senators on the Judiciary Committee seemed unaware that Haynes had interviewed Dunlavey in February 2002 and concurred in the appointment of the man he now referred to as the "aggressive" major general, but whose name he did not mention—or that he had visited Guantánamo in September 2002, accompanied by Gonzales and Addington, and that they had discussed interrogations with Dunlavey and Beaver. They could have questioned him about the decision on aggressive interrogations that followed interagency efforts as a result of which he had knowledge of the contents of the Yoo/Bybee memo, or about the aggressive interrogation of al-Qahtani that began on November 23, 2002. They could have asked if he had been aware of specific concerns before November 27, or whether he was part of the group that failed to provide an accurate account when they said that al-Qahtani's interrogation ended on January 12 .

This was a weak performance by a man who had made the wrong call in seeking to persuade the Senators that he was suitable for high judicial office. There was no hint of a suggestion that errors had been made, or of regret, or that a different approach might have been less damaging.

These were points I would put to Mr. Haynes when we met. And we did meet, in June 2007 at the Pentagon, sitting at the same round desk that Alberto Mora had described to me, with Kelly Wheaton and someone from the DoD press office. A few days later I sent off some quotations with a request for his approval, as we'd agreed. I waited for the answer.

After a period of deliberation, an email arrived from his office. "The GC has made his decision," it said, "he doesn't want any quotes." I expressed regret, but at the same time appreciation for his consideration of my request. "I hope that Mr. Haynes feels I have been fair in providing him with a decent opportunity to set out his views," I wrote.

Some weeks later he came through London, and left a message. "Interested in getting a beer later?" I was away, so we missed each other. A few weeks after that we met again in his office in the Pentagon, this time just the two of us. Only after that second meeting did I write the final chapter. Of the many people I spoke with, he was the only one to decline the request to allow me to refer to any part of our conversation. My conclusions take full account of everything that he told me.

28

President George W. Bush invoked the "finest traditions of valor" when he visited the Pentagon on December 2, 2002. What happened to those traditions, to the spirit of Abraham Lincoln's order outlawing cruelty even in the face of necessity? By the time Bush addressed his audience they'd already gone, as Bush, Donald Rumsfeld and Dick Cheney already knew. Those traditions had been cast aside with the decision to ignore the Geneva Conventions, embrace aggressive interrogation and approve the special interrogation plan for al-Qahtani. The primary responsibility rests with those who signed the orders and took the decisions, but they were not alone. In removing the obstacles to aggressive interrogation, the lawyers lent their active support and became willing accomplices.

A common theme that emerged from many of my conversations and interviews was the pervasive sense of threat that hung in the air a year after the September 11 attacks. I've no doubt that the fear that motivated the decisions may have been palpable and real and that many people on the ground at Guantánamo acted in good faith. But did it justify the actions that were taken? If I'm honest, I have to recognize a certain empathy with Cal Temple, the man who headed al-Qahtani's Exploitation Team, that there may be some extreme circumstances in which some might want to take extreme action. But the law is clear that torture is never permitted, and it is also clear that al-Qahtani was not the "ticking time bomb scenario" or anything close to it. Al-Qahtani had been in captivity for a year by the time his abuse began, and there was never any possibility that his treatment would produce any meaningful material. Spike Bowman and Mike Gelles made that clear at the time, but they were ignored. Now, it seems, they were proved right. The U.S. Army Field Manual was set aside, but the cruelty that followed did not produce meaningful intelligence. In any event, neither Geneva nor the Torture Convention allowed the total constraints on cruelty to be undone by necessities, real or imagined.[1]

A new culture of cruelty had been unleashed. The bar was raised, the lines were blurred. The dogs had slipped their leashes and run. It is not possible to identify precise cause and effect. At the very least, however, it is clear that the pictures of abuse that emerged from Abu Ghraib would have been less likely without the Haynes memo and the culture of ill-considered aggression it embraced. The CIA's program of "extraordinary rendition" was the product of the same mindset, and it seems to have ensnared various European and other countries in a culture of complicity.[2] Once freed, it proved difficult to bring the dogs back under control. A recent Pentagon battlefield survey in Iraq found that more than a third of the U.S. troops questioned believed that torture was acceptable.[3]

The corrosive effects of the decisions taken are now widely recognized. Following the Supreme Court's decision in *Hamdan v. Rumsfeld,* the Pentagon acted to restate the applicability of Common Article 3 to all detainees in this conflict. It was notable that the order was not signed by Rumsfeld but by his deputy, Gordon England. Efforts to remove Common Article 3 from revisions to the *U.S. Army Field Manual* failed.[4] In its current version it applies once more to all detainees and interrogators in military facilities. Congress has therefore gone a long way toward reinstating the international constraints, although the international definitions of Common Article 3 have not yet been applied, so as to give the CIA "flexibility" in interrogations.[5] (On March 8, 2008, President Bush vetoed a bill that would have outlawed the use by the CIA of any of the interrogation techniques set out in the Haynes memo.)

Public pressure, the media, friends and allies of the United States, the courts and the legislature have all played a part. But what about the lawyers? "A violation of the law is a violation of the law," said John Rizzo in hearings before the Senate for his nomination as CIA General Counsel.[6] He is right. If there have been violations of the law then responsibility must follow. The lawyers advising the Administration played a decisive role in subverting the system of international rules that should have protected all detainees from cruel and degrading treatment, a system that the United States had done so much to put in place. This was no mere accident or oversight. Nor was it a case of responding to a legitimate request that came up from the ground-level interrogators at Guantánamo, as the Bush Administration would have us believe. September 11 gave rise to a conscious decision to set aside international rules constraining interrogations. That decision was motivated by a combination of factors, including fear and ideology and an almost visceral disdain for international obligations. The decision was never subjected to critical scrutiny: if anyone asked what the incidental consequences might be, the answers were ignored.

As early as December 2001, White House Counsel Alberto Gonzales acted to take that decision forward. Even if David Addington was the more likely architect of the ideas, Gonzales's role as compliant bag-carrier would not absolve him of responsibility. As American forces captured individuals believed to be associated with the Taliban and al-Qaeda, it was decided that the Geneva Conventions would not cover these individuals—and this was before full legal advice was obtained from the Justice Department a month later. Even at this stage, Jim Haynes was authorizing U.S. forces to "take the gloves off." Whatever that instruction meant, it reflected an early and clear violation of the international rules.

Within days of Haynes's instruction, the process of decoupling Geneva and Guantánamo was underway. It crystallized with the President's decision on February 7, 2002, which set aside Geneva and opened the door to abusive interrogation in the name of security and "necessity"—a clear policy decision that had been authored and signed off by the lawyers. The Administration sought to portray the decision as an application of the law. It was not. Doug Feith, himself a lawyer, could not have been clearer when he told me that the intention was to remove constraints on interrogation. The policy should have been drawn up around the law: instead, the legal advice was fitted around the policy. For that alone, the most senior lawyers involved, the members of the "War Council," bear a direct responsibility for all that flowed: David Addington, Alberto Gonzales, John Yoo, Jim Haynes.

The Geneva decision created a legal black hole, and into that hole were cast a great number of detainees, some hapless, some dangerous. Mohammed al-Qahtani was among them. I hold no brief for him. If the facts are established, he must take responsibility for his acts, although that becomes more difficult after his treatment. But these detainees were not the only people to be cast into the blackness: Mike Dunlavey and Diane Beaver were also hurled into the lawlessness that was Guantánamo. The unfortunate Mike Dunlavey seems to have been chosen by Rumsfeld because he could be relied upon to do what he was told. On his own account, he was Rumsfeld's point of contact, reporting directly to his office, picking up the signals, responding to the pressures, supportive of the new approach. "Maximize the information" Rumsfeld told him, and he did the necessary.

The discovery of al-Qahtani was catalytic. The initiative for the new techniques was the result of pressure from Washington in the void created by the abandonment of Geneva. The idea for the techniques and their design reflected input from Washington, through the DIA and the CIA and with the benefit of creative ideas such as the reverse engineering of SERE. "Many of the techniques I would not authorize," General Hill had told me. Nevertheless, Ivy League sustenance for the principle of aggressive interrogation was provided by Alan Dershowitz and other high-brow legal commentators. Cultural sensitization came with Fox's 24 and other television programs that normalized violence and justified aggression, beamed directly into Guantánamo where they were lapped up by an enthusiastic audience.

Diane Beaver was put in the impossible situation of finding a substitute for Geneva. Her legal advice was poor and it was wrong, manifestly so, as I said to her on several occasions. But she should never have been in the position of having to write such an advice, on a blank sheet of paper, at short notice, and without any assistance from the senior lawyers at Southern Command or the Joint Chiefs. A more seasoned lawyer might not have given the advice she did. Indeed, faced with a request to give oral advice she chose not to. If she had not acted as she did, no paper trail would have existed and an Administration that was uncomfortable with written records might not have been unmasked. You can't un-write what has already been written, Jim Haynes might say. Diane Beaver achieved honor in an unlikely way: by insisting on written advice she made it more likely that the true story would emerge, unleashing a chain of events that placed the responsibility squarely at the feet of the most senior lawyers.

Those senior lawyers visited Guantánamo as a group: David Addington, Alberto Gonzales, Jim Haynes and John Rizzo. The fact of that visit and its attendant meetings and conversations bears witness to their collective enterprise, their interest, their knowledge. They met the "aggressive Major General," as Haynes later described Dunlavey. New interrogation techniques were on the agenda, so was al-Qahtani. By the time they visited, Gonzales and Rizzo had received and digested the legal memos from Jay Bybee and John Yoo at the Justice Department that advised that abusive interrogation, including many of the techniques used on Detainee 063, was lawful. Addington and Gonzales contributed to those memos. Any remaining suggestion that Haynes might have been the only member of the "War Council" who did not know the contents of those legal advices in September 2002 lacks all credibility.

Armed with the Justice Department memoranda, Diane Beaver's advice was, to all intents and purposes, irrelevant even before it was written.

Having insisted on putting her views in writing, however, Beaver's advice would later provide a useful point of reference and deflection for Haynes and Gonzales when the issue blew up. Haynes could have blacked out her name when her advice was declassified. He didn't do so.

What Haynes did do, however, when Dunlavey's request reached Washington a couple of weeks after he had signed off on it, was short-circuit the decision-making process. General Myers and the Joint Chiefs were not allowed to complete their assessment. The result was preordained and that is why the Haynes memo didn't follow the usual route. The authorization process wasn't even complete when the abuse began: that came with Rumsfeld's early VOCO, supported by the lawyers. Concerns expressed even before the early VOCO were ignored, and later objections overridden. Al-Qahtani's interrogation extended into an eighth week because he was thought to be on the verge of "breaking." When Dan Dell'Orto told the media that the Secretary of Defense had suspended the use of the authorized Category II and III techniques on January 12, Jim Haynes was there, so he must have known that what Dell'Orto was saying was not true, that the techniques had been used for a further three days in the hope of breaking al-Qahtani. It was only after Alberto Mora confronted him with a draft memo on the afternoon of January 15 that the use of the techniques ended.

It's instructive to look back to the days after Abu Ghraib, to the narrative that was presented on June 22, 2004. Alberto Gonzales led a group of lawyers that included a relatively unknown Jim Haynes. By releasing some documents, they hoped to snuff out any lingering suggestion that the Administration might have some responsibility for the events at Abu Ghraib. That initiative failed. A draft report from the Pentagon's Inspector General reached a damning conclusion. The push for "aggressive interrogations," said the draft, had "created an atmosphere in which the pressure to produce actionable intelligence overwhelmed the primacy of the Geneva Conventions."[7] The result was that the "interrogation ideas proved difficult to contain and had unintended consequences." Cully Stimson, Deputy Assistant Secretary of Defense for Detainee Affairs, responded on behalf of Rumsfeld. These paragraphs of the report would "lead the reader to the erroneous conclusion that the Secretary and some senior DoD officials have direct responsibility," Stimson wrote, "or in the alternative that the policies developed by DoD detainee operations were responsible for the abuses that occurred in . . . Guantánamo." He did not concur with the conclusion, adding that "its release would cause irreparable harm to the Department." The removal of the draft text from the final version of the

Pentagon's Inspector General's report cannot obscure the power of the conclusion, which is also my conclusion: the most senior DoD officials have direct responsibility, together with the President and the Vice-President, who were, through their most senior lawyers, directly implicated.

When Alberto Gonzales and Jim Haynes stood in the media room in June 2004 the narrative they spun was based on a foundation of untruths. Rumsfeld did not merely respond to a request from Guantánamo: he and his office were actively involved from an early stage, pressuring and bullying so that a request came. The supporting "multi-page, single-spaced legal review" was a fig-leaf: the real but undeclared legal advice that was relied on came from Bybee and Yoo. General Hill didn't indicate approval of the request. A careful reading showed it to be conditional upon further legal advice from the Justice Department, the contents of which was known by Haynes and Gonzales by the time the request arrived. Yet they have never been willing to confirm that fact, because it destroys another part of their story. The Justice Department memos played a significant role; they did reflect policies adopted by the Administration in approving the abuse of al-Qahtani.

In the Administration's narrative, the Pentagon's involvement only really began after General Hill's memo arrived in late October 2002. In truth, the involvement was active and constant from February onward, through Mike Dunlavey and his successor, Geoffrey Miller. Without access to the interrogation log nobody could challenge the claim that the new techniques didn't go beyond a bit of poking and light shoving that was mentioned. With the benefit of access, the log shows that to be a lie. As applied to al-Qahtani the new techniques systematically violated the rules reflected in Common Article 3 and reasonable people believe their use on that individual amounted to torture.

On February 11, 2008, more than six years after he was first caught and then detained at Guantánamo, the Department of Defense announced that al Qahtani was being charged with a range of offenses, including murder, violation of the laws of war, attacking civilians, and terrorism, and that the death penalty was being sought. The details were thin but nevertheless striking: the Department of Defense's public announcement referred only to the fact that he had attempted to enter the United States in August 2001, that he carried $2800 in cash, and that he had an itinerary that listed the name of another detainee who was being charged with assisting and preparing the 9/11 hijackers. All of this information was available to interrogators well before the Haynes memo was written or used. The Department of Defense announcement was consistent with what I was told: the abusive interrogation of al Qahtani produced nothing of value.

The authorization of the Haynes memo did not follow a "thorough" or "deliberative" process, at least in the sense Gonzales suggested. It was the result of a pre-ordained policy of aggression that came from the very top, which the most senior lawyers approved: they gave their names as jurists to cloak the policy with a veneer of legality. No doubt it will be said that these lawyers acted in what they thought to be the best interests of the country. But can that be enough?

It is difficult to escape the conclusion that these most senior lawyers bear direct responsibility for decisions that led to violations of the Geneva Conventions. They failed to provide independent advice and instead became advocates for a cause. Legal opinions became expressions of policy, to paraphrase the U.S. Military Tribunal in the case of *Altstötter*.[8] Whether this was aided by ideology or driven by other ambitions matters not: a violation of the law is a violation of the law. Despite the responsibility they bear, it cannot be said that their careers have suffered unduly.

David Addington continues to work for Vice President Dick Cheney. In October 2005 he was promoted to Chief of Staff, following the resignation of "Scooter" Libby. He remains an unabashed leader of efforts to limit the reach of international rules, including Common Article 3.

Since March 2003 Jay Bybee has served as a Circuit Judge on the U.S. Court of Appeals for the Ninth Circuit, which is headquartered in San Francisco. When he was confirmed, his role in the events leading to the adoption of the Haynes memo was not known to the U.S. Senate. The Bush Administration continues to refuse to release the memo bearing his name (the memo referred to as Bybee II), on the grounds that its release would threaten national security.

Doug Feith occupies the same office where I visited him, in the garret of the Edmund A. Walsh School of Foreign Service at Georgetown University, where he is a Distinguished Practitioner in National Security Policy. In February 2007 he launched a new website, www.dougfeith.com. It makes no mention of his role in the Geneva decision or the authorization of the eighteen techniques.

In February 2005 Alberto Gonzales managed to squeeze through confirmation hearings to be appointed as the eightieth Attorney General of the United States, despite being constantly mired in controversies, including the surveillance of American citizens without proper warrants and the dismissal of U.S. Attorneys for political reasons. The fact that he survived as long as he did was a result of his poor memory and the personal support of the President. "Your credibility has been breached to the point of being actionable," the ranking Republican on the Senate Judiciary Committee finally told him, and a few weeks later, in September 2007, he resigned.[9]

Jim Haynes was not confirmed as a federal judge. In the face of strong opposition from a number of Democrat and Republican Senators, he asked for his name to be withdrawn from nomination to the U.S. Court of Appeals. President Bush decided not to re-nominate him. On February 24, 2008, the Department of Defense announced that Haynes would leave the DoD and return to private life the following month.

John Yoo left the Justice Department in 2003 and returned to the Boalt Hall School of Law at the University of California at Berkeley, where he teaches international law and constitutional law. He is also a Visiting Scholar at the American Enterprise Institute, and remains a strong believer in the arguments he put forward, the adequacy of his legal opinions and the error into which the U.S. Supreme Court has fallen.

Thanks to the immunity from criminal process that has been built into U.S. law, and to which several of these lawyers contributed, they are presently free from criminal investigation at home. That immunity does not, however, extend beyond the shores of the United States. The members of this distinct group of six lawyers, and perhaps others, may decide wisely to think carefully about where they travel in the future.

What of the other people I met during the course of my investigations?

Ludwig Altstötter has retired from legal practice and lives in Nuremberg. I continue to receive occasional and kind letters from him, pointing out aspects of his father's case that I might not have been aware of.

Mike Dunlavey remains in Erie, Pennsylvania, and sits on the Court of Common Pleas. He hasn't yet taken up my invitation to take him to an Arsenal game at the Emirates Stadium in north London, but the offer remains open. I know he worries about the issues we talked about, he has told me so. Our conversations had caused him to reflect more about the events. He had wanted to go back down to Guantánamo, but his request was turned down. He would also have liked to have gone back to the daily diaries and schedules that were kept on the computer system, together with reports that were sent out on a daily basis, and details of the videoconferences that had taken place with the Pentagon. "I need to see that stuff," he mused, "how am I going to get to it?" It seemed doubtful that he would. "They were backed up at SOUTHCOM," he explained, but "a couple of months after I left there was a SNAFU and all was lost." I now wonder whether there was any link to the CIA's destruction of videotapes depicting other abusive interrogations. Nevertheless, he remained resolute in his belief that he had done the right things, would do them again, and was willing to take full personal responsibility for his actions. I appreciated his willingness to engage in discussion with me. At no point in our conversations did he ever seek to deflect blame, and he stood up for those below him, including Diane Beaver. I doubt he really needs to worry about his association with the Haynes memo: his good fortune was to be removed from Guantánamo before the memo was approved or the aggressive interrogations began.

As for Diane Beaver, the last time I saw her she was still in Washington. We had a fine dinner together at the Tabard Inn. The sky above her was almost cloudless. She'd decided to leave the military and move back to St. Louis with her mother; she was thinking of taking on a franchise with a company called Dogtopia that provides daycare and overnights for canine friends. It even has a daily spa service, shampoo and conditioning in a hydrosurge massaging tub, followed by a full fluff dry and brush-out. A long way from the eighteen techniques.

CHRONOLOGY OF EVENTS

(SOME DATES ARE APPROXIMATE)

2001

November	Detainee 063 captured in Afghanistan.

2002

January	Detainee 063 transferred from Afghanistan to Guantánamo.
February 7	President Bush decides detainees at Guantánamo have no rights under the Geneva Conventions.
March	Major General Mike Dunlavey arrives at Guantánamo as Commander of JTF-170.
June	Lieutenant Colonel Diane Beaver arrives at Guantánamo as Staff Judge Advocate.
June	Identity and background of Detainee 063 emerges (Mohammed al-Qahtani).
August 1	Bybee/Yoo memo completed. Bybee II completed.
August 8	al-Qahtani separated from other detainees and put in isolation.
August 14	Publication of *Why Terrorism Works: Understanding the Threat, Responding to the Challenge,* by Alan Dershowitz.
September 11	First anniversary of attacks on World Trade Center and Pentagon and downing of Flight 93.
September 25–26	David Addington, Alberto Gonzales, Jim Haynes and John Rizzo visit Guantánamo.
October 11	Major General Dunlavey requests new interrogation techniques. Lieutenant Colonel Beaver provides supporting legal advice.
October 25	General Hill forwards Dunlavey's request to General Myers.

October 29	Second series of 24 airs on Fox TV.
November	Assessment of new interrogation techniques by Joint Chiefs is cut short; Jim Haynes discusses new techniques with General Myers, Paul Wolfowitz and Doug Feith.
November 8	Major General Dunlavey ends term as commander of JTF-GTMO.
	Major General Geoffrey Miller takes over.
November 10 (or 12)	Spike Bowman calls Bob Deitz.
November 12	DIA interrogation plan for al-Qahtani completed.
November 19	Spike Bowman calls Dan Dell'Orto.
November 21/22	Alternative interrogation plan for al-Qahtani rejected.
November 23	Secretary Rumsfeld gives VOCO and aggressive interrogation of al-Qahtani begins.
November 27	Jim Haynes recommends approval of new interrogation techniques (Haynes memo).
December 2	Secretary Rumsfeld signs and approves Haynes memo.
December (early)	Spike Bowman calls Jim Haynes.
December 7/8	Mohammed al-Qahtani hospitalized.
December 17	Dave Brant tells Alberto Mora of aggressive interrogation.
December 20	First meeting between Alberto Mora and Jim Haynes.

2003

January 9	Second meeting between Alberto Mora and Jim Haynes.
January 12	Secretary Rumsfeld telephones General Hill; interrogation continues.
January 15	Third meeting between Alberto Mora and Jim Haynes.
January 15	Aggressive interrogation of al-Qahtani suspended.
August	Major General Miller visit Baghdad and Abu Graib.
September 14	General Sanchez signs memorandum authorizing new interrogation techniques (Iraq)
October 17	Photographic evidence shows abuse beginning at Abu Graib

2004

March	Bybee/Yoo memo suspended.
March	Major General Dunlavey returns to bench at Court of Common Pleas, Erie, Pennsylvania.
April	Major General Miller appointed deputy commanding general for detainee operations for multinational forces in Iraq.
April28	CBS broadcasts images of abuse at Abu Ghraib.
June	Bybee II memo suspended.
June 22	Alberto Gonzales, Jim Haynes and Dan Dell'Orto hold press conference at Eisenhower Executive Office.
June 29	*Rasul v. Bush,* judgment of Supreme Court opens door to legal representation for al-Qahtani.
August	Schlesinger report published.

| August 23 | Fay-Jones report published. |
| December 30 | Bybee/Yoo memo replaced by new OLC memo. |

2005

February 14	Alberto Gonzales becomes eightieth Attorney General of United States.
June 1	Paul Wolfowitz takes office as President of World Bank.
April 1	Schmidt-Furlow report published
June 12	*Time* magazine publishes extracts of al-Qahtani interrogation log.
August 8	Doug Feith resigns as Under secretary of Defense for Policy.
September 30	General Myers ends term as Chairman of Joint Chiefs of Staff.
October	David Addington appointed Chief of Staff to Vice President Dick Cheney.
November 9	General Myers awarded Presidential Medal of Freedom.

2006

March 3	*Time* magazine publishes 84- page interrogation log of Detainee 063 on its website.
June 29	Hamdan v. Rumsfeld, Supreme Court rules that Guantánamo detainees have rights under Common Article 3.
July 7	DoD issues memorandum directing the application of Common Article 3 at all DoD facilities, including Guantánamo.
July 11	Jim Haynes's confirmation hearings before Senate Judiciary Committee for nomination to U.S. Court of Appeals.
August 25	DoD Inspector General, Review of DoD-directed Investigations of Detainee Abuse published.
December 18	Donald Rumsfeld resigns as Secretary of Defense.

2007

January 10	Jim Haynes withdraws nomination to U.S. Court of Appeals.
June 30	Paul Wolfowitz resigns as President of World Bank.
September 17	Alberto Gonzales resigns as Attorney General.

2008

| February 11 | U.S. Department of Defense announces that al Qahtani has been charged with a number of criminal offences, including murder in violation of the law of war, attacking civilians, and terrorism, and that it is seeking the death penalty. |

February 24   DoD announces resignation of Jim Haynes
March 8   President Bush vetoes a bill that would prohibit the CIA
                     from using interrogation techniques in the Haynes memo.

NOTES

KICK-OFF

Chapter 1

1. "Rumsfeld's opening remarks at the signing of the Defense Authorization Bill," December 2, 2002, http://www.defenselink.mil/transcripts/transcript.aspx?transcriptid=2799.
2. The documents are available at http://www.gwu.edu/~nsarchiv/NSAEBB/NSAEBB127/02.12.02.pdf. For background, see Philippe Sands, *Lawless World* (Viking, 2005), especially Chapters 7 and 9.
3. Dan Heggen, "Cheney Remarks Fuel Torture Debate," *Washington Post*, October 27, 2006, p. A9.
4. Testimony of Lieutenant General Schmidt, taken August 24, 2005 at Davis-Monthan Air Force Base, Arizona, for Department of the Army Inspector General, Virginia, at p. 21, on file with author.

Chapter 2

1. Vice Adm. John D. Stufflebeem. Briefing January 28, 2002, http://www.defenselink.mil/news/newsarticle.aspx?id=43813.
2. U.S. DoD briefing, January 11, 2002, http://www.defenselink.mil/transcripts/transcript.aspx?transcriptid=2031.
3. *Ibid.*
4. Common Article 3 provides:

   > In the case of armed conflict not of an international character occurring in the territory of one of the High Contracting Parties, each Party to the conflict shall be bound to apply, as a minimum, the following provisions:
   >
   > (1) Persons taking no active part in the hostilities, including members of armed forces who have laid down their arms and those placed 'hors de combat' by sickness, wounds, detention, or any other cause, shall in all circumstances be treated humanely, without any adverse distinction founded on race, colour, religion or faith, sex, birth or wealth, or any other similar criteria.
   >
   > To this end, the following acts are and shall remain prohibited at any time and in any place whatsoever with respect to the above-mentioned persons:
   >
   > (a) violence to life and person, in particular murder of all kinds, mutilation, cruel treatment and torture;
   >
   > (b) taking of hostages;
   >
   > (c) outrages upon personal dignity, in particular humiliating and degrading treatment;
   >
   > (d) the passing of sentences and the carrying out of executions without previous judgment pronounced by a regularly constituted court, affording all the judicial guarantees which are recognized as indispensable by civilized peoples.

(2) The wounded and sick shall be collected and cared for. An impartial humanitarian body, such as the International Committee of the Red Cross, may offer its services to the Parties to the conflict. The Parties to the conflict should further endeavour to bring into force, by means of special agreements, all or part of the other provisions of the present Convention. The application of the preceding provisions shall not affect the legal status of the Parties to the conflict.

5. *U.S. Army Field Manual 34–52*, Chapter 1, under the heading "Prohibition against Use of Force."

6. Limited extracts covering the period November 23, 2002 until December 21, 2002 were published in *Time* magazine on June 12, 2005 (http://www.time.com/time/magazine /article/0,9171,1071202,00.html). An 84-page copy of the interrogation log was published on the website of *Time* magazine on March 3, 2006 (http://www.time.com/time/nation /article/0,8599,1169322,00.html).

Chapter 3

1. DoD briefing December 3, 2002, http://www.defenselink.mil/transcripts/transcript.aspx ?transcriptid=2803.

2. "Working Group Report on Detainee Interrogations in the Global War on Terrorism: Assessment of Legal, Historical, Policy and Operational Considerations," March 6, 2003, in K. Greenberg and J. Dratel, *The Torture Papers: the Road to Abu Ghraib* (Cambridge, 2005), ("*The Torture Papers*") p. 241.

3. Hearing, Senate Armed Services Committee, May 13, 2004, Federal News Service.

4. Hearing, Senate Judiciary Committee, on the Federal Government's Counterterrorism Efforts, June 8, 2004, Federal Document Clearing House, transcript, p. 35.

5. Press Conference of the President after the G8 Summit, International Media Center, Savannah, Georgia, June 10, 2004, http://www.whitehouse.gov/news/releases/2004/06 /20040610–36.html.

6. See http://www.gwu.edu/~nsarchiv/NSAEBB/NSAEBB127/02.12.02.pdf

7. Jack Goldsmith, *The Terror Presidency: Law and Judgment Inside the Bush Administration* (W.W. Norton and Company, 2007) ("The Terror Presidency"), p. 22.

8. *Ibid.*

9. Press Briefing by White House Counsel Judge Alberto Gonzales, DoD General Counsel William Haynes, DoD Deputy General Counsel Daniel Dell'Orto and Army Deputy Chief of Staff for Intelligence General Keith Alexander, Eisenhower Executive Office Building, June 22, 2004 ("Eisenhower Office Press Briefing, June 22, 2004"), transcript at http://www.whitehouse.gov/news/releases/2004/06/20040622–14.html.

10. The "Manchester Manual" is available at: http://www.fas.org/irp/world/para/manualpart1 _1.pdf.

11. Hearing, Senate Judiciary Committee on Confirmation Hearings of William Haynes II, July 11, 2006, http://frwebgate.access.gpo.gov/cgi-bin/useftp.cgi?IPaddress=162.140.64 .184&filename=30496.pdf&directory=/diska/wais/data/109_senate_hearings.

12. *Ibid.*, p. 49.

13. *Ibid.*, p. 50.

14. *Ibid.*, p. 50.

Chapter 4

1. United Nations War Crimes Commission, Law Reports of Trials of War Criminals (HMSO, 1947) Vol III p. 32; also at http://www.mazal.org/archive/nmt/03/NMT03-T0032.htm.

2. U.S. Military Tribunal III, Case No. 3, *U.S. v Josef Altstötter et al*, Closing Argument for the Prosecution, Appendix 1.

3. Spencer Tracy as Chief Judge Dan Haywood in *Judgment at Nuremberg;* unofficial transcript of the film at http://www.script-o-rama.com/movie_scripts/j/judgment-at-Nuremberg-script-transcript.html.

THE PATH

Chapter 5

1. Jeffrey Goldberg, "A little learning: what Doug Feith knew, and when he knew it," *The New Yorker,* May 9, 2005, http://www.newyorker.com/archive/2005/05/09/050509fa_fact.
2. Secretary Rumsfeld in a farewell speech for Doug Feith, Pentagon Auditorium, Washington D.C., August 8, 2005, http://findarticles.com/p/articles/mi_m0PAH/is_2005_August_8/ai_n15384426.
3. Bob Woodward, *Plan of Attack* (Simon & Schuster, 2004), p. 281.
4. 1 *National Interest* 36 (1985).
5. Jason DeParle, "Out of the frying pan, into the freezing cold," *International Herald Tribune,* May 26, 2006; http://www.iht.com/articles/2006/05/25/news/teach.php.
6. Letter from Paul J. McNulty, U.S. Attorney, to James J. Brosnahan and others, June 12 2002, obtained from www.talkingpointsmemo.com/docs/lindh-rumsfeld/. See also http://www.tpmmuckraker.com/archives/003522.php.
7. John Yoo and Robert Delahunty, Memorandum for William J. Haynes II, Part II, January 9, 2002, in Greenberg and Dratel, *The Torture Papers,* p. 38.
8. Secretary Rumsfeld, Memorandum for Chairman of the Joint Chiefs of Staff, January 19, 2002, in Greenberg and Dratel, *The Torture Papers,* p. 80.
9. Alberto Gonzales, Memorandum for the President, Decision re Application of the Geneva Convention on Prisoners of War to the Conflict with al-Qaeda and the Taliban, January 25, 2002, in Greenberg and Dratel, *The Torture Papers,* p. 118.
10. Barton Gellman and Jo Becker, "Pushing the Envelope on Presidential Power," *Washington Post,* June 25, 2007, p. A1.http://blog.washingtonpost.com/cheney/chapters/pushing_the_envelope_on_presi/.
11. Rumsfeld Memo, January 19, 2002, in *The Torture Papers,* p. 119.
12. William H. Taft IV, Memorandum to Counsel to the President, February 2, 2002, Insert A, para. 2, in Greenberg and Dratel, *The Torture Papers,* p. 129.
13. Ibid.

Chapter 6

1. Hearings, Senate Judiciary Committee on Confirmation Hearings of William Haynes II, July 11, 2006, p. 49.
2. Carol Rosenberg, "Gen. Dunlavey offers look at Guantanamo Interrogations," *Erie Times-News,* March 28, 2002.
3. Bill Gertz and Rowan Scarborough, "Notes from the Pentagon," *The Washington Times,* October 4, 2002.
4. *Erie Times-News,* June 24, 2004, http://www.goerie.com/archives/.
5. See *Erie Times-News* articles between June 24, 2004 and July 3, 2004. http://www.goerie.com/archives/.
6. The suit was filed on October 27, 2004, *Shafiq Rasul et al. v. Donald Rumsfeld et al.,* Civil Action No. 04−1864 (RMU), U.S. District Court for the District of Columbia, (*Rasul v. Rumsfeld*) February 6, 2006, 414 F. Supp. 2d 26, at p. 29.
7. Report of Brigadier General John Furlow Lieutenant General Randall M. Schmidt ("Schmidt-Furlow Report") on the "Investigation into FBI Allegations of Detainee Abuse at Guantánamo Bay, Cuba Detention Facility," published on April 1, 2005 (amended June 9, 2005); http://www.defenselink.mil/news/Jul2005/d20050714report.pdf.
8. *Rasul v. Rumsfeld* supra note 6 above.

9. Matthew Purdy and Lowell Bergman, "Unclear Danger: Inside the Lackawanna Terror Cell," *New York Times,* October 12, 2003.

10. Schmidt-Furlow report, p. 18.

11. Josh White and Barton Gellman, "Defense Espionage Unit to Work With CIA," *Washington Post,* January 25, 2005, p. A3.

Chapter 7

1. See Instructions for the Government of Armies of the United States in the Field, prepared by Francis Lieber, LL.D., originally issued as General Orders No. 100, Adjutant General's Office, 1863 (Government Printing Office, 1898) Article 16 provides: "Military necessity does not admit of cruelty—that is, the infliction of suffering for the sake of suffering or for revenge, nor of maiming or wounding except in fight, nor of torture to extort confessions. It does not admit of the use of poison in any way, nor of the wanton devastation of a district. It admits of deception, but disclaims acts of perfidy; and, in general, military necessity does not include any act of hostility which makes the return to peace unnecessarily difficult."

2. *U.S. Army's Operational Law Handbook* JA 422, sections 18–20, cited in A. Roberts, "Counter-Terrorism, Armed Forces and the Laws of War," *Survival,* vol. 44, no. 1 (Spring 2002), pp. 7–32, note 46 and accompanying text.

3. See generally Alfred W. McCoy, *A Question of Torture: CIA Interrogation from the Cold War to the War on Terror* (Metropolitan Books, 2006).

4. National Security Archive, at http://www.gwu.edu/%7Ensarchiv/NSAEBB/NSAEBB122/index.htm#hre.

5. Memorandum for the Secretary of Defense from Werner E. Michel, Assistant to the Secretary of Defense (Intelligence Oversight), March, 10, 1992, available at: http://www.gwu.edu/%7Ensarchiv/NSAEBB/NSAEBB122/920310%20Imporper%20Material%20in%20Spanish-Language%20Intelligence%20Training%20Manuals.pdf

6. *Los Angeles Times,* November 8, 2001, Part 2, p. 19.

7. MSNBC, *Alan Keyes Show,* February 4, 2002.

8. MSNBC, *Hardball with Chris Matthews,* April 5, 2002.

9. Alan Dershowitz, *Why Terrorism Works* (Yale University Press, 2002).

10. CBS News, *60 Minutes,* September 22, 2002.

11. Eisenhower Office Press Briefing, June 22, 2004.

Chapter 8

1. The full text said: "Issues for LTC Beaver: MSU-tracking/screening criteria; ICRC Access; Command Relationships/Tasking authority; Personnel; Litigation Support; Repatriation?/prosecution?/ Relationship with CITF and Military Commissions; Training; C2 assessment/mobile detachment screening teams; Distribution of info."

2. Summarized Witness Statement of the Intelligence Control Element (ICE) Chief for *JTF-170,* given to Schmidt-Furlow Investigation on March 3, 2005, p.2, on file with author.

3. Mark Benjamin, "The CIA's torture teachers," Salon.com, June 21, 2007, www.salon.com/news/feature/2007/06/21/cia_sere/

4. Supra note 2 above, pp. 2–3.

5. Ibid., p. 3.

6. Statement of former psychiatrist with the BSCT, sent by email on February 25, 2005, to Schmidt-Furlow Investigation, p. 1.

7. See *Washington Post,* January 21, 1968, p.1, showing a photograph of a U.S. soldier supervising the questioning of a captured North Vietnamese soldier, who is being held down as water was poured over his face while his nose and mouth were covered with a cloth; also W. Pincus, "Waterboarding Historically Controversial," *Washington Post,* October 5, 2006, p.A17.

Chapter 9

1. Goldsmith, *The Terror Presidency*, p. 167. On the traditional role of the OLC see Dawn Johnsen, "Faithfully Executing the Laws: Internal Legal Constraints on Executive Power," unpublished draft (July 2007), to be published in the *UCLA Law Review*, available at: http://papers.ssrn .com/sol3/papers.cfm?abstract_id=1002111; see also Guidelines for the President's Legal Advisors, 81 *Indiana Law Journal* 1345 (2006).

2. Jay Bybee, "Memorandum for Alberto R. Gonzales Counsel to the President Re: Standards of Conduct for Interrogation under 18 U.S.C. §§ 2340–2340A," August 1, 2002; in Greenburg and Dratel, *The Torture Papers*, p. 172.

3. Goldsmith, *The Terror Presidency*, p. 169.

4. Quoted in *Sydney Morning Herald*, May 17, 2002.

5. B. Gellman and J. Becker, "Pushing the Envelope on Presidential Power," *Washington Post*, June 25, 2007, p. A1.

6. D. Johnston, N. Lewis and D. Jehl, "Nominee Gave Advice to CIA on Torture Law," *New York Times*, January 29, 2005, p. A1.

7. Paul Farhi, "Calling on Hollywood's Terrorism Experts; Homeland Security Chief Compares Reality and '24,'" *Washington Post*, June 24, 2006, p. C1.

8. http://www.youtube.com/watch?v=UNKG2a7JDgM; see also http://transcripts.cnn.com /TRANSCRIPTS/0701/17/sbt.01.html.

9. Dan Froomkin, "No Checks, No Balances—No Supervision?," washingtonpost.com, June 25, 2007; http://www.washingtonpost.com/wp-dyn/content/blog/2007/06/25/BL20070 62500874.html.

10. Hearing, Senate Select Intelligence Committee, Nomination of John Rizzo to be CIA General Counsel, June 19, 2007, ("Rizzo hearing"), Federal News Service transcript, p. 7, and also p. 10.

11. Letter from John Yoo to Alberto Gonzales, regarding "the views of our Office concerning the legality, under international law, of interrogation methods to be used on captured Al Qaeda operatives," August 1, 2002, in Greenberg and Dratel, *The Torture Papers*, p. 218.

12. Ibid., p. 220. The understanding entered by the United States (October 21, 1994) and the notification by Germany (February 26, 1996) are at: http://www.unhchr.ch/html/menu2 /6/cat/treaties/convention-reserv.htm.

13. See *ACLU and others v. DoD and others*, U.S. District Court Southern District of New York, Case 04 Civ. 415 (AKH), Sixth Declaration of Marilyn A. Dorn, Information Review Officer, CIA, August 5, 2005.

14. Rizzo Hearing, supra. note 10 above, transcript p. 11.

15. Barton Gellman and Jo Becker, "Pushing the Envelope on Presidential Power," *Washington Post*, June 25, 2007.

16. Rizzo Hearing, supra. note 10 above, transcript p. 11.

17. *Ibid.*

18. Bill Dedman, "Gitmo interrogations spark battle over tactics," October 23, 2006, available at: http://www.msnbc.msn.com/id/15361458/ ("Senior lawyers from the Bush administration toured Guantanamo on Sept. 25, 2002, while the plan for the aggressive interrogation of al-Qahtani was being formed"). The article mistakenly includes John Yoo in the group, and omits Jack Goldsmith.

Chapter 10

1. Carol Rosenberg, "Germany to Consider Probe of Rumsfeld," *Miami Herald*, November 15, 2006.

2. Testimony of General James T. Hill to the Schmidt-Furlow Investigation, on October 7, 2005, to the Department of the Army Inspector General, Investigations Divison, "Testimony of General James T. Hill," p. 30, (on file with the author).

Chapter 12

1. The Vice President appeared on *Meet the Press* with Tim Russert, Camp David, Maryland, September 16, 2001; http://www.whitehouse.gov/vicepresident/news-speeches/speeches/vp20010916.html.
2. Hearing, Senate Armed Services Committee regarding Contingency Reserve Fund Request for FY05, Washington, D.C., May 13, 2004, transcript Federal News Service.
3. Second Report of the Ad Hoc Group, World Bank, May 14, 2007, available at: http://siteresources.worldbank.org/NEWS/Resources/secondreportoftheheadhocgroup.pdf.

Chapter 13

1. Schmidt-Furlow report, p. 18.
2. See letter from T.J. Harrington, FBI Deputy Assistant Director, Counterterrorism Division, to Major General Donald J. Ryder, Department of the Army, Criminal Investigation Command, July 14, 2004, p. 2; http://aclu.org/torturefoia/released/FBI_4622_4624.pdf.
3. Testimony of Lieutenant General Randall M. Schmidt, Davis-Monthan Air Force Base, Arizona, August 24, 2005, pp. 33–34.
4. Schmidt-Furlow report, p. 15.
5. Summarized witness statement of Major General Geoffrey D. Miller, Arlington, Virginia, March 18, 2005, p. 6, statement taken by Lieutenant General Randall M. Schmidt for the Schmidt-Furlow Investigation, on file with the author.
6. *Ibid.* pp. 1–2.
7. *Ibid.*
8. *Ibid.* p. 2.
9. *Ibid.*, p. 3.
10. Email dated May 30, 2003, from the FBI Behavioral Analysis Unit of the Critical Incident Response Group (on file with the author).
11. Testimony of General James T. Hill, October 7, 2005, p. 12.
12. Testimony of Lieutenant General Randall M. Schmidt, Davis Monthan Air Force Base, Arizona, August 24, 2005, p. 14.

COMEBACK

Chapter 14

1. See Positive Response no. 3, Responses–36, investigation September 14, 2004, concerning observed treatment of Guantanamo detainees, at http://www.aclu.org/pdfs/safefree/torturerelease_20070102_p150.pdf, p. 35.
2. Positive Response no. 3, Responses–38, investigation September 14, 2004; the electronic communication was approved by SAC Wiley and forwarded to CTD Executive Management; at http://www.aclu.org/pdfs/safefree/torturerelease_20070102_p150.pdf, p. 37.
3. Hearing, Senate Judiciary Committee on Confirmation Hearings of William Haynes II, July 11, 2006, response to written questions by Senators Durbin and Feingold, pp. 179 and 189.
4. Jess Bravin, "The Conscience of the Colonel," *Wall Street Journal*, March 31, 2007, available at: http://online.wsj.com/article_email/SB117529704337355155-lMyQjAxMDE3NzM1M TIzOTE3Wj.html.
5. Email dated May 30, 2003 from the FBI Behavioral Analysis Unit of the Critical Incident Response Group (on file with the author).
6. Jerry Markon, "Defense Analyst Guilty in Israeli Espionage Case," *Washington Post*, October 6, 2005.
7. See http://www.humanrightsfirst.org/us_law/etn/pdf/fbi-brief-inter-analysis–112702.pdf.

Chapter 15

1. M. Gregg Bloche and Jonathan Marks, "Doctors and interrogators at Guantánamo Bay," *New England Journal of Medicine* 353(2005) p. 1633; Jane Mayer, "The Experiment," *The New Yorker*, July 11 and 18, 2005. http://www.newyorker.com/archive/2005/07/11/050711fa _fact4.

Chapter 16

1. Jane Mayer, "Annals of the Pentagon: the Memo," *The New Yorker*, February 27, 2006; http://www.newyorker.com/archive/2006/02/27/060227/fa_fact.

Chapter 17

1. Eisenhower Office Press Briefing, June 22, 2004.
2. Voice of America News, December 8, 2005, http://www.voanews.com/english/archive /2005-12/2005-12-08-voabb.cfm.
3. Testimony of General James Hill, October 7, 2005, p.19.
4. Summarized witness statement of Major General Geoffrey D. Miller, Arlington, Virginia, March 18, 2005, p. 8, taken by Lieutenant General Randall M. Schmidt for the Schmidt-Furlow Investigation.

Chapter 18

1. Eisenhower Office Press Briefing, June 22, 2004. See also the executive summary of the Report of the Review of the Department of Defense detention operations and detainee interrogation techniques (the Church Report), http://www.defenselink.mil/news /Mar2005/d20050310exe.pdf.
2. Media Availability with Commander, U.S. Southern Command General James T. Hill, June 3, 2004. Transcript available at http://www.defenselink.mil/transcripts/transcript .aspx?transcriptid=3153.
3. Testimony of General James Hill, October 7, 2005, supra. Chapter 17, note 3, p.19.
4. Testimony of Lieutenant General Randall M. Schmidt, Davis-Monthan Air Force Base, Arizona, August 24, 2005, p. 21.
5. Josh White, "Interrogation Research Is Lacking, Report Says," *Washington Post*, January 16, 2007, p. A15; Report of the Intelligence Science Board, *Educing Information—Interrogation: Science and Art, Foundations for the Future*, December 2006, at: http://www.fas.org/irp /dni/educing.pdf.

Chapter 19

1. Eisenhower Office Press Briefing, June 22, 2004.
2. *Ibid.*, p. 8.
3. Testimony of Lieutenant General Randall M. Schmidt, Davis-Monthan Air Force Base, Arizona, August 24, 2005, p. 18.
4. *Working Group Report on Detainee Interrogations in the Global War on Terrorism: Assessment of Legal, Historical, Policy and Operational Considerations,* April 4 2003, in Greenberg and Dratel (eds), *The Torture Papers,* p. 286.
5. *Memorandum from the Secretary of Defense for the Commander, U.S. Southern Command on Counter-Resistance Techniques in the War on Terrorism,* April 16, 2003, in Greenberg and Dratel (eds), *The Torture Papers,* p. 360.
6. Hearings, Senate Judiciary Committee, on Confirmation Hearings of William Haynes II, July 11, 2006, p. 52.

7. See Memorandum Opinion for the Deputy Attorney General, Legal Standards Applicable under 18 U.S.C. §§ 2340–2340A, December 30 2004, at: http://www.usDoJ.gov/olc /18usc2340234oa2.htm.

8. Detainee Treatment Act of 2005, Section 1002(a), at: http://jurist.law.pitt.edu/gazette /2005/12/detainee-treatment-act-of–2005-white.php.

9. Eisenhower Office Press Briefing, June 22, 2004.

10. *Memorandum on CJTF-7 Interrogation and Counter Resistance Policy,* from Lieutenant General Ricardo Sanchez, Commander, Joint Task Force Seven, September 14 2003: http://www .aclu.org/safefree/general/17561lgl20050329.html. These techniques were superseded with a new memorandum on October 12: *Memorandum on CJTF-7 Interrogation and Counter Resistance Policy,* from Lieutenant General Ricardo Sanchez, Commander, Joint Task Force Seven, October 12 2003, at: http://www.aclu.org/FilesPDFs/october%20sanchez%20memo.pdf.

11. Hearing, Senate Armed Services Committee, May 19 2004: http://transcripts .cnn.com/TRANSCRIPTS/0405/19/se.03.html. Colonel Warren was later the subject of a preliminary screening inquiry conducted by the Department of the Army's Office of the Judge Advocate General for allegations of (1) professional impropriety under lawyers ethics rules and (2) dereliction in the performance of his duties. In May 2005 the Office of the Judge Advocate General found the allegations to be unsubstantiated: http: //www4.army.mil/ocpa/read.php?story_id_key=7293.

12. *Memorandum on CJTF-7 Interrogation and Counter Resistance Policy,* from Lieutenant General Ricardo Sanchez, Commander, Joint Task Force Seven, October 12 2003, at: http://www .aclu.org/FilesPDFs/october%20sanchez%20memo.pdf.

13. J. Yoo, *War by Other Means: An Insider's Account of the War on Terror* (New York: Atlantic Monthly Press, 2006), p. 168.

14. The Church report concluded that none of pictured abuses at Abu Ghraib bore "any resemblance to approved policies at any level," p. 3 of the Executive Summary to the Report, at http://www.defenselink.mil/news/Mar2005/d20050310exe.pdf.

15. Report by Major General George Fay and Lieutenant General Anthony Jones, Investigation of Intelligence Activities at Abu Ghraib, August 23, 2004 ("Fay-Jones report"), http://www.defenselink.mil/news/Aug2004/d20040825fay.pdf.

16. *Ibid.,* p. 117.

17. *PBS Frontline,* "A Question of Torture," October 18, 2005; transcript at: http://www.pbs .org/wgbh/pages/frontline/torture/etc/script.html.

18. The Schlesinger report, *Final Report of the Independent Panel to Review DoD Detention Operations,* in Greenberg and Dratel (eds), *The Torture Papers,* p. 908 at 914–15 and 941.

19. *Ibid.*

20. Inspector General for the Department of Defense, Review of DoD-Directed Investigations of Detainee Abuse, August 25, 2006, p. ii and 23; available at http://www.DoDig .mil/fo/Foia/DetaineeAbuse.html.

21. *Ibid.,* pp. 27–8. As discussed in the Church report, the CJTF-7 Staff Judge Advocate stated that its September 14, 2003, Interrogation Policy (supra. note 10) was influenced by multiple factors, including the *U.S. Army Field Manual* (FM 34–52) and the Interrogation Policy also incorporated the Guantanamo counter-resistance policies. The CJTF-7 Staff Judge Advocate attributed the "genesis of this product" to the JTF-Guantanamo assessment team. The new techniques included "Sleep Management: Detainee provided minimum 4 hours of sleep per 24 hour period, not to exceed 72 continuous hours."

22. *R. v. Donald Payne et al.,* Live note, February 13 2007, 11:30 a.m., on file with the author, at paras. 36 and 37. Transcript available at http://www.geocities.com/aspals_legal_page s/mendoncajudge.pdf.

23. On the acquittal of the six soldiers, see http://news.bbc.co.uk/1/hi/uk/6446649.stm. On the sentencing of Corporal Payne see http://www.guardian.co.uk/uk/2007/may/01/iraq.

24. Cross-examination of Brigadier Duncan, on file with the author.

RESPONSIBILITY

Chapter 20

1. Testimony of Lieutenant General Randall M. Schmidt, 24 August 2005, supra. Chapter 1, note 4, p. 21. The Schmidt-Furlow Report states that a medical examination of Al Qahtani on January 16th 2003 "found no medical conditions' of note," supra. Chapter 6, note 7 p. 20.
2. Interview with Sir David Frost, June 27, 2004. A transcript of the interview is available at http://news.bbc.co.uk/1/hi/programmes/breakfast_with_frost/3844047.stm.
3. *Shafiq Rasul, et al. v George W Bush, et al.* 124 S.Ct. 2686, judgment of the U.S. Supreme Court (2004).
4. Declaration of Vice Admiral Lowell E. Jacoby dated January 9, 2003, at http://www.pegc.us/archive/Padilla_vs_Rumsfeld/Jacoby_declaration_20030109.pdf.
5. Letter from William J Haynes II to Alfred P. Carlton Jr., President, American Bar Association, September 23, 2002. http://www.defenselink.mil/releases/release.aspx?releaseid=3492.
6. "Guantanamo Provides Valuable Intelligence Information," DoD News Release, June 12, 2005. The press release is available at http://www.defenselink.mil/Releases/Release.aspx?ReleaseID=8583.
7. Adam Zagorin and Michael Duffy, "Inside the Interrogation of Detainee 063," *Time*, June 12, 2005, http://www.time.com/time/magazine/article/0,9171,1071284-1,00.html.
8. Letter re: Suspected Mistreatment of Detainees, from T.J. Harrington, Deputy Assistant Director, Counterterrorism Division, FBI, to Major General Donald R. Ryder, Criminal Investigation Command, Department of the Army, July 14, 2006, at http://www.aclu.org/torturefoia/released/FBI_4622_4624.pdf.

Chapter 21

1. Steven H. Miles, "Medical Ethics and the Interrogation of Guantanamo 063," *American Journal of Bioethics* (4) (2007) p. 1; *Oath Betrayed: Torture, Medical Complicity, and the War on Terror* (New York: Random House, 2006).
2. Summarized Witness Statement of Major [███████] Former Psychiatrist with the BSCT, email response of February 28, 2005, to Schmidt-Furlow Investigation.
3. World Medical Association, Guidelines for Medical Doctors concerning Torture and other Cruel, Inhuman or Degrading Treatment or Punishment in Relation to Detention and Imprisonment, Declaration of Tokyo, 1975.
4. Testimony of Lieutenant General Randall M. Schmidt, supra. Chapter 1, note 4, p. 32.
5. Schmidt-Furlow Report, p. 20; see also testimony of Testimony of Lieutenant General Randall M. Schmidt, supra. Chapter 1, note 4, p. 45.
6. Conclusions and Recommendations of the Committee Against Torture, CAT/C/U.S.A /CO/2, May 18, 2006 (advance unedited version), at p.3 ("the U.S. should ensure that 'acts of psychological torture, prohibited by the Convention, are not limited to "prolonged mental harm" as set out in [its] understandings lodged at the time of ratification of the Convention, but constitute a wider category of acts, which cause severe mental suffering, irrespective of their prolongation or its duration.'")
7. Statement of John Bellinger, Legal Adviser, State Department, before the Committee Against Torture, Geneva, May 8, 2006, at: www.state.gov/g/drl/rls/68562.htm

Chapter 22

1. *Hamdan v Rumsfeld*, 126 S. Ct. 2749, judgment of the U.S. Supreme Court, June 29, 2006.
2. Jack Goldsmith, *The Terror Presidency: Laws and Judgement Inside the Bush Administration* (New York: W.W. Norton & Company, 2007), p. 136.
3. "Application of Common Article 3 of the Geneva Conventions to the Treatment of Detainees in the Department of Defense," memorandum from Gordon England, Office of

the Secretary of Defense, July 7, 2006, http://www.washingtonpost.com/wp-srv/nation/nationalsecurity/genevaconvdoc.pdf.

4. Hearings, Senate Judiciary Committee on Confirmation Hearings of William Haynes II, July 11, 2006, Response to written questions by Senator Leahy, at p. III.

5. Hearing on military commissions in the light of the Supreme Court's decision in *Hamdan v Rumsfeld*, July 13, 2006.

6. Final Report and Recommendations of the Working Group to assess the Legal, Policy and Operational Issues Relating to Interrogation of Detainees Held by the US Armed Forces in the War on Terrorism; Memorandum for SAF/GC from AF/JA Jack L Rives, Major General, USAF Deputy Judge Advocate, dated February 5, 2003 at para 3.

7. Memorandum to General Counsel of the Air Force, dated February 27, 2003, Subject: Working Group Recommendations on Detainee Interrogations from Kevin M. Sandkuhler, Brigadeer General USME, Staff-Judge Advocate.

8. Draft Report and Recommendations of the Working Group to Access the Legal and Policy Operational Issues Related to Interrogations of Detainees Held by the US Armed Forces in the War on Terrorism; para 4, Memorandum to the General Counsel of the Department of the Air Force from Thomas J. Romig, Major General, US Army Judge Advocate, March 3, 2003, para 4.

9. Sir William Holdsworth, *A History of English Law*, (London: Methuen, 1903–1972), Vol. 5, 3rd ed., p. 195.

10. David Hope, "Torture" (2004) 53 *ICLQ* 807.

11. *Ireland v United Kingdom* (1978) 2 *EHRR* 25, judgment of the European Court of Human Rights.

12. Neil Lewis, "Red Cross Finds detainee Abuse in Guantanamo," *New York Times*, November 30, 2004, A1.

13. UN Doc. CAT/C/U.S.A/CO/2, May 18, 2006, paras. 22 and 24.

14. Commission on Human Rights, Situation of the detainees at Guantanamo, Report of the Chairperson of the Working Group on Arbitrary Detentions and five Special Rapporteurs, UN Doc. E/CN.4/2006/120, February 15, 2006, para. 51.

15. José Alvarez, "Torturing the Law" (2005) 37 *Case W. Res. J. Int'l L.* 175.

Chapter 23

1. George Tenet, *At the Center of the Storm: My Years at the CIA* (New York: HarperCollins, 2007), p. 241.

2. Geoffrey C. Hazard Jr. and William W. Hodes, *The Law of Lawyering 3rd Edition* (New York: Aspen Publishers, 2000), Section 3.2 at 3–5.

3. Kathleen Clark, "Ethical Issues Raised by the OLC Torture Memorandum," 1 *Journal of National Security Law and Policy* (2005), 455, 465

4. *Ibid.*, p. 458.

5. CAT/C/USA/co12, May 18, 2006, p.5.

6. Clark, supra. note 3, p. 462.

7. Stephen Gillers, "Tortured Reasoning," 26 *American Lawyer*, July 2004, p. 65.

8. Jeffrey K. Shapiro and Lee A. Casey, "Let lawyers be lawyers," *American Lawyer*, vol. 26, September 2004.

9. See Colin Freeze, "What would Jack Bauer do? Canadian jurist prompts international justice panel to debate TV drama 24's use of torture," *Globe and Mail*, June 16, 2007, p. A9. ("The real genius, the judge said, is that this is primarily done with mental leverage." 'There's a great scene where he told a guy that he was going to have his family killed,' Judge Scalia said. 'They had it on closed circuit television—and it was all staged. . . . They really didn't kill the family.')

10. Shapiro and Casey, supra note 8.

11. Scott Horton, "Through a Mirror Darkly: Applying the Geneva Conventions to 'A New Kind of Warfare'," in Karen J. Greenberg, ed. *The Torture Debate in America* (New York: Cambridge University Press, 2005).

12. Jose Alvarez, "Torturing the Law," supra. Chapter 22, note 15.
13. *Ibid.*, note 11, 178.
14. *Ibid.*, 176.
15. *Ibid.*, 191.
16. Yoo, *War by Other Means: An Insider's Account of the War on Terror* (New York: Atlantic Monthly Press, 2006), 235.
17. *Ibid.*, 237.
18. *Ibid.*, p. 182.
19. *Ibid.*, 183.

Chapter 25

1. UN War Crimes Commission, *Law Reports of Trials of War Criminals,* (London:HMSO, 1947), Volume VI, *The Trial of Josef Altstotter and Others,* p. 69.
2. *Ibid.,* p. 71.
3. Closing Argument for the Prosecution *U.S. v Altstötter et al,* p. 45.
4. On file with the author.
5. See official transcription of Altstötter's interrogation before the Military Tribunal (September 15 and 16, 1947) at p. 8491 (on file with author). I was directed to an article that Altstötter wrote in 1943 in which he wrote about the need for Nazi legal reforms to be safeguarded ("Die nationalsozialistische Rehtserneuerung auf dem Gebiete des Bürgerlichen Rechts und der Bürgerlichen Rechtspflege," reproduced in Deutsche Justiz, 1943, p. 83 ff, in Martin Hirsch, Diemut Majer, Jürgen Meinck (eds), *Recht, Verwaltung und Justiz im Nationalsozialismus* [Cologne: Bund-Verlag, 1984) pp. 383–4). He wrote: "Since the legal profession was strongly infiltrated and governed by Jews at the time of the seizure of power, the main objective in reforming the rules for the legal profession, was the exclusion of Jews and Communists" (translation by Mirja Trilsch, using the word "exclusion" rather than "elimination" to translate "Ausschaltung").
6. On file with the author.
7. On file with the author.
8. On file with the author.
9. Letter from Charles Lafollette, Director, Office of Military Government, Land Wurttemburg-Baden, to Dr. Hermann Orth, June 8, 1948.

Chapter 26

1. See http://www.niemanwatchdog.org/index.cfm?fuseaction=ask_this.view&askthisid=00 214.
2. See http://www.defenselink.mil/news/Mar2005/d20050310exe.pdf.
3. *Ibid.,* p. 10.
4. *Ibid.,* pp. 1, 3.
5. *Ibid.,* pp. 9, 13 and 14.
6. See Chapter 6, note 7 above; http://www.defenselink.mil/news/Jul2005/d20050714report.pdf.
7. *Ibid.,* p. 15.
8. *Ibid.,* p. 16.
9. *Ibid.,* p. 20.
10. Schmidt-Furlow, p. 20, Recommendation No. 16.
11. Testimony of Lieutenant General Randall M. Schmidt, Davis-Monthan Air Force Base, Arizona, August 24, 2005, p. 26.
12. See http://www.pbs.org/newshour/bb/military/july-dec05/gitmo_7–13.html.
13. See D. Brown, "Coercive Methods Prompted Sept. 11 Figure to Talk, General Testifies," Knight Ridder, July 14, 2005, at http://www.commondreams.org/headlines05/0714–05.htm.

14. See http://www.washingtonpost.com/wp-dyn/content/graphic/2005/12/06/GR2005120 600044.html.

15. "Spain orders arrest of U.S. troops," *BBC News Online,* October 19, 2005, http://news.bbc.co .uk/1/hi/world/middle_east/4357684.stm.

Chapter 27

1. Hearing, Senate Judiciary Committee on Confirmation Hearings of William Haynes II, July 11, 2006, p. 53.

2. Yoo, *War by Other Means,* p. 32.

3. William J. Haynes II, "The War on Terrorism and the Rule of Law," Speech to the Federalist Society, October 17, 2002, p. 1. (on file with author).

4. Jane Mayer, "The Hidden Power: the legal mind behind the White House's war on terror, *The New Yorker,* July 3, 2006, at: http://www.newyorker.com/archive/2006/07/03 /060703fa_fact1.

5. Haynes "The War on Terrorism and the Rule of Law" speech to the Federalist Society, supra. note 3, pp. 8 and 9.

6. Jane Mayer, "The Hidden Power," supra. note 4, quoting Bradford Berenson, who worked under Alberto Gonzales as an Associate Counsel at the White House. See also Andrew Cockburn, *Rumsfeld: An American Disaster* (London: Verso, 2007), p. 152, referring to Haynes as a protégé of David Addington, who "supervised a government-wide chain of command through fellow members of the ideologically hard-line Federalist Society."

7. Haynes "The War on Terrorism and the Rule of Law," speech to the Federalist Society, pp. 2, 3.

8. See Philip Heymann and Juliette Kayyem, *Protecting Liberty in an Age of Terror* (Cambridge: The MIT Press, 2005).

9. Eisenhower Office Press Briefing, June 22, 2004, p. 12.

10. Note from William Taft IV to William J. Haynes, "The 1949 Geneva Conventions: The President's Decisions under International Law," March 22, 2002, in Karen Greenberg ed., *The Torture Debate in America,* p. 283.

11. Gellman and Becker, "Pushing the Envelope on Presidential Power," *Washington Post,* June 25, 2007, p. A1. See Chapter 5, note 10.

12. Tom Golden and Eric Schmitt, "Detainee Policy Sharply Divides Bush Officials," *New York Times,* November 1, 2005.

13. Gellman and Becker, "Pushing the Envelope on Presidential Power." Above note 11.

14. Letter addressed to the Hon. Arlen Specter, Chairman and the Hon. Patrick Leahy of the Senate Judiciary Committee, July 7, 2006.

15. See http://www.committeeforjustice.org/contents/reading/091406a.shtml.

16. See generally, Goldsmith, *The Terror Presidency.*

17. *Ibid.,* pp. 155–6.

18. *Supra.* note 15.

19. Yoo, *War by Other Means,* p, 32.

20. Hearing, Senate Judiciary Committee on Confirmation Hearings of William Haynes II, July 11, 2006, response to written questions by Senator Kennedy, p. 208.

21. *Ibid.,* p. 209.

22. Goldsmith, *The Terror Presidency,* p. 173.

23. *Ibid.,* p. 88.

24. *Ibid.,* pp. 154–5; this comment refers to the March 2003 memo.

25. *Ibid.,* p. 67.

26. *Ibid.,* p. 110.

27. *Ibid.,* p. 195.

28. *Ibid.,* p. 193.

29. *Ibid.,* p. 194.

30. *Ibid.,* p. 161.

31.   *Ibid.,* p. 203.
32.   *Ibid.,* p. 163.
33.   *Ibid.,* p. 164.

Chapter 28

1.   I recognize the balanced approach put by Michael Ignatieff: "Those of us who oppose torture should also be honest enough to admit that we may have to pay a price for our own convictions. Ex ante, of course, I cannot tell how high this price might be. Ex post following another terrorist attack that might have been prevented through the exercise of coercive interrogation—the price of my scruple might simply seem too high. This is a risk I am prepared to take, but frankly, a majority of fellow citizens is unlikely to concur"; in Kenneth Roth and Minky Worden (eds.), *Torture: Does it Make Us Safer? Is it Ever OK?,* (New York: The New Press, 2005).

2.   "Secret detentions and illegal transfers of detainees involving Council of Europe states," Second Report of Special Rapporteur Dick Marty, Council of Europe Parliamentary Assembly, June 11, 2007, at http://www.coe.int/t/e/legal_affairs/legal_co-operation/fight _against_terrorism/doc11302%20E.pdf.

3.   BBC News, "U.S. Iraq troops 'condone torture'," May 4, 2007, http://news.bbc.co.uk/1 /hi/world/middle_east/6627055.stm.

4.   See *FM 2–22.3,* Human Intelligence Collector Operations, September 2006 (replacing *FM 34–52*), Appendix A. http://www.fas.org/irp/doddir/army/fm2–22–3.pdf.

5.   "Interpretation of the Geneva Conventions Common Article 3 as Applied to a Program of Detention and Interrogation Operated by the Central Intelligence Agency," Executive Order signed by President George W. Bush, July 20, 2007, http://www.whitehouse.gov /news/releases/2007/07/20070720–4.html.

6.   Hearing, Senate Select Committee on Intelligence, June 19, 2007, p. 14; see also Senator Feinstein, at pp. 16 and 18.

7.   Letter from Cully Stimson, Deputy Assistant Secretary of Defense for Detainee Affairs, to the Deputy Assistant Inspector General for Intelligence Evaluation, July 29, 2006, http://www.fas.org/irp/agency/dod/abuse.pdf, at p. 106.

8.   UN War Crimes Commission, *Law Reports of Trials of War Criminals,* Volume VI, *The Trial of Josef Altstotter and Others,* at p. 14, note 1.

9.   See http://www.bloomberg.com/apps/news?pid=20601087&sid=amoeIdSanAzw&refer =home.

INDEX

A

Abbassi, Ferroz, 158
Abu Ali, 110
Addington, David, *17*
    al-Qahtani and, 216–217, 222, 226–227
    Beaver and, 227
    Bybee/Yoo memos and, 74–75, 77, 220
    Cheney and, 230, 235
    Dunlavey and, 53
    Geneva Conventions and, 31–32, 34, 182
    at Guantánamo, 47, 49, 53, 64, 78, 84, 137,
        233
    Haynes and, 19, 49, 95, 135, 137, 210–213,
        215–217
    interrogation techniques and, 176
    Torture Convention and, 177, 184
    War Council and, 16
    Wilkerson and, 203
al-Qahtani, Mohammed, 43, 99, 109, 158–159,
        161, 173, 184, 204, 218, 226, 233, 234
Alito, Samuel (Justice), 174
Altstötter, Josef, 194
Altstötter, Ludwig, Jr., 194–201, 231
Alvarez, Jose (Professor), 177, 183–184
Ashcroft, John, 15, 18, 116, 168

B

Baccus, Rick (Brig. Gen.)
    Beaver and, 60
    Dunlavey and, 37–38, 42–43, 107–108, 133
    Hill and, 80–81
    Phifer and, 63
Bauer, Jack, 61–62, 74, 245n
Beaver, Diane (Lt. Colonel), *56*
    al-Qahtani and, 145, 147, 168
    Bybee/Yoo memos and, 3, 76–77

Dunlavey and, 48–50, 107–109, 232
Feith and, 103
Gelles and, 124, 126, 128–129
Geneva Conventions and, 52, 56–67, 138,
    203, 226–227
Haynes and, 22, 23, 98, 211, 215–216,
    220–222
Hill and, 78, 81, 83–85, 91, 113
interrogation techniques and, 55, 68–71, 72,
    75, 173, 175–177, 184
Miller and, 151
Mora and, 133–136, 140, 142
Myers and, 95–97
Becker, Dave, 61
Begg, Moazzem, 158
Bellinger, John, 244
Billingslea, Marshall, 127, 137
Bin Laden, Osama, 86, 143, 144, 148, 158–160,
    173
Boggs, Paula, 218
Brant, Dave (Director, NCIS), 123, 129–130,
    132–133, 137–138, 234
Bush, George W., 2, 9, 15, 18, 19, 27, 31, 32, 33,
    34, 35, 173, 208, 224, 231
Bybee, Jay, *73*
    al-Qahtani and, 151, 227
    Altstötter case and, 202
    Bybee/Yoo memos and, 19, 23, 49, 71,
        74–77, 113, 120, 178–179, 184, 186,
        204–205, 214–215, 218–222, 229, 233,
        234, 235
    Gonzales and, 73
    Haynes and, 177, 230
    Hill and, 78, 85
    Mora and, 135
    Myers and, 95
    Rives and, 175
    Supreme Court and, 173

C

Cambone, Stephen, 99, 137, 215, 216
Cheney, Dick, 4, 16, 19, 32, 47, 53, 64, 95, 102,
    135, 177, 211, 212, 220, 224, 230, 235, ii
Chertoff, Michael, 74
Church, Albert (Vice Admiral), 206, 220, 243n
Clark, Kathleen (Professor), 179–180, 186
Clifton, Russell (Major), 153
Craddock, Bantz (General), 92–93, 208
Custer, John (Brig. General), 80, 82

D

Dalton, Jane, 47, 65, 70, 87, 88, 90, 91, 92, 93,
    96, 98, 134, 139, 140, 179, 215
Delahunty, Robert, 31, 180
Dell'Orto, Dan
    al-Qahtani and, 141–143, 144
    Bowman and, 114–115, 117, 234
    Guantánamo and, 150
    Haynes memo and, 228
    Mora and, 139
    War Council and, 16–18, 20–22
Dershowitz, Alan, 54, 72, 127, 227
Dietz, Bob, 114
Duncan, Ewan (Brigadier), 154
Dunlavey, Michael E. (Maj. General)
    Altstötter case and, 184
    Beaver and, 56–57, 60, 63–66, 68–70, 177
    Bowman and, 113, 116–117
    Gelles and, 123–129
    Geneva Conventions and, 203
    Guantánamo and, 37–51, 53–55, 87, 233
    Haynes and, 213–215, 219–222, 226–229
    Haynes memo and, 4, 5, 22–23
    Hill and, 78–85
    interrogation techniques and, 72, 77,
        99–102, 145, 147
    Miller and, 107–108
    Mora and, 133
    Myers and, 93, 95–97
    post-Guantánamo career, 231, 234
    Rumsfeld and, 36, 136
Durnan, Jamie, 138–9

E

England, Gordon, 136, 138, 174, 216, 225
England, Lynndie, 14

F

Fallon, Mark, 123, 129

Fay, George (Maj. General), 152
Feinstein, Diane (Senator), 221
Feith, Doug, *28*
    al-Qahtani and, 128, 134
    Altstötter case and, 184, 187, 201
    Beaver and, 48, 56, 60
    Bowman and, 117
    Bybee/Yoo memos and, 214
    Dunlavey and, 42–43, 45, 83
    Geneva Conventions and, 27, 29–36,
        88–90, 154, 158, 173, 180–182, 214, 226,
        230
    Haynes memo and, 3, 92
    interrogation techniques and, 22, 98–104,
        106, 142, 189–190, 234
    Iraq War and, 14
    Myers and, 92, 97
    resignation, 235
Flanigan, Tim, 16, 74
Franks, Tommy (General), 30

G

Gebhardt, Karl, 193, 200–201
Gelles, Mike, 43, 62, 122–130, 133, 146–147,
    152–153, 212, 224
Gibbons, John, 158, 159
Gillers, Stephen (Professor), 180–182, 186
Goldsmith, Jack Landman, 16, 74, 174, 218,
    220–221
Gonzales, Alberto
    al-Qahtani and, 141–143, 144–145
    Bybee/Yoo memos and, 178, 180,
        219–220
    Dunlavey and, 38, 56
    Geneva Conventions and, 22–23, 31, 34, 35,
        184
    Guantánamo and, 47, 49, 64, 78, 215, 222,
        227
    Haynes and, 26, 32, 44, 71, 83–84, 89,
        150–151, 174, 177, 227–230
    Torture Convention and, 73–77
    War Council and, 16–21, *17*, 226
Graham, Lindsay (Senator), 175, 219–220
Gutierrez, Gita, 158–162

H

Hamdan, Salim Ahmed, 174
Harrington, T.J., 161
Haynes, William J., *17, 28*
    Addington and, 213
    al-Qahtani and, 157, 213–214
    Beaver and, 56–57, 64, 70, 71, 227–228

Bowman and, 117–118, 119–120
Bybee/Yoo memos and, 177, 178, 180
Dell'Orto and, 114–115, 117
Dunlavey and, 37, 40, 42, 44–45, 47, 49–50,
   54, 99
Feith and, 102–103
Gelles and, 127
Geneva Conventions and, 31–32, 34, 36, 177,
   217, 226
Gonzales and, 144–145, 150
Guantánamo and, 19–23, 55, 74–75, 78,
   84–85, 151, 215
Haynes memo, 3, 5–6, 10, 12–13, 16–18, 23,
   26, 29, 73, 96, 100, 108–109, 131–135,
   152–153, 172, 184, 203, 204–206,
   208–209, 225, 229–232
Hill and, 98, 141–143
interrogation techniques and, 76–77, 83,
   101, 128–129, 144–145, 210, 214–216
Iraq War and, 14
Judiciary Committee and, 214–223
McMillan and, 211
Mora and, 136–140
Myers and, 88–93, 95
Rumsfeld and, 36, 107
Supreme Court and, 173–176
Taft and, 214
Wolfowitz and, 104–106
Yoo and, 212
Heymann, Phillip, 213
Hicks, David, 31
Hill, James T. (General)
   2002 memo, 87, 90, 91, 93–94
   al-Qahtani and, 145, 160
   Beaver and, 60, 64, 103
   Dunlavey and, 47, 49–50, 101
   Geneva Conventions and, 173
   Guantánamo and, 78–86, 208
   Haynes memo and, 4, 5, 23
   interrogation techniques and, 21,
      107–109, 113, 127–128, 141–143, 215, 227,
      229
   Mora and, 133–134
   Myers and, 98–99
Holdsworth, William Searle, 176
Hope, David (Lord), 176
Horton, Scott, 182–184, 187, vii
Hussein, Saddam, 2, 14
Hutson, John (General), 175

I

Ignatieff, Michael, 248

J

Jacoby, Lowell (Vice-Admiral), 46, 135, 136,
   156, 157, 213, 214
Jessen, Bruce, 62
Jones, Anthony (lt. General), 152
Judgment at Nuremberg (1961), 26, 192, 238

K

Kennedy, Anthony (Justice), 174, 182
Kennedy, Edward (Senator), 219
Kern, Paul (General), 152

L

LaFollette, Charles, 26, 201
Leahy, Patrick (Senator), 174–175, 221
Leso, John (Major). 125
Lincoln, Abraham, 2, 22–23, 52, 224
Lindh, John Walker, 31, 189
Lindlaw, Scott, 17
Livingstone, Susan, 138

M

McCain, John (Senator), 208
McMillan, James (Judge), 211
Margulies, Joseph, 158
Memory of Justice (1976), vii, 26
Mendonca, Jorge (Colonel), 153
Miles, Stephen (Dr), 163
Miller, Geoffrey D. (Maj. General)
   FBI and, 107–109, 116
   Guantánamo and, 38, 49, 81, 85, 129, 234
   Gutierrez and, 160
   Haynes memo and, 5, 151–153
   Hill and, 143, 229
   Myers and, 93
   Schmidt-Furlow report and, 207–208
Milosevic, Slobodan, 193
Mohammed, Khalid Sheikh, 144
Mora, Alberto
   Geneva Conventions and, 131–140
   Haynes and, 157, 176, 214–216, 218, 222, 228
   interrogation techniques and, 130, 141–143,
      234
   Myers and, 92
   Schmidt-Furlow report and, 169
Morello, Steve, 133, 139
Moussaoui, Zacarias, 44
Myers, Richard (General)
   Beaver and, 65

Dunlavey and, 42, 47–49
Feith and, 32–33
Geneva Convention and, 128, 134, 173
Guantánamo and, 7
Haynes and, 210, 213–215
Haynes memo and, 3, 5, 98–100
Hill and, 80, 82–85
interrogation techniques and, 22, 87–97,
    103, 109, 117, 184
Rumsfeld and, 31–33

O

Orth, Hermann, 194–195, 196, 201
Owen, Tim, 153

P

Pace, Peter (General), 42, 142–143
Padilla, José, 144–145, 156–157, 160, 189, 213
Payne, Donald (Corporal), 153
Phifer, Jerald (Lt. Colonel), 4, 45, 48, 63, 66,
    67, 69, 107, xi
Pierce, George, 215
Pinochet, Augusto, 184, 204
Powell, Colin, 32, 34, 89, 94, 102, 203, 214

Q

Qaed Salim Sinan al Harethi. *see* Abu Ali

R

Reed, Jack (Senator), 104–105
Reid, Richard, 144, 160
Rives, Jack (Maj. General), 109, 194
Rizzo, John
    Bybee/Yoo memos and, 76, 178, 215
    Dunlavey and, 77
    Geneva Conventions and, 225
    at Guantánamo, 64, 75, 215, 227, 233
Romig, Thomas (Maj. General), 32, 59,
    175–176, 194, 212, 214
Roosevelt, Eleanor, 72
Roosevelt, Theodore, 29
Rumsfeld, Donald
    al-Qahtani and, 7, 10, 12–13, 113, 128, 129,
        147, 156, 160, 216
    Beaver and, 71
    Billingslea and, 127
    Dunlavey and, 36, 38–39, 42–48, 50, 54, 81,
        102, 123–124, 226–227
    England and, 174

Feith and, 29
Geneva Conventions and, 31–33, 35, 80, 89
Hamdan v. Rumsfeld 173, 181, 186, 225, vii
Haynes memo and, 2–3, 5–6, 70, 85, 96,
    98–99, 103, 109, 133, 172, 203, 208,
    212–213, 221, 229
Hill and, 82–83, 142–143
interrogation techniques and, 19, 21–23, 64,
    68, 85–86, 107–108, 150–152, 189
Iraq War and, 14
Mora and, 135–139
Myers and, 84, 91–93, 215
War Council and, 16
Ryder, Donald J. (Maj. General), 123, 129

S

Sanchez, Ricardo (General), 151, 153
Sandkuhler, Kevin (Brig. General), 175
Scalia, Antonin (Justice), 181, 245n
Schlegelberger, Franz, 191, 195
Schlesinger, James R., 152
Schmidt, Randall M. (Lt. General), 39, 107,
    109, 145, 169, 170
Seltzer, Abigail, 163–172, 176, 204, 210, 221
Shimkus, Albert J (Captain), 168
Shinseki (General), 79
Slahi, Mohammedou Ould, 115
Smith, Cynthia, 211
Specter, Arlen (Senator), 219
Stevens, John Paul (Justice), 174
Stimson, Cully, 228
Supervielle, Manny, 59, 65, 70, 78, 83–84, 91,
    93, 134

T

Talalay, Susan, 132
Taylor, Charles, 193
Taylor, Telford (Brig. General), 25–26, 187, 193
Temple, Caleb, 112, 146–148, 224
Tenet, George, 179
Thomas, Clarence (Justice), 173, 181, 186
Trilsch, Mirja, 195, vii

W

Walker, John, 31, 139, 175
Walker, Mary, 139, 175
Wallace, Mike, 54
Warren, Marc (Colonel), 151
Waxman, Matthew, 216, 217
Wedgwood, Ruth, 218

Wheaton, Kelly (Colonel), vii, 88, 210, 222
White, Thomas E., 134
Wilkerson, Lawrence, 203
Wolfowitz, Paul, *105*
  Dunlavey and, 42
  Durnan and, 138
  Feith and, 3
  Geneva Conventions and, 15
  Haynes and, 22, 98, 104–105, 134, 213, 234
  Hill and, 83, 91
  Iraq War and, 14
  Myers and, 92
  World Bank and, 235
Wright (Lord), 192

Y

Yoo, John, *73*
  2003 memo, 151
  AEI and, 231

  al-Qahtani and, 229
  Altstötter case and, 184–186, 187, 202
  Bowman and, 113
  Bybee/Yoo memos and, 23, 49, 71, 73–76,
    78, 85, 175, 178–180, 203–205, 214–215,
    219–220, 222, 233, 234, 235
  Geneva Conventions and, 184–186
  Goldsmith and, 220–221
  Haynes and, 177, 212
  memo for Haynes, 31, 180
  migration theory and, 152
  Mora and, 135
  Myers and, 95
  Supreme Court and, 173
  Torture Convention and, 19
  War Council and, 16, 226–227

Z

Zubaydah, Abu, 54, 178